THE SEVEN NATIONS
OF CANADA
1660-1860

**Solidarity, Vision and Independence
in the St. Lawrence Valley**

JEAN-PIERRE SAWAYA

Translated by Katherine Hastings

Copyright © Septentrion 1998
Publié avec l'autorisation du Septentrion (Québec)
Original title: *La fédération des sept feux de la vallée du Saint-Laurent* XVIIᵉ-XIXᵉ *siècle*

Translation © Katherine Hastings

ISBN 978-1-77186-332-2 pbk; 978-1-77186-343-8 epub; 978-1-77186-344-5 pdf

Cover: Illustration by Alfred Worsley Holdstock, *Indian Encampment On Desert And Gatineau Rivers (near Maniwaki, Quebec)*, c. 1870. Watercolour, National Archives of Canada C-40098.

Photo of the Seven Nations Flag courtesy of Patricia Culliford.

Cover and Book Design by Folio infographie
Editing and proofreading: Robin Philpot, Anne Marie Marko

Legal Deposit, 4th quarter 2023
Bibliothèque et Archives nationales du Québec
Library and Archives Canada

Published by Baraka Books of Montreal

Printed and bound in Quebec

TRADE DISTRIBUTION & RETURNS
Canada – UTP Distribution: UTPdistribution.com

UNITED STATES
Independent Publishers Group: IPGbook.com

We acknowledge the support from the Société de développement des entreprises culturelles (SODEC) and the Government of Quebec tax credit for book publishing administered by SODEC.

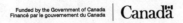

To my parents, Marie and Jean

I would like to express my gratitude to all those who had a hand in getting this book to print. First, my family for their unflagging support and encouragement. Special thanks also to Denys Delâge for his invaluable guidance and advice throughout my research journey, Alain Beaulieu at the Université Laval Department of History for his much-appreciated input, and the staff at CELAT for their assistance and kindness. Additional thanks to Baraka Books publisher Robin Philpot; Patricia Culliford, Anishinabeg researcher, for her interest in my work; and Katherine Hastings, for her rigorous translation.

Contents

Abbreviations

DRCHNY	O'Callaghan, ed., *Documents Relative to the Colonial History of the State of New York*
HAINM	Hodge, ed., *Handbook of American Indians North of Mexico HNAI* Sturtevant, ed., *Handbook of North American Indians*
HP	*Sir Frederick Haldimand: Unpublished Papers and Correspondence 1758-84*
IIADH	Jennings, ed., *Iroquois Indians: A Documentary History of the Diplomacy of the Six Nations and their League. The Microfilm Collection*
JCA	Quebec, *Journals of the House of Assembly of Lower-Canada*
JP	Sullivan *et al.*, ed., *The Papers of Sir William Johnson*
JR	Thwaites, ed., *The Jesuit Relations and Allied Documents: Travels and Explorations of the Jesuit Missionaries in New-France, 1610- 1791*
MG 1, C11A	NAC, *Manuscript Group 1*: Archives nationales, Paris, série *C11A*, archives des colonies
MG 19, F 1	NAC, *Manuscript Group 19: Fur Trade and Indians 1763-1867*, series *F 1*, *Claus Papers*
MG 23, GII1	NAC, *Manuscript Group 23: Late Eighteenth Century Papers*, series *GII1*, *James Murray*
NAC	National Archives of Canada, Ottawa
RAAQ	*Recherches amérindiennes au Québec*
RAPQ	*Rapport de l'archiviste de la province de Québec*
RG 8	NAC, *Record Group 8: British Military and Naval Records RG 10* NAC, *Record Group 10: Indian Affairs*

Foreword by Patricia Culliford

In May of 2017, Denys Delâge, myself and my assistant were brought by boat to a meeting with Chief Mike Thomas at his home in St. Regis. We were greeted by elders, a traditional Iroquois feast, wampum belts and the keepers of St. Kateri's relic. They told us that they were what was left of the Seven Nations Confederacy leadership (also known as the Seven Feathers Confederacy). They were involved in fighting for their rights to participate in treaty land claims in Akwesasne and told me their stories. These stories were recorded. I was also asked to send a letter to Her Majesty the Queen on their behalf. I did so.

In our discussions with them and other community members, we learned that there was a lack of archival and historical information about the Seven Nations of Canada in English. I promised them to try to fill this gap so that they (and their children) would have a chance to learn their history.

A year later Chief Thomas passed on. And his wife Charlene Thomas graciously sent me the flag of the Seven Nations Confederacy. I have since received the rights to the flag and all that it represents.

The flag's green background represents the land. (See the flag on the cover.) The diamonds represent six of the nations and the rectangle in the centre represents Kahnawake, which was both the seventh nation and the Central Council Fire of this an many other confederacies. The white lines at either edge represent the St. Lawrence River and delineate both sides of the continent, Canada and the United States.

We wish to express our deepest gratitude towards Baraka Books for making the elders' wishes a reality.

Niawen Megwitch, Merci.

We dedicate this book to Chief Mike Thomas, last of the "longhairs."

Patricia Culliford, Feb. 1, 2023

Patricia Culliford is an Anishinabe member of the Seven Nations Confederacy. She is a historical researcher whose focus is on the uses of wampum belts in Indigenous/settler relations. She has reached out to Baraka Books to request this translation in order to fulfill a promise made to Chief Mike Thomas.

INTRODUCTION

History of an Ancient Political Culture

In the days of Canada's French and British regimes, Quebec's Indigenous Peoples forged a singular political alliance known in the Euro-American written tradition as the Seven Nations of Canada. The alliance consisted of Catholic Indigenous Peoples from the villages in the St. Lawrence River Valley—Wendake, Pointe-du-Lac, Wôlinak, Odanak, Kahnawake, Kanehsatake, and Akwesasne. This confederacy represented an alliance between nations, i.e., between the Indigenous councils or governments of each village.[1] It was a federative pact because there was a central political organization, the Grand Council of Kahnawake, which shared various jurisdictions with the different member nations who, in principle, were guaranteed cohesiveness and self-determination, without compromising the identity of the allied communities. Consequently, when these Indigenous Peoples looked to the Confederacy, they sought unity and shared representation. The political organization of the Indigenous Peoples of Quebec began to take shape in the 17th century, around 1660, and continued into the 19th century when, in about 1860, the alliance fell apart.

The examination of the Seven Fires is part of a new field of research, that of the political and diplomatic history of the Indigenous Peoples of North America. Since very few researchers have studied this political organization, its historiography is virtually non-existent.[2]

In Quebec, Georges Boiteau was doubtless one of the first to shed light on its existence in his 1954 master's thesis on the history of the Huron of Lorette.[3] Since 1989, three other studies on the Seven Fires Confederacy have been conducted. The first by Lawrence Ostola, in 1989, deals with events in the history of the Seven Nations of Canada during the American Revolution.[4] The other two studies consist of reports tabled in 1995 and 1996 to the Royal Commission on Aboriginal Peoples: one by Jean-Pierre Sawaya on the political traditions of the domiciled nations and the way their organization operated,[5] and the other by Denys Delâge and Jean-Pierre Sawaya on the treaties between the Confederacy and the British in the 18th and 19th centuries.[6] These latter two studies were based on a systematic review of the colonial archives.

The history of the political organization of the Indigenous Peoples in Quebec was therefore still somewhat of a mystery because, while a number of researchers had examined—at least in part—one or other of the federated nations, none of their studies dealt with the alliance those nations formed within the Seven Fires. Although numerous studies have looked at Indigenous communities in Quebec from the standpoint of economics, family, ethnic makeup, politics, and the role of priests, among other perspectives, as well as certain aspects of their political alliances, none has delved into the composition and diplomatic role of the communities allied with the Seven Fires. Furthermore, while some of these studies cover Indigenous politics in a general fashion, particularly those of the Iroquois League of Six Nations, none has drawn a parallel between its practices and the Seven Fires Confederacy.[7]

In order to reconstruct the history of this alliance as it existed between the 17th and 19th centuries, we consulted a host of French and British colonial archives:[8] the National Archives of Canada in Ottawa, the C11A series of Archives des Colonies, which contain the official correspondence of the government of New France, and the RG 8 and RG 10 series featuring the military archives and those of the Department of Indian Affairs. The RG 10 series, the most exhaustive with regard to Indigenous Peoples under the British Regime of Canada, includes all the administrative archives of the imperial government and the departments related to Indian Affairs, as well as those of the regional offices and archives dealing with Indigenous lands. They contain all the correspondence between the official representatives of the British Crown and the colonists and Indigenous Peoples, as well as documents created or collected by the "Northern Department," which was tasked, among other things, with running the Province of Quebec starting in 1760. We also consulted the archives of various superintendents of the Department of Indian Affairs, including those of Sir William Johnson, released in 1953 under the title *The Papers of Sir William Johnson*, as well as those of his successors, Guy Johnson and John Johnson.[9] In addition we consulted a documentary corpus edited by the Newberry Library of Chicago under the direction of American historian Francis Jennings entitled *Iroquois Indians: A Documentary History.*[10]

The archival material we perused contains documents related to a range of actors, both Indigenous and colonial, who played a key role in the historical development of North America, including civilian and military officers, politicians, diplomats, members of the clergy, traders, entrepreneurs, and merchants. While some of the archival documents are of a more private nature (accounts of travel and exploration, military expedition journals, tales of battle), generally speaking they are official, public records that fulfilled a specific political and administrative role. These include correspondence, journals of the Department of Indian Affairs, memorandums, investigative reports, the proceedings from Euro-Indigenous conferences, treaties, petitions, bills of sale or lease, expenditure lists, accounts, demographic surveys, geographic maps, and more.

The documents in the archives also contain the details of conferences between Indigenous Peoples and Europeans, which in some cases resulted in the signing of treaties, although more often consisted of the renewal of pacts between the parties. Given the secret nature of some meetings between Indigenous Peoples or, in other cases, the presence of only certain Indigenous representatives at such meetings, the records of some diplomatic events are not included. For example, Sir William Johnson noted in a letter to London, in 1770, that some Indigenous people held secret negotiations and that he was therefore unable to provide the proceedings from these meetings to the British authorities.[11] In a number of instances, the proceedings of these private meetings were transcribed by the Indigenous parties to the meeting. One such example was the Congress of the Grand Council of the Iroquois League of Six Nations in Onondaga (present-day New York State) in the winter of 1774, where Thayendanegea, a Mohawk chief of the League, transcribed the speeches made there. In fact, Thayendanegea was specifically appointed by Superintendent Guy Johnson to do so, and was accepted in this role by the chiefs present at the Council.[12] Chief Thayendanegea also kept a journal in which he transcribed other Indigenous-only conferences.[13]

While the conferences were multilingual events, the proceedings of these gatherings were usually written in only one language, either English or French. The diplomatic sources of these proceedings were therefore re-transcriptions of the interpretation of what was actually said at the conferences. As for the interpreters tasked with transcribing the speeches made by the Indigenous speakers, were they really qualified to do so? American anthropologist William N. Fenton, who consulted these colonial archives extensively in his research on the Iroquois, noted that those interpreters, who played a vital role in producing archives for the Department of Indian Affairs, were, sadly, not sufficiently "schooled" to fulfill that role, adding that one Princeton-educated interpreter who had devoted his life to learning was incompetent to infuse the fire of Indian Oratory into his expressions.[14]

There is certainly reason to criticize certain translations and question their value. We know it was in the political interest of the Europeans to report the words of the Indigenous parties as accurately as possible: the better they understood them, the easier it was to control them. In a document dated February 13, 1759, the governor of Pennsylvania demanded that the secretary tasked with transcribing the speeches of certain Great Lakes Indigenous ambassadors take great care in reporting the speeches of the Indigenous delegates, specifically that he be very precise with regard to the replies they gave to the questions asked by the Pennsylvania commissioners.[15] On November 8, 1764, Sir William Johnson wrote to the military governor, Thomas Gage, that the conference transcriptions were perhaps not as faithful as hoped: in some instances entire written speeches differed from what the Indigenous interlocutors had actually said, including the words contained in a treaty with the Sandusky Wyandot in Detroit.[16] In a letter dated August 24, 1829, Louis-Juchereau Duchesnay, then superintendent of Indian Affairs in Quebec, sent military secretary George Couper the transcription of a French translation of the speeches given by a number of Indigenous chiefs from Lower Canada. In it he warned Couper: "I send the translation of the Indian speech in French as sent to me, to deviate as little as possible from the original speech in Indian, unavoidable by a second *traduction*."[17] On August 18, 1830, William Mackay, Superintendent of Indian Affairs in Montreal, received from the Sulpician priest at Lake of Two Mountains the proceedings of a council of the Iroquois in the village. In it, the missionary noted the inherent challenges he faced translating them, given the limited capacity of the French language to accurately convey the Indigenous "verve." He wrote: "I felt it my duty to report this speech, at the very least with regard to its substance, and to render it as close as possible to the 'Indian' language, insofar as the French language allows."[18]

The councils and conferences between Indigenous and European parties were systematically translated by translators or interpreters working for the colonial government, in conjunction with secretaries or scribes tasked with recording the near-entirety of the speeches and the gestures made on these occasions. In some transcriptions, they intentionally left out certain details, while occasionally noting such omissions. In other cases, the meeting proceedings appear to be more summary than actual systematic re-transcriptions. As a result, such documents sometimes contain general abbreviations and vague references to certain mores and customs, without any further description, as if the scribes, having grown used to forest diplomacy and the customs of the Indigenous Peoples, felt it unnecessary to describe the ceremonies, referring to them merely in passing and in a general fashion. Nothing in the documents clearly explains how these conferences were recorded, aside from a 1756 reference dating from the French regime, in which a French officer notes in his war memoirs that, at a conference between Governor Vaudreuil and the Indigenous Peoples of Canada and New England, "the words of the five nations were rendered, one after the other, by the interpreter; they were noted by the governor's secretary, and the wampum were numbered, in the order they were received."[19] One might well imagine that even the lengthiest reports of proceedings could not provide a record of all that may have been significant to the many participants in the discussions.[20]

The documents were usually drafted in person by the signatories, interpreters, or others. However, the impeccable calligraphy of some of the sources suggests they were likely the work of copyists, given their immaculate appearance, with no stains or deletions. In most of the archival fonds consulted, the documents were accompanied by the original. If the original was in French and had been copied from an archive into English, there was a note to that effect. If the archived documents were originally in an Indigenous language, this was specified, and a translated copy provided. In one such instance, on May 24, 1809, the Indian Affairs agent assigned to the Abenaki of Saint-François and Bécancour, on the orders of the Indian Superintendency, sent the military government a number of documents relating to the colonial history of the Abenaki. In them the agent mentions that he enlisted the services of an interpreter to translate some of the original documents into the Abenaki language.[21]

Our research into the political history of the Indigenous Peoples required a specific methodology for several reasons. For the most part, the documents consulted were European texts dealing with relations between Indigenous and non-Indigenous peoples, as well as with colonial policies in the northeastern part of North America. The point of view of the colonizers is therefore often clearly stated. However, that of the Indigenous Peoples, who have an oral tradition, poses a problem: their viewpoint, as reported by the Europeans, is filtered through a discourse that is often ethnocentric, direct, and simplistic. Nevertheless, despite the lack of objectivity of the colonial documentation, it was possible to extract from it the strategies of the Indigenous Peoples and identify the characteristics of their political culture. Doing so required decoding, in an exhaustive fashion, all references to their political traditions, organization, and government operations.

It also meant identifying every mention of Indigenous diplomatic and political protocol, and of those dealing with inter-nation relations, which are often alluded to by the European and Indigenous parties alike in their speeches on the state of their alliances. Furthermore, in order to gain a better understanding of the elements of this political culture, it was important to decrypt the speeches, especially with regard to the terms of kinship expressed by the Indigenous Peoples, terms that referred to the different diplomatic partners. It was therefore crucial to decode the language, since it is this diplomatic kinship that allowed each group to identify itself in relation to the others (the expressions related to kinship specify the nature of the alliances by determining the role and status of the individuals and nations).

This task was particularly challenging when the European translation of an Indigenous term altered its meaning; it was nonetheless important to attempt to provide its value and significance while keeping these nuances in mind. It was important to keep this discursive analysis in perspective, as we also needed to pay special attention to the symbolic gestures that were reported, for example, when wampum or gifts were exchanged, and to the different ritualized ceremonies practised by the Indigenous Peoples. As for the importance of the objects that were exchanged, they allowed us to differentiate between what was essential—and what was less so—to the Indigenous Peoples at specific meetings.

CHAPTER ONE

Peoples of the St. Lawrence River Valley

The political alliance of the domiciled Indigenous people took shape under the government of New France around 1660, and was dissolved in the 1860s. This organization, known in the British colonial archives as the "Confederacy of the Seven Nations" or the "Federation of the Seven Fires," included the Huron, Iroquois, Algonquin, Nipissing, and Abenaki nations, which were all Catholic. The French referred to them as "domiciled Indians" due to the fact they lived in villages close to the colonial settlements of Montreal, Trois Rivières, and Quebec, and also to differentiate them from nomadic peoples.

The Confederacy represented the Huron who hailed from Huronia, on the shores of Georgian Bay. They arrived in Quebec in 1650 and settled permanently in Lorette in 1697. As early as 1667, Oneida Iroquois and Mohawks from the Mohawk and Connecticut rivers settled in the Montreal area, on the south shore of the St. Lawrence River, first in Laprairie then, as of 1716 (after several relocations), in Sault-Saint-Louis, near the Lachine Rapids. From there, some migrated to two other areas. One group left Sault-Saint-Louis and settled on the Island of Montreal, at the Sulpician Mission of La Montagne du Mont-Royal (which was then located near what is now Atwater and Sherbrooke streets). They subsequently resettled near Rivière des Prairies, at the Sault-au-Récollet Mission near Boulevard Gouin and rue Papineau, until eventually moving to the current region of Lac-des-Deux-Montagnes, where they founded a village in 1721.

A third Iroquois village was founded in Saint-Régis just prior to 1740 by men and women from Sault-Saint-Louis together with others from Iroquoia, the Iroquois territory south of Lake Ontario. Several years later, in 1749, other Iroquois, mostly Onondaga, as well as some Oneida, Cayuga, and Seneca peoples, founded a village known as Oswegatchie, on the current-day site of Ogdensburg, New York. The village was subsequently dismantled, and the Iroquois community living there relocated to Saint-Régis, which would also become home to Oneida, Mohawk, and, for a time after 1759, Abenaki people.

Two other communities lived on the shores of Lake of Two Mountains—the Algonquin and Nipissing—and were known as the first occupants of Old Canada, as they had been present in the Ottawa and St. Lawrence rivers region between Lake Nipissing and Quebec. Between 1650 and 1700, they left the La Montagne mission in Montreal and relocated to Rivière des Prairies and, from there, to Lake of Two Mountains. They were followed by a group of Nipissing from Île-aux-Tourtes as well as some Algonquin from the Sainte-Anne-du-Bout-de-l'Île (Sainte-Anne-de-Bellevue) mission. The Algonquin also had another village in Pointe-du-Lac, near Trois-Rivières. Around 1676, a number of Abenaki from the region between the Merrimack River and Lake Champlain arrived at the mouth of the Chaudière River before eventually settling, in 1680, in Saint-François-du-Lac, Bécancour, and on the shores of Missisquoi Bay on Lake Champlain.[1]

It appears that the settlement of these villages was the result of an initiative by the French colonial power and, in particular, the desire of the authorities in Montreal to create an "Indian barrier"[2] between New France and the British colonies.[3] With the exception of the Algonquin and Nipissing, the members of the Seven Fires were Indigenous communities who had been displaced from their traditional territories.[4] The colonial wars in

New England had forced many of the Abenaki to flee, while the Iroquois Wars had dispersed the Huron. The tensions between Catholics and traditionalists in Iroquoia, combined with economic factors, also contributed to the migration of the Iroquois. There is absolutely no doubt that at the time the St. Lawrence communities were being established, in Laprairie, Lorette, and Saint-François, for example, the Indigenous Peoples considered themselves refugees among the French and, especially, the Jesuit missionaries. The reason these Indigenous Peoples aligned themselves with the French was that they shared a religious allegiance to the same God.[5] It is also possible that the groups' traditional hunting territories now intersected with the new settlements, which would have implied a trade and economic alliance, as well as a military alliance.[6]

Who were the Seven Fires?

In the beginning, the Confederacy included Huron, Algonquin, and Nipissing, with Iroquois and Abenaki members joining later. On October 7, 1791, an Iroquois chief from Kahnawake reminded the Superintendent of Indian Affairs, John Campbell, that in the early days of the French Regime, the alliance consisted of "the Huron, the Algonkin, and the Nipissing," who, at that time, "were one." A short time later, it came to encompass the "Kanawageronon, Huron, Algonkin, Nipissing,"[7] that is, the domiciled Iroquois of Sault-Saint-Louis, Huron of Lorette, Algonquin, and Nipissing. The Abenaki subsequently joined the Confederacy.[8] By the end of the French Regime in Canada, the Indigenous Peoples of the Seven Fires Confederacy were grouped in eight villages:

— Jeune Lorette or Wendake (Huron)[9]
— Saint-François or Odanak (Abenaki)[10]
— Bécancour or Wôlinak (Abenaki) [11]
— Pointe-du-Lac, near Trois-Rivières (Algonquin)[12]

— Sault-Saint-Louis or Kahnawake (Iroquois)[13]
— Lake of Two Mountains or Kanehsatake (Iroquois, Algonquin, Nipissing)[14]
— Saint-Régis or Akwesasne (Iroquois)[15]
— La Présentation or Oswegatchie (Iroquois)[16]

In early September 1760, after negotiating with the Huron chiefs from Lorette in Longueuil, British general James Murray met with eight representatives of the Seven Fires Confederacy.[17] Several days after the Capitulation of Montreal, on September 15 and 16, 1760, the British authorities gathered in Kahnawake to meet with representatives of the Seven Fires Confederacy, referred to at that time as the "Eight Nations of Canada."[18] On August 25, 1763, on behalf of the "Confederacy of Canada," eight nations sent a message to the Great Lakes nations who were rebelling against the British presence in the region.[19] While there is scarce documentation from the French about the political ties binding the domiciled people of the St. Lawrence Valley villages, the British, who had perceived those ties in the early years of the Seven Years' War, spoke of the alliance as a "confederacy." In 1763, Sir William Johnson described them as the "confederated nations" of Canada and, seven years later, as the "Canadian Confederacy."[20] Several documents from the British Regime in Canada explicitly mention a link between this "Canada Confederacy" and the names "Seven Nations," "Seven Villages," or "Seven Fires."[21] The name "Seven Nations" appears for the first time in documents from the British Regime. One of the earliest mentions is dated 1761, and appears in the correspondence between Daniel Claus, the Indian Affairs agent in Montreal, and Sir William Johnson. In it, Claus explains to the superintendent that the "Seven Nations of Canada" received a proposal for an alliance from the Iroquois of the League of Six Nations in the form of a "Treaty of Alliance and Friendship."[22] This mention was followed by several others in subsequent years.

In 1770, a delegation from the Seven Nations of Canada attended a diplomatic congress in German Flats, New York. The proceedings of the meeting include a list of domiciled nations present at the gathering: "Cagnawageys" and "the Indians of St. Regis," "Algonkins," "Ganagsadagas," "Abenaquis St. Francis Abenaki," "Hurons of Lorett," and "Nipisinks." Superintendent Johnson addressed the "Canada Confederacy" consisting of "seven nations."[23]

In 1779, Colonel John Campbell received a request from the chiefs of the "Seven Villages" asking that the British dispatch missionaries to their communities, in accordance with the pledges made in August 1760, shortly before the Capitulation of Montreal. Campbell, who passed the petition on to Governor Frederick Haldimand, wrote that it had been presented to him by delegates from several villages of domiciled Indians: Sault-Saint-Louis, Lake of Two Mountains, Saint-Régis, and Saint-François.[24]

In 1794, the proceedings of a meeting between representatives of the "Seven Villages of Lower Canada" and Governor Guy Carleton (Lord Dorchester) included a list of ambassadors of the domiciled nations: the Iroquois of Saint-Régis, Algonquin and Nipissing of Lake of Two Mountains, Iroquois of Sault-Saint-Louis, Abenaki of Saint-François, and Huron of Lorette.[25]

In 1829, Nicolas Vincent Tsaouenhohoui, Grand Chief of the Huron of Lorette, responded to the questions of a committee of the Assembly of Lower Canada. When the representatives of the Assembly asked him to state the names of the Seven Nations, Tsaouenhohoui replied: "Iroquois of Sault Saint Louis, (Great Fire or Council); Huron, Lorette; Iroquois and Algonquin, Lake of Two Mountains; Iroquois, Saint-Régis; Abenaki, Saint-François; and Abenaki, Bécancour."[26]

In 1837, Governor Gosford received a petition from Sault-Saint-Louis on behalf of the chiefs of the "Sept Nations de Sauvages du Bas Canada, assemblées en conseil" represented by the Iroquois of Sault-Saint-Louis, Lake of Two Mountains, and Saint-Régis, as well as by the Algonquin and Nipissing of Lake of Two Mountains.[27]

In 1850, Governor Elgin was sent a petition by the Iroquois chiefs of Sault-Saint-Louis on behalf of the "Savages of Canada," specifically "the Indian Tribes of Sault-Saint-Louis, Saint Régis, and Lake of Two Mountains in the District of Montreal, and Saint-François, in the District of Trois-Rivières."[28]

In 1856, representatives from the villages of Sault-Saint-Louis, Lake of Two Mountains, Saint-François, and Bécancour submitted a request to the Legislature of United Canada. The petition begins: "We, the Indians of Lower Canada assembled in Caughnawaga, delegated by each of our Indian tribes and villages, named the Seven Indian Nations of Lower Canada."[29] The Seven Fires alliance was flexible, and the composition of its members varied. It could, at times, present itself and be presented as an alliance consisting of six, seven, or eight nations. The rules governing the way member villages were tallied are somewhat unclear. If the Confederacy represented various villages and nations, it was because their numbers fluctuated, and the way in which they were counted changed over the course of time. We do know, however, that each member nation of the Confederacy corresponded to a specific village. In other words, village and nation were interchangeable. At the core of the political organization of the domiciled people was the council, and the fire was the symbol, or basic unit, of that council. But the fire did not necessarily refer to the village, because a fire could represent more than one village, and a village, more than one fire. However, the fire was always ethnic, in other words, the Iroquois and Algonquin never shared the same council. Within a single language family, each nation had its own village council. Generally speaking, seven councils gathered around a central great fire, i.e., the grand council of all the allied villages, which is why the political organization of seven nations came to be referred to as the Confederacy of Seven Fires.

The manner in which the alliance members and villages were calculated is problematic. Depending on the period, the domiciled Abenaki counted for one, two, and sometimes three fires, since they occupied three villages, including the one at Mississquoi Bay. When the Abenaki village councils reached a consensus on a particular problem that was of interest to them all, they could speak with a single voice. For instance, on October 26, 1829, in Trois-Rivières, at a congress between the domiciled Abenaki, Algonquin, and Huron, and in the presence of the superintendent of Indian Affairs, the chief of the Abenaki of Saint-François spoke on behalf of all the domiciled Abenaki, that is, those of both Saint-François and Bécancour.[30] On other occasions, the chiefs of Saint-François represented all the domiciled Abenaki, including the Socoki of the same village and the Abenaki of Mississquoi Bay.[31] If, for example, in 1829, it was referred to as the "Six Nations Council" of Kahnawake, it was because the problem in question primarily concerned six member nations of the Confederacy of Seven Fires.[32] Oswegatchie also posed a problem. Founded in 1759, the village was gradually dismantled in the 1760s, and its inhabitants displaced to the village of Saint-Régis.[33] As for the village of Lake of Two Mountains, where three distinct Indigenous communities resided, they could be counted as one, two, or even three fires since there were Iroquois, Algonquin, and Nipissing living there.[34] On a number of occasions the village's ambassadors spoke on behalf of their respective nations, while on others, they spoke in the name of the lake's three nations.[35] With regard to the village of Pointe-du-Lac, certain documents attest to the presence of several domiciled nations: Algonquin, as well as Nipissing, Têtes-de-Boule (Attikamekw), and Montagnais.[36] The Algonquin of Pointe-du-Lac, in some instances, spoke on behalf of the Têtes-de-Boule of Rivière Saint-Maurice whom, in the 19th century, they had the mandate to represent before the colonial government.[37] The Algonquin of Pointe-du-Lac were not always distinguished from the Algonquin of Lake of Two Mountains,[38] in the same way the Iroquois of Saint-Régis were not systematically differentiated from the Iroquois of Sault-Saint-Louis[39] and from the other Iroquois of the village of Saint-Régis, which was split in two in 1815 with the creation of the border between Canada and the United States.[40]

There is no doubt that some Indigenous communities in Quebec were not part of the Seven Nations of Canada. These included nomadic groups or nations that were members of other political organizations: the Mi'kmaq of Gaspésie, the Maliseet of Témiscouata, the Montagnais of Saguenay–Lac-Saint-Jean and the Lower St. Lawrence, the Cree of James Bay and Hudson Bay, the Naskapi of Northeastern Quebec, and the Inuit of Nunavik. Although they were represented a number of times in Kahnawake at the grand diplomatic gatherings of the Seven Fires,[41] the Mi'kmaq of Rivière Restigouche and the Maliseet of Île-Verte were not part of the Seven Nations.[42] As for the Attimatekw (Têtes-de-Boule) and Montagnais, it is difficult to ascertain their membership, as it boils down, once again, to the way the Confederacy members were calculated. These peoples had diplomatic relations with the member nations of the Seven Fires Confederacy, by way of its Grand Council in Kahnawake. The Attimatekw were not directly represented at the Grand Council, meaning they did not constitute a fire. However, the Algonquin of Pointe-du-Lac were, and they spoke on behalf of the Attimatekw, as there were frequently Attimatekw living at Pointe-du-Lac alongside the Algonquin.[43] Unlike the Montagnais, the Attimatekw, like the other members of the Confederacy, had military obligations.[44] Given the cultural proximity between the Algonquin and Attimatekw, it is possible that the two names actually referred to the occupation by the same group of two, adjacent geographic areas. Nevertheless, it is impossible to state with certainty whether they were members of the Seven Fires because, as we will see, they, like all the other Indigenous Peoples of North America who were allied with the British after 1760, were able to go through the Grand Council of the Seven Fires before addressing the representatives of the King of England.

   Insofar as population size is generally an important variable in the history of the population in question, it is worth putting the population of the Seven Fires into perspective. The demographic fate of the peoples in the Confederacy reflected that of the Indigenous Peoples in general, which is to say, it was in decline. Although the data we consulted are incomplete, partial, and not always reliable, one general trend emerged: the domiciled Indigenous population grew, likely primarily due to immigration, peaking at around 4,000 between 1737 and 1755. After that, it declined, remaining stable at about 3,600 from 1820 to 1858.[45] What is remarkable is the decline in relation to the colonial population: In the late 17th century, the Iroquois population of the two domiciled villages of Kahnawake and La Montagne was roughly equivalent to that of Montreal, with approximately 1,500 inhabitants.[46] The 600 Abenaki living in the village near the Chaudière Falls in 1689 exceeded the total number of French immigrants who arrived in Quebec City between 1680 and 1689,[47] at a time when the city had a population of around 1,200. In 1763, British civil servants compiled a list of warriors that, when extrapolated to the total population, suggests there were approximately 5,000 of them, which represented about 8% of the colonial population of Canada at the time.[48] One century later, the number of domiciled people had shrunk by 28 percent to 3,600, however their weight in relation to the population of Quebec (1.1 million) had dropped 25-fold.

The obvious conclusion is that the colonial population doubled with each generation, while the Indigenous population continued to decline. But why was that so? The weaker immunity of Indigenous populations against European diseases was likely one contributing factor, however migration was certainly the determining factor. Migration was caused in large part by farmland being taken over by colonists and, in the 19th century, by famines stemming from the loss of hunting grounds caused by logging and the expansion of the colonial territory.[49] War was a third factor explaining the decline in population, given the strategic importance of Indigenous warriors in the colonial conflicts, however it was a factor only in the period prior to 1815. In short, in the 18th century, domiciled Indigenous people made up less than 10 percent of the population. However, their military and economic value was greater, particularly since they had a network of alliances both in the Maritimes and around the Great

Lakes. But by 1860, the domiciled people no longer carried any demographic, economic, or military weight.[50]

An Alliance of Ethnic and Linguistic Diversity

The Seven Fires Confederacy consisted of two linguistic communities: Iroquoian and Algonquian. Generally speaking, in the villages, each community kept its own language.[51] Communication was obviously not a problem between groups belonging to the same language family, such as the Nipissing and Algonquin of Lake of Two Mountains, who shared a virtually identical language.[52] In Kahnawake, where several Iroquoian groups lived among the Mohawk majority, the Mohawk language was used by all the members of the community.[53]

Within the Confederacy, interpreters played a key role in discussions not only between the member nations but also between the other Indigenous nations and representatives of the colonial power. Interpreters were tasked with translating their words, in principle without altering their meaning. These language professionals would swear a solemn public oath to faithfully interpret the interlocutors' speeches. An archival document from September 1, 1829, describes the process surrounding a council attended by a justice of the peace from Montreal and a number of Iroquois delegates from Lake of Two Mountains. It explains how the Iroquois gave their speech "through the medium" of their interpreter François Duain, who had previously sworn on the Gospels to interpret "accurately and honestly" the entire substance of their words and meaning.[54] The choice of these interpreters fell to those persons who had personal contacts with the groups who designated them. The interpreters would therefore accompany the diplomatic delegations, as they had a fundamental role to play in the operations of the Confederacy.

A note dated March 28, 1762, in the *Journal of Indian Affairs* states that Jean-Baptiste alias Wadongemit is the "designated" interpreter for certain domiciled Abenaki and that he shall translate their speeches and act as intermediary in discussions between the superintendent and the delegation.[55]

The Indigenous parties selected their own interpreters. On July 9, 1764, in Niagara, the Odawa ambassadors requested that the superintendent consider an individual they had chosen to interpret their discussions since he spoke English and Odawa.[56] In the summer of 1770, at a conference in the presence of the superintendent of Indian Affairs, the domiciled Abenaki petitioned Sir William Johnson to have a man named John-Jacob Hertell serve as their interpreter in discussions with the British and the domiciled Iroquois. Hertell was a multilingual interpreter who understood and spoke the language of all the negotiating parties.[57] In February 1786, a group of ambassadors from the Odawa of Mackinac (Michilimackinac) travelled to the Iroquois village of Kahnawake to meet with the chiefs of the Seven Fires. The delegation was accompanied by its own interpreters, while the Iroquois engaged the services of another individual.[58] These interpreter-translators facilitated discussions since they were multilingual—a prerequisite for their position. On September 19, 1811, the Kahnawake chiefs petitioned Governor George Provost to appoint Bernard Saint-Germain as interpreter since he had the full trust of the chiefs and, what's more, he was fluent in Iroquoian and Nipissing.[59] On October 8, 1828, the chiefs of the councils of Lake of Two Mountains, Saint-Régis, Saint-François, Bécancour, and Lorette submitted a petition to Governor Kempt asking him to appoint, for the benefit of the Iroquois of Lake of Two Mountains, an interpreter who spoke and understood not only the language of the Algonquin and Nipissing.[60] On June 28, 1841, the secretary of Indian Affairs submitted a request to the civil secretary asking the governor to allow Jean-Baptiste Delorimier to accompany them to Albany, at their own cost, to interpret the words of the Iroquois to the Americans.[61] Several years later, on March 11, 1848, Ignace Giasson wrote to Governor Elgin asking the colonial government to appoint him as Department of Indian Affairs interpreter for the Iroquois of Kahnawake. In his request, he explained that he spoke three languages: English, French, and Iroquoian.[62] These interpreters had access to reference documents such as those of the Iroquois of Kahnawake missionary, Joseph Marcoux.[63]

Interpreters were generally paid by the British Crown.[64] A number of names pop up frequently in the archives, including that of Louis Pertuis, who appears to have been at most of the conferences the Iroquois of Canada attended between 1756 and 1765.[65] Another recurring name is Delorimier, with both father and son occupying the position of interpreter at the Department of Indian Affairs.[66] In 1795, the Abenaki petitioned the governor to appoint Basile Bellisle, their interpreter for the previous 40 years.[67]

Some of the domiciled people spoke and understood French or English. On September 8, 1764, Daniel Claus reported to Sir William Johnson that the Iroquois of Akwesasne had complained about some French officers and soldiers with whom they had been conversing in French, a language they understood "perfectly."[68] In a report dated March 12, 1828, Superintendent James Hughes wrote of a visit he made to the Iroquois village of Kahnawake in the presence of a war chief who spoke and understood French very well.[69] In a letter he wrote to British Secretary of State George Murray on May 20, 1830, Governor James Kempt mentions that most of the Indigenous people living in Canada spoke French, and a "considerable" number of them spoke English.[70] Some of these bilingual Indigenous people were chosen as interpreters[71]. On October 7, 1843, the superintendent of Indian Affairs requested that a Nipissing chief who was proficient in French answer the department's questions and subsequently relay them to his colleagues who were not in attendance.[72]

Some domiciled people learned these foreign languages by attending prestigious Dartmouth College in New Hampshire. They included certain Huron from Lorette who studied there in the 18th century. In a letter dated February 27, 1773, Eleazar Wheelock, the school's founder, informed Sir William Johnson that two "most promising" Huron students had decided to make a visit to see the superintendent. In his letter he praises the two students, Basteen and Lewis, noting that they "have an uncommon thirst for Learning, have been diligent in their Studies and have made good Proficiency." He goes on to say "They appear to be rational, Manly Spirited, courteous, graceful and Obliging, far beyond what I have found to be common to Indians."[73] Sir William Johnson replied to Wheelock on March 23, 1773, mentioning among other things the arrival of four other young students from the village of Kahnawake, and noting that the Huron had long maintained a close relationship with the French, and that they were "esteemed an orderly People" and that he was "hopefull that the inclination they Manifest for Study may thro your care be productive of good Consequences."[74]

"All brothers, all of the same colour, and, praise be to God, all of the same religion"

These words are attributed to the King of France who, in the mid-17th century, acknowledged that the domiciled people of the St. Lawrence Valley were all "related," that they were "of the same political colour" as the French, and that they shared with them the same religion.[75] Indeed the members of the Seven Fires Confederacy were Indigenous Peoples who self-identified and referred to themselves as Catholic Amerindians. The term "domiciled" was initially used by the French to differentiate between the Indigenous Peoples from the missions and other peoples, and by the "sedentary" Indigenous Peoples in the St. Lawrence Valley to distinguish themselves from others.[76] Under the British Regime in Canada, the people living in these St. Lawrence River Valley villages continued to be referred to as "domiciled."[77] The same term was also used to designate all of the allied villages, which were known as the "Seven Domiciled Villages."[78]

The Huron, Algonquin, Nipissing, Iroquois, and Abenaki were Catholics who, from the outset, shared, "thanks be to God," the same religious beliefs as the French,[79] since being a member of the Seven Fires or holding a position as a chief of the alliance's councils meant one had to be of the same "prayer" as the other domiciled members.[80] These Indigenous Peoples willingly accepted the Catholic religion. Officer Bougainville's observations in this regard are explicit: On July 9, 1757, he noted in his journal that the Indigenous Peoples of Lake of Two Mountains attended church to pray three times a day.[81] After conquering Canada and observing the religious practices and customs of the domiciled people, the British remarked that the "French Indians" were "prodigiously attached to their Priests & religion" and were fervent Catholics.[82] In a brief submitted to the Department of Indian Affairs in the first half of the 19th century, reference is made to the religious fervour of the Indigenous Peoples of Lake of Two Mountains:

> Their character reveals a stalwart sense of freedom, and they bow only to the religion of their priests, to whom they are strongly attached. They receive religious instruction every Sunday, and their Children receive it every day: the boys from the Missionaries and the girls from the nuns who reside there for that purpose. Evening and morning there is a public prayer where the "*Sauvages*" [Algonquin, Nipissing, Iroquois] sing psalms, hymns, etc. in their own language.[83]

The Seven Nations of Canada were Catholic communities, and there are multiple references in the literature to the privilege of being—and remaining—Catholic, of being able to freely practice their religious devotions, and of enjoying the guidance and assistance of Roman Catholic missionaries in this regard. Documents dating from both the French and British regimes in Canada contain numerous mentions of the Catholic nature of the nations. This was in fact one of the conditions of the alliance between the Confederacy and the British Crown, and one of the clauses of the neutrality and non-aggression treaty signed in Oswegatchie in August 1760 between the Seven Nations of Canada, on one side, and Sir William Johnson and Jeffery Amherst on the other. The domiciled people were Catholic Amerindians, and were allied to the British as such. It is worth recalling that at that time they were up against British Protestants for whom papists were their sworn enemies. That is why they insisted on negotiating with the British to obtain guarantees of the free exercise of their religion. Under Article 40 of the Capitulation of Montreal of September 8, 1760, they received additional guarantees similar to those agreed upon with the Oswegatchie agreement: that the Indigenous Peoples could maintain their freedom of religion, which by implication meant their Catholic religion, as the article goes on to pledge that they could keep their missionaries.[84] Over the course of history, the members of the Seven Nations of Canada often referred to the Oswegatchie treaty and to Article 40 to promote and protect their religious practices and customs.[85]

In the eyes of all of the domiciled nations belonging to the Seven Fires, the presence of missionaries was essential, as emphasized by Osseragoa, a grand chief of Kahnawake, to Lieutenant-colonel John Campbell, the superintendent of Indian Affairs, at a meeting in Montreal on October 20, 1779. As part of their "support for the Seven Villages," the British pledged to provide the domiciled people with the missionaries required to ensure they were able to conduct their devotions properly. The domiciled Indigenous people saw this as a logical aspect of the alliance: as their adoptive father, the King of England should allow the domiciled people to remain true Catholics. The following excerpt makes reference to the 1760 agreements between the Confederacy and the Crown:

> You see in this Necklace the Person of the King who holds our Hand, who consequently adopted us as his Children. At the time he presented it to us, we adopted it, but on the Condition that we would be given permission to always follow the Religion in which we were born (such were our Agreements in the past). Today, we are virtually all deprived of Missionaries, and we beg you, who we consider the Tree bearing the Seven Branches, to act in our favour, as it is you who holds up the Seven Villages.[86]

The presence of missionaries was considered fundamental, not only to uphold good moral standards, but also to maintain political ties. Without missionaries by their side any longer, the domiciled people felt lost, noting: "what concerns us, and we are extremely sensitive in this regard, is that our Young People become debauched and blinded, and that they stray from the Tree."[87] The "Tree" symbolized peace and loyalty towards the political alliance with the British, and to avoid such debauchery, i.e., any failure to respect the alliance, the domiciled people insisted they be able to keep their missionaries, who would encourage them to stay "on the right path." In so doing, they sought to convince a Protestant governor that papist missionaries had a good influence on their youth and on the rest of the community. However, once the British took control of the country, there were fewer and fewer members of the Catholic clergy available to fill this position: "We don't expect our request to be met promptly, given the very few missionaries in this country."[88]

Indeed, after 1760, the British tolerated the Jesuits only for a short time, prohibiting any new recruitment. Yet, the Jesuits were responsible for conducting religious services for the Huron of Lorette, the Abenaki of Saint-François and Bécancour, as well as the Iroquois of Sault-Saint-Louis and Saint-Régis. The disappearance of the priests constituted a further risk for these communities, given the ambiguity surrounding the titles of the so-called seigneurial lands concerning the Jesuits. The members of the Confederacy of the Seven Fires therefore felt that it was their British ally's duty to agree to their request. To stress the imperative nature of their petition, the Seven Nations asked that it be submitted to King George III of England: "which is why we wish you to Deliver the Subject of our Requests together with our Belts to our Grandfather of England."[89] Although the king was leader of the Anglican Church, the domiciled people believed that their father had a duty to guarantee the conditions of their religious practice. In other words, it was the Christian Indigenous Peoples who, as per the treaties and the alliance, asked to remain Catholics and to have missionaries by their side.

As guarantors of the agreements with the domiciled people, the British would provide financial support for the members of the clergy in the Indigenous villages in Canada. In a letter he wrote to the Minister of Colonial Affairs in London dated August 14, 1770, Sir William Johnson described the complaints of the Mohawk of the Iroquois League of Six Nations regarding the shortage of Anglican missionaries in their villages. These Mohawk lamented the fact that their brothers in Canada, who were their former shared enemies, were provided a regular supply of missionaries at the expense of the government.[90] Whenever any dispute or problem arose between the missionaries and the domiciled people, the latter could also address their concerns to another intermediary, the Bishop of Quebec, leader of the Roman Catholic Church in Canada.[91]

The British, who were convinced of the political value of religion in the alliance with the domiciled Indigenous Peoples of Canada, used it as a means to serve their own political ends. In a brief dated October 1, 1771, that he submitted to the authorities in London, the military governor noted that the Indigenous Peoples in Canada were highly attached to the religion taught them by the French. Thomas Gage concluded that the most important thing was that the Indigenous-Peoples of Canada be Christians, and that it was of little matter that they were Papist Catholics. In his capacity as governor and representative of a Protestant Crown, he stressed that, in this instance, papism did not pose a problem.[92] In a letter dated May 24, 1761, written by Daniel Claus, the deputy agent in the British Indian Department wrote that there is no better way than converting the Indigenous Peoples to manipulate them, noting "if they once take to it they are zealous and can be brought to any thing."[93] On June 11, 1761, Sir William Johnson replied that, while he, too, believed that converted Indigenous people were easier to manipulate than pagans, he nevertheless feared Catholicism because, at the end of the day, the actions of the papists could alter the pro-British sentiments of the domiciled people.[94] Unlike Gage, Johnson saw Catholicism as a threat to the interests of the Crown.

The domiciled Indigenous people were devout Catholics. In a letter dated March 30, 1762, Sir William Johnson wrote in the *Journal of Indian Affairs* at Johnson Hall, New York, that a number of Abenaki had come from Canada to complain that there was no "divine service" available in their village since they no longer had any missionaries available to provide it. They stressed the fact that, prior to the destruction of their village by Major Robert Rogers in 1759, two men of the Church had occupied the position and that they had practised their devotions three times a day.[95] They insisted that their "spirit" would be "appeased" only once their request was accepted.[96] In a study on the Christian Iroquois, Denys Delâge emphasizes the importance and veracity of conversion: "by encouraging followers to completely forsake alcohol, by bringing new meaning to their lives through a commitment to religion, and by recreating solidarity and obligations, Catholicism played a role similar to that of contemporary fundamentalist sects in fractured settings, i.e., it gave a new sense of meaning to life."[97]

The Catholic religion served as a beacon for the actions of the Seven Nations. On a political level, Christianity was a means to ensure "proper conduct" within the alliance. On August 21, 1755, a number of Mohawk representatives from the Iroquois League of Six Nations relayed the response of the Iroquois of Canada to Sir William Johnson's proposal of neutrality in the war between France and England. The Iroquois reportedly replied that the French priests, "by throwing Water upon our Heads, subject us to the Will of the Governor of Canada."[98] The domiciled people shared the same religious instruction as the French, and therefore the same expectations. Their religious convictions were firm, and similar to those of the French: like them, they believed in Heaven and in the resurrection. When it came to politics, their identical religious relations helped maintain the allies in a similar state of mind and encouraged them to fight for the same cause. In matters of religion, they were brothers.[99] Sir William Johnson replied to the Seven Nations ambassadors in a letter dated May 6, 1762, stating that a Christianized society like that of the domiciled people could not allow any deviation from the alliance.[100] Since their religious and political alliances were connected, the former was expected to inspire the latter. And on August 30, 1765, in his correspondence with Sir William, Daniel Claus narrates a discussion with the "Cognawageys" in which he describes how the chiefs declared they "had the advantage of being taught the *Christian Religion*, which wou'd banish the Devil from among them..."[101]

On June 15, 1775, representatives of the Stockbridge Abenaki in New England appeared before the Continental Congress to present the conclusions of their meeting with the Confederacy of Seven Fires in Kahnawake. The chiefs had reportedly insisted on the fact that, since the arrival of the white man, Stockbridge and Iroquois had unanimously shared the same religious convictions, i.e., the belief in the same Christian God, and since two Christian nations could not aggress one another, they accepted the neutrality proposal presented by the Stockbridge on behalf of the Americans in the conflict with the King of England.[102] On May 23, 1796, during talks with the American agents tasked with negotiating the land claims of the Seven Nations of Canada in the State of New York, the ambassadors of the domiciled Iroquois offered the following advice on how to conduct a dialogue between Christianized groups: justice must be obtained not by force, but through a diplomatic approach based on Christian values. Through this form of interaction alone could the Christian people of the Seven Fires hope to settle their disputes with their fellow Christians from New York.[103]

The Same Dish, Spoon, and Bowl

The Seven Nations were a Roman Catholic people, and they were bound, through their alliance, to a peaceful, communal life. Nicolas Vincent Tsaouenhohoui, Grand Chief of the Huron of Lorette, described in 1824 what it meant for his people to "live together in peace": "which is to say they must eat with the same '*micoine*' (wooden spoon) from the same dish; they must hunt together on the same lands, to avoid any arguments amongst themselves." The Grand Chief also explained that one of the reasons that led to this sharing agreement was the fact that, in earlier times, his people would kill any "foreigner who ventured out to hunt on their lands."[104] The agreement, it was hoped, would bring an end to that bloody conflict.

According to the tradition of the Iroquois of Saint-Régis, before the white man arrived in the Americas, the Indigenous nations did not wage war over territory that was used and shared by all Indigenous communities. The domiciled Iroquois added that it was only after contact between the Indigenous peoples and Europeans that disputes arose, explaining that "it should not then appear so very strange that when two kings will often expose the lives of a great many white Men, for the sake of a very small piece of ground that two red Brothers should contend for a Beaver Skin."[105]

The domiciled Iroquois of Sault-Saint-Louis also pointed out to Superintendent John Campbell in 1791 that it was "the King of France" who initiated the plan to share and pool together the hunting grounds:

> So the king of France summoned to council all the Indians of the continent: Kanawageronon, Huron, Algonkin, Nipissing. He brought a large dish in which there was a piece of meat, broth, a wooden spoon, a knife, and he said to us:
> "My children! You are all brothers, all the same colour, and, thanks be to God, all of the same religion. Until this day you have made war for your hunting grounds; what I desire of you, today, is that you make peace for all time. Here is a dish with meat, broth, a wooden spoon, and a knife with which you shall take care not to harm one another. Take it without fighting over it. He who has greater appetite shall eat more, without the other objecting."[106]

The domiciled Iroquois explained the king's metaphorical language, saying, "My Father! This parable signified our hunting grounds being amalgamated by the King of France."[107] The king then set down a dish that symbolized the sharing of land in the village of the Iroquois of Sault-Saint-Louis so that they could preserve it. This land agreement was concluded after the Christian Iroquois were incorporated into the alliance, apparently encouraged to join by the French colonial authorities. Was this political organization then a one-off, circumstantial, and reactive treaty initiated by the governors of New France? It appears so. Following the lead of one of the governors of the colony, the French authorities called an important political council to which all of the domiciled people in the St. Lawrence Valley were summoned, specifically the Iroquois, Huron, Algonquin, and Nipissing. The French and Indigenous attendees agreed to a proposal to pool together the hunting grounds and share the resources found on them. On June 4, 1760, four Mississauga chiefs travelled to Fort Lévis to hold a council with the Iroquois of La Présentation. The fourth speech pronounced by the Mississauga orator was addressed to these domiciled Iroquois, and in it he proposed that the hunting grounds on an island in the St. Lawrence River opposite the Iroquois village be shared. The speaker for the domiciled Iroquois, charmed by the Mississauga spokesman's metaphorical language, replied to his speech by referring to the former alliance forged between the Seven Fires and a governor of New France, and to the resulting agreement regarding the sharing of hunting grounds: "I am delighted that you have made mention of the expression of having a single dish and sharing the same spoon. That reminds me of the words of our forebears. Onontio used this same expression to appeal to the members of all the nations to see one another as brothers and as his children."[108]

Jean-Baptiste Delorimier, an interpreter for the Iroquois, transcribed on August 13, 1796, the speeches of the leaders of the Seven Nations who addressed Governor Robert Prescott at a council in Kahnawake in the presence of representatives of the Odawa of Michilimackinac, Mi'kmaq, and Maliseet. The speaker reminded the audience that the King of France had agreed to and encouraged the alliance between Indigenous peoples and the sharing of hunting grounds.[109] The domiciled Iroquois stressed to General Prescott that the Indigenous people were the original inhabitants of the "country," that they were the first to occupy it, and that it was in this "country" that their ancestors, with a view to preserving the peace, had agreed to eat from the same dish and the same plate, and share the same utensils. In their view, the parable meant that the entire "country" would be free for all.[110] This was a metaphor that had been long familiar to the British. On January 10, 1797, Jean-Baptiste Destimauville, an agent at Indian Affairs, recalled the words of Sir William Johnson about the lands of the domiciled people: Around 1763, as part of the application of the terms of the Royal Proclamation of October 7, 1763, regarding First Nations and British lands, he is said to have used the same parables as the domiciled people in reference to the hunting grounds, and to have affirmed to their ancestors that the domiciled people would be treated the same way as in the days of their French father, which is to say that "far from reducing their dish, we would increase it."[111]

The Indigenous Peoples frequently referred to the "dish" as being symbolic of this land agreement. The "dish" is often associated, in the words of the domiciled people, with the metaphors of the shared "pot" and "dish" which, likewise, symbolize the joining together of hunting grounds and the sharing of the resources found there. On October 4, 1767, at a council in the village of Kanehsatake, the Iroquois Chief Assarigoa of Kahnawake referred to the nature and terms of the alliance of the domiciled people. According to tradition, this sharing dated back to the forefathers of the Seven Nations and was established so as to prevent any discord between the member nations of the alliance with regard to the use of hunting grounds. It appears the founding ancestors clearly set out the ground rules for the Seven Fires regarding the sharing of the grounds: each nation could use the woods for hunting in order to feed themselves. Each must also be inspired by the same sense of hospitality and sharing they

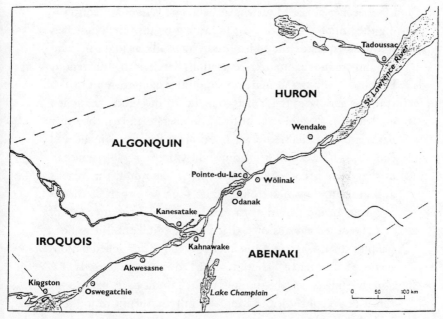

Map 1. Seven Fires Hunting Grounds

felt during a feast among friends. One domiciled nation could
not refuse access to hunting grounds by another nation that was
larger and whose "appetite" was greater. No nation could claim
exclusive ownership of the grounds. Sharing was a matter of eth-
ics. Assarigoa recalled the advice of the forefathers of the Seven
Fires to "use the Wood with the same freedom as they would a
Kettle with Victuals when invited to a feast and with one Spoon
and one Knife to eat all together sociably & without begrudging
those that had a better appetite & eat more than others."[112]

It is likely that this sharing of lands between members of the
Confederacy dates back to the Great Peace of Montreal signed
in 1701, or at the latest, to the first 20 years of the 18th century.
On August 30, 1765, Daniel Claus reported to Sir William the
response of the Iroquois of Kahnawake with regard to the words
of the Iroquois of the League of Six Nations, and specifically to

the speeches of the Mohawk, Oneida, and Onondaga concerning the limits of each of their hunting grounds. The domiciled Iroquois requested the assistance of Sir William Johnson, who was duly mandated to oversee relations between the Indigenous Peoples. They beseeched the superintendent to remind the Iroquois nations of the "old agreement" made before the French governor, in the presence of five Confederate and all the other nations in Canada, that "when a general Peace was made and concluded between these Nations, the Governor told them that, as they were become one body, and of one mind, the Woods and Hunting Grounds could be no otherwise than common, and free to one nation as to another..."[113] Did the mention of "all the other nations of Canada" refer to all the Indigenous peoples allied with the French, or only to the domiciled nations of the St. Lawrence Valley? It's hard to know for sure. If that agreement between the Iroquois of the League dates back to the Great Peace concluded in Montreal in 1701, then it would have included all the protagonists in attendance, i.e., the delegates from the Great Lakes, the Maritimes, and the domiciled nations of the St. Lawrence Valley. We do know, however, that the Great Peace of Montreal granted the Iroquois of the League access to the hunting grounds of the Indigenous allies of the governor of New France, specifically those to the north and west of Lake Ontario and Lake Erie.[114]

In a letter dated 1798 from the chiefs of the Iroquois of Sault-Saint-Louis to those of the Mohawk of the League of Iroquois Six Nations of Ontario, the chiefs refer to an earlier sharing of hunting grounds and to the conclusion of an ancestral peace:

> You know, Brothers, that our forefathers, according to those we call 'birds of ill omen,' claimed that there were many on both sides who stayed on our lands. It was in those days that our forebears perceived the evil they were committing and attempted to reconcile them. It was then that they made our paths free and shared our lands or hunting grounds and, in our expression, they made the deep hole that leads to Rivière Rapide and threw into the

current all that aversion they all had so it would never reappear. It is down that path of peace that our grandfathers forged for us that we must go, and serve ourselves from that dish of friendship that our ancestors insisted we eat from together, without harming one another.[115]

Yet, in a speech the Sault chiefs gave on April 6, 1798, to Superintendent Sir John Johnson, the domiciled Iroquois refuted all the territorial claims of the Iroquois of the Six Nations of Ontario. They accused them of fomenting dissent and reigniting "old divisions" that had once separated their forefathers but that had since eased, after "much spilling of blood," when they reached a permanent agreement that divided—according to the Sault Iroquois—our "Hunting Grounds to the satisfaction of the interested Nations."[116]

The sustenance of the Indigenous Peoples of Canada was dependent on two specific areas—the fields and the woods. The lands on which the villages stood were essentially a matter for the village councils and did not concern the Confederacy of the Seven Fires. The fields within the village were the responsibility of that particular village council. The lands of the Seven Fires, therefore, were not limited to the specific areas of the domiciled villages; rather they included all the hunting grounds. Essentially, each person was free to hunt, fish, or trap on any these lands. Without going into specific detail, we will simply mention that these grounds were located, for the most part, in the states of Vermont and New York, and in the provinces of Ontario and Quebec, that is, in the St. Lawrence River Valley, north of the river, between Kingston and Tadoussac, all the way up to the Hudson Bay drainage basin, and in the regions of the Eastern Townships, the Ottawa River Valley, and the Laurentians,[117] a vast territory over which possession was guaranteed, at least for certain areas, by either the French or the British. In some cases, guarantees were granted to a nation, and in others, to the Confederacy. These hunting grounds, while huge, were sparsely populated by the members of the Confederacy, and as such, we cannot conclude that the Confederacy formed a political superstructure governing specific populations and territories, as a number of ambiguities arose over the course of the history of the Seven Fires with regard to the claims of the different parties over these lands.

The rules established under the French Regime and that applied to the member nations regarding the use and sharing of the lands and their natural resources were very difficult to enforce. In fact, this policy of pooling and sharing of lands never really worked and never led to making the Seven Fires a harmonious alliance. While the agreement was originally drawn up to prevent discord between the Indigenous nations, in reality the policy never sat well with the members of the alliance. Throughout the history of the Seven Fires, several disputes arose surrounding the sharing of these grounds and the claims of some groups over the grounds of others. In such disputes over land between members of the Confederacy, the Grand Council of the Seven Nations, as the central authority, never managed to create a strong and lasting consensus among its members. In 1791, in reaction to intertribal conflicts surrounding access to the hunting grounds of the domiciled Iroquois, Algonquin, and Nipissing, the domiciled Iroquois affirmed that the Iroquois could, with pleasure, give the Algonquin and Nipissing "fire and dish," and that they could "warm and feed themselves, drink the broth in peace, without snatching it from our hands, without bringing their complaint to you daily that we are taking meat from the same dish."[118] They added that, from that time on, the domiciled Iroquois of Sault would content themselves with the "small parcel of land" that their father, the governor, had given them to ensure the subsistence of their wives and children which "until this time had only served the good of the seven villages, and most often, for the good and the service of the king."[119] The speech from the Iroquois contained an ultimatum:

> …but also that our brothers shall not believe they can come to our
> village to conduct their business, eat our supplies and more; then
> go and kill the animals while we have not the freedom to set foot

there. No, my Father! No, we are not their cooks, and even less so, their slaves! It is already enough that they are our elders.[120]

The Iroquois of the Grand Council of the Seven Fires decided to defer to the decision of the governor and his representative in charge of Indian Affairs: "Your decision shall be our wish," they said, "so long as the great fire and the dish do not go one without the other."[121] The fact they turned to the colonial authorities to settle their dispute points to the failure of the inter-ethnic Indigenous institution and the rules put in place to preserve it. On July 14, 1791, the Algonquin and Nipissing of Lake of Two Mountains declared to the superintendent that they wanted nothing to do with the lands that did not belong to them. When they received an invitation from the Iroquois of Sault-Saint-Louis to accompany them to the United States in order to claim lands around Lake Champlain, the domiciled Algonquin and Nipissing chose to ignore it, since "we did not want to have any involvement in lands that have never been ours."[122]

In 1829, the Huron of Lorette advised the agents at Indian Affairs of the boundaries of the territorial agreement, at least insofar as the domiciled Huron and Algonquin were concerned:

We, the Huron of Lorette, have always been friends with our brothers the Algonquin of Trois-Rivières and still are today. [...] We, or our forefathers on our behalf, have maintained with the Algonquin that we shall always hunt together, so long as no difficulties should arise, however should such case unfortunately arise, then our hunting rights shall be limited [the chief goes on to define the geographical limits of the agreement].[123]

On August 25, 1827, at a conference in Montreal in the presence of Algonquin and Nipissing from Lake of Two Mountains, these two domiciled peoples warned the representative from Indian Affairs that their nations sought only to maintain peace and good relations with their brothers (the other domiciled Indigenous Peoples, and in particular, the Iroquois), but that the chiefs could not guarantee the reaction of their young people if they should "detect" Iroquois or other domiciled peoples on their hunting grounds.[124] As for the Iroquois of the Lake, they defended their position at a Grand Council of the Seven Nations in the village of Kahnawake on October 5, 1827: "We live in the same Village as the Algonquin and the Nipissing, and we are Jealous that they claim to be Superior to us, and claim all the Hunting Grounds for their sole use." To bring an end to this discord and have their own needs met, they petitioned the British government for land for planting.[125] The superintendent, in response to the speeches of the domiciled leaders and the many petitions and requests presented regarding hunting grounds, gave this reply on behalf of the governor to the members gathered at the Grand Council: "Let not the Iroquois interfere with the Hunting Grounds of the Algonquins and Nepissingues nor must the Algonquins kill Bears or Beavers on the Grounds of the Iroquois or Abenaquois, but each hunt on the grounds allotted to his Tribe."

The governor intervened again in 1830, urging the domiciled nations to put an end to the many interminable disputes among themselves about the use of their hunting grounds, suggesting that each group hunt on their own grounds without encroaching on that of the others,[127] which was problematic for the Iroquois of the Lake, who had no hunting grounds. They explained that "if we go to hunt on the lands of our brothers at Sault and St Régis, we will not be welcomed, and if we hunt on the lands of our brothers the Algonquin, we shall be equally repelled."[128]

Beginning in the early 1830s, colonial expansion considerably shrunk the hunting grounds of the Indigenous Peoples. Further complicating matters, some communities like the Abenaki and the Iroquois had lost more than others, prompting their men to go and hunt on the grounds of their allies, and thereby exerting too much pressure on the hunting grounds. The members of the Confederacy discussed the matter without arriving at a solution. The Algonquin and Nipissing wanted to refuse the Abenaki access to the hunting grounds north of the St. Lawrence and refuse the Iroquois access to those along the Ottawa and Mattawa rivers.[129] The Abenaki contested the Algonquin and Nipissing claims of having exclusive rights to occupy the land.[130] As a result, the Grand Council of Kahnawake, unable to reach a consensus,[131] submitted the problem to the governor who, in his role as father in the alliance, abolished the policy of shared hunting grounds.[132]

CHAPTER TWO

Rules, Operations, and Political Relations

The literature makes no mention of a written constitution governing the Confederacy of the Seven Fires. However, based on the actions that were taken, we are able to identify the rules followed by the members of the alliance and establish how the Confederacy operated. We will see the positions that certain member-villages occupied, the kinds of relationships that were forged between the members, and the inner workings of the Seven Fires in their diplomatic efforts with other Indigenous organizations. The decrypting of the metaphorical terms of familial diplomacy is a significant element of those relations.

The Great Fire of Gana8age

The members of the Confederacy were grouped around a central authority, the Great Fire of the Iroquois of Kahnawake, which is to say that this village played the role of grand council of the member nations. The chiefs of the Council of the Iroquois sat on this council and were also, as we shall see, chiefs of the Seven Nations. It was also in the village of these domiciled Iroquois that the other Indigenous chiefs of the Confederacy's villages would gather for discussions. Representatives of the colonial government and other Indigenous political organizations would also come to meet there. The Grand Council was a special place—a place for debate and diplomacy.

The Iroquois chiefs of Kahnawake held diplomatic initiative, a privilege resulting from an agreement which the other members of the Confederacy had signed on to. As such, they were considered the representatives of the Seven Nations. In other words, when reference is made to the spokespersons for the Great Fire of Kahnawake, it was usually to the domiciled Iroquois of Kahnawake, the official representatives of the Seven Nations. In the proceedings of a conference held at Johnson Hall in March 1768, the secretary of the Department of Indian Affairs tasked with transcribing the speeches took pains to note that the "Caugnawagas spoke on behalf of the Seven Nations of Canada."[1] This was an observation that stemmed also from the desire of the Indigenous people to be properly identified when addressing an assembly. For example, in the transcription of a conference held on September 18, 1798, at Credit River attended by Iroquois chiefs from the League of Six Nations of Grand River and those of the Mississauga of Lake Simcoe, the Mississauga speaker specifically mentioned to the assembly that his speech was aimed at the "Caughnawaga," meaning the Indigenous Peoples of Lower Canada.[2]

The village of the Iroquois of Kahnawake was the largest of the domiciled Indigenous villages and was considered the "seat of all the villages of Canada;"[3] the "Grand Fire of all the domiciled Indigenous nations."[4] In a letter addressed to Sir William Johnson dated October 30, 1761, Pierre Roubaud, a missionary with the domiciled Abenaki, described to the superintendent the diplomatic events that took place around the Great Fire of the Seven Nations. He wrote that the Abenaki chiefs of Saint-François had spent the summer in Kahnawake where, in the presence of the Iroquois of the village, they held several councils with a view to discussing the diplomatic initiatives of the peoples of Ohio, who had proposed an alliance with them. These proposals were passed on at the Grand Council of the Seven Nations by "some Ottawas & even by the Cherokees from Carolina."[5]

As the keepers of the alliance's great fire, the Iroquois of Kahnawake were tasked with speaking on behalf of the other members of the Confederacy. The reply of an Iroquois spokesman from the League of Six Nations to the speeches of the Iroquois of Kahnawake is significant in this regard. At a gathering in Montreal in the summer of 1778, the League's spokesman mentioned to his brothers from "Cachnawaga" that they were the ones who should answer on behalf of the other domiciled nations since theirs was the "main Village of Canada."[6] As keepers of the "Great Fire of the Seven Villages," the domiciled Iroquois were mandated to speak for and represent the other members of the Confederacy. Military officer Jean-Baptiste Destimauville reminded the Baron of Rottenburg of that fact in a letter dated February 26, 1811, that he sent from the village of Lorette, describing how the Huron were demanding formal recognition from the British government for their military support during the revolution of the American colonies.[7]

On October 1, 1816, Officer Louis de Salaberry, who was in charge of Indian Affairs in the Quebec City area, presented to Sir John Sherbrooke a report of an assembly held in Beauport in the presence of "Representatives of the Seven Nations, sent on behalf of said Nations by the Great Fire of Sault S[t] Louis." In it, de Salaberry describes this "Great Fire" as the "Metropolis" of the Seven Nations, and explains that the main purpose of the representatives of the Seven Fires was to submit to the governor the fact that the crops of the Iroquois of Kahnawake and Akwesasne had been destroyed by the cold and that they were petitioning the colonial authorities for assistance in accordance with the promises made by the British during the War of 1812-1814 with the United States.[8]

When the British conquered Canada in 1760, they "ratified" the King of France's actions by creating and "establishing the Great Council Fire" in the village of the Iroquois of Sault. The Iroquois chiefs of Kahnawake reminded the British officials of that fact on October 7, 1791, at a Grand Council in the presence of Superintendent Campbell: "the king of France placed the Great Fire in the village known as Gan8age."[9] By accepting the statement, the British acknowledged the existence of an organized Indigenous world as it existed under the French Regime. After all, if the British were to be successful in their colonialist endeavours, it was important that they understand the nature of the relationship between the French and the Indigenous nations, so as to carry on or modify the French policy. When they captured Quebec and Montreal, the British replaced the French at the heart of a vast network of longstanding alliances. It was therefore in the interest of the victorious power to be aware of the established traditions and practices—a condition on which the success of their policies would hinge. From then on, Kahnawake would find itself at the very centre of the British Empire in Eastern North America and its influence on the Indigenous world. To understand the position that Kahnawake held at that time, we must set aside our contemporary perspective, as it was a whole different time, both in reality and in the minds of the main players.[10]

The British officials therefore acknowledged the central role of the Iroquois of Kahnawake and took much the same approach as the French did when they wished to speak with the domiciled nations. On June 2, 1762, Daniel Claus informed Sir William Johnson that he had extended an invitation to the "Caneghsadageys" of Lake of Two Mountains to attend the meeting at "Caghnawago" which would be held a few days thereafter.[11] Daniel Claus noted to Sir William Johnson on August 25, 1769, that the Iroquois of Akwesasne had invited him to Kahnawake to communicate to him a speech addressed to the superintendent.[12] On July 19, 1781, Lieutenant Colonel Campbell informed Frederick Haldimand that he had summoned all the chiefs and warriors from the villages of the domiciled nations to Kahnawake, to advise them of Governor Haldimand's instructions regarding the war with the American colonies.[13]

A "council house" was erected for this purpose under the British Regime by the colonial government. On August 9, 1824,

Map 2. Geopolitical Organization of the Indigenous World

Sir John Johnson reported to Peregrine Maitland, the colonial administrator, that the talks must be held in Kahnawake when negotiating with the Seven Nations, as this was the custom.[14] And it was at the council house of the Iroquois of Sault-Saint-Louis that discussions concerning the Seven Fires were held.

On February 3, 1837, the members of the Seven Nations of Lower Canada sent a petition to Governor Gosford on behalf of the Iroquois of Kahnawake, Akwesasne, and Kanehsatake, as well as the Algonquin and Nipissing of Kanehsatake: "We, the principal chiefs of the Seven Nations of Lower Canada, are assembled today in the village of Sault St. Louis, in a house atop which we have hoisted the British flag."[15]

On September 1, 1827, the superintendent of Indian Affairs asked his secretary to assemble the department's interpreters in Kahnawake, where the Grand Council of the Fires was usually held.[16] In a letter dated October 27 to his counterpart at Indian Affairs in Toronto, Superintendent Darling noted that the complaints expressed by the Indigenous Peoples of Upper Canada regarding the intrusion of certain domiciled people from Lake of Two Mountains onto the hunting grounds of the Mississauga had been discussed in Kahnawake in the presence of the Indigenous chiefs of Lower Canada and, specifically, Algonquin and Nipissing chiefs from Lake of Two Mountains, Iroquois from Sault-Saint-Louis and Saint-Régis, as well as Abenaki of Saint-François.[17] At that same gathering the superintendent would deliver the governor general's speech on the matter to the members of the Confederacy.[18] In a report on the administration of the Department of Indian Affairs that he dispatched to London on July 24, 1828, Henry C. Darling wrote that that "the grand councils of the fires" were held in the Iroquois village of Kahnawake, adding that the opinion of the chiefs of that village prevailed over that of the other chiefs.[19] A report dated March 31, 1845, on the lands of the Indigenous Peoples of Quebec noted that the village of Caughnawaga was the site of gatherings of domiciled peoples from other villages and that "Caughnawaga" was the "Grand Council Fire of the 7 Nations of Lower Canada."[20]

The Grand Council of the Seven Nations was also the meeting place for Indigenous ambassadors from other political systems, including the Wabanaki from the Maritimes, and the Odawa from the Great Lakes and New York Iroquois. Every friendly and allied delegation was welcomed around the Great Fire. The oral tradition of the Wabanaki of the Maritimes in the 20th century is eloquent in this regard: According to tradition, the Wabanaki ambassadors used to go to Kahnawake when they needed to speak with the members of the Seven Fires. According to Wabanaki traditionalists, the Iroquois village Kahnawake also served as a place for discussions and diplomacy at meetings between members of their confederacy and the Odawa of the Great Lakes.[21] The colonial archives confirm this: On August 25, 1822, Louis de Salaberry informed Governor Dalhousie and Superintendent Johnson that a delegation of Indigenous chiefs from the Maritimes was headed to a general assembly of Indigenous Peoples around the Great Fire of the Iroquois of the St. Lawrence. Salaberry wrote:

> I believe, My Lord, that it is my duty to inform you that several Indian chiefs from New-Brunswic and from eastern parts of this country have been summoned by the Great Fire (the Capital of all the Indian nations of Canada) and recently travelled to Quebec for a general assembly of these nations, which is expected to be held shortly at Sault-Saint-Louis, the Great Fire or Capital.[22]

On August 17, 1844, the secretary of Indian Affairs was advised that a delegation of 15 Passamaquoddy, that is, the spokes-people for the Wabanaki Confederacy, were on their way to the region of Montreal for talks with the different nations of Lower Canada, the Huron of Lorette, the Abenaki of Saint-François, and the Iroquois of Sault-Saint-Louis.[23] And on September 14, 1850, a group of Passamaquoddy travelled again to Kahnawake to take part in a great pacific conference of all the "British Indians."[24] As for the representatives of the Iroquois League of Six Nations, they, too, attended the Great Fire of Kahnawake to speak with the Seven Nations. On October 22, 1793, Jean-Baptiste Delorimier, the interpreter of the domiciled Iroquois, described to Governor Dorchester the events surrounding a diplomatic meeting between the Iroquois of the Seven Fires and the Oneida of the League, who had come to the Grand Council of Sault-Saint-Louis to "renew an alliance with the nations of Lower Canada."[25]

Village Councils versus the Grand Council of the Confederacy

The creation of the Confederacy did not mean that each member community ceased to pursue its own particular interests; rather, each council of the alliance enjoyed political and military autonomy. The village councils managed their own internal politics and oversaw decisions regarding village affairs. Take, for example, the dispute that arose between the British and the Indigenous people about the titles to the seigneurial lands they occupied. When the lands of the missions were in dispute, the Confederacy or Grand Council did not intervene. It was up to the councils of each of the villages involved in the dispute to negotiate with the colonial authorities. The dispute between the Huron of Lorette and the British Crown was significant in this regard as the Huron chiefs never called on the Grand Council of the Seven Nations in their negotiations, any more than did the Iroquois of Sault-Saint-Louis and Saint-Régis, or the Abenaki of Saint-François or Bécancour when their village lands were threatened. On January 21, 1819, the Huron chiefs sent a petition to the governor denouncing the unjust condition of their community as compared to the other domiciled communities. The Huron Council did not address the Seven Nations, but rather each of the nations occupying seigneur-ial land: "Your Humble Petitioners note that the other Indians of this country have not been deprived of their possessions, and that the Iroquois of St Régis and Sault St Louis, and the Abenaki of St François are in peaceful possession of the seigneuries that the King of France allowed them to retain in their country."[26]

The village councils consisted of recognized authorities. They appointed their political and military leaders based on the opinion of the community and with the unanimous consent of the entire village. On August 25, 1767, Daniel Claus attended the election of a new Iroquois chief in Kahnawake who had been selected, in a unanimous decision, to take over the position left vacant upon his predecessor's death. The deputy agent at Indian Affairs subsequently approved the election by means of the "usual ceremony" as per tradition. And so, the old chief Tharough-wandats was replaced by a young warrior called Takanundye, and the medal of the deceased was put about his neck.[27]

The reason Daniel Claus was involved in the ceremony was that, under the British Regime of Canada, the village councils were obliged to seek the approval of the colonial authorities when appointing a leader. This practice appears to be in keeping with the "ancient customs" of the Indigenous Peoples. On July 29, 1768, the Abenaki of Saint-François presented to Superintendent Sir William Johnson two individuals they had chosen to lead them. Several days later, Sir William approved their choice, according to the established custom.[28] On July 26, 1773, the Huron of Lorette recommended to the deputy agent of Indian Affairs in Montreal the choice of "Simonet alias Onhegtiidarrio, who by the unanimous Opinion & Consent of the whole Village was looked upon equal to the Task being a sensible Man & well acquainted with their Affairs."[29] The council of the Huron obtained the approval of the Indian Affairs deputy agent, who noted in his journal on July 28, 1773, that he would respect the village's choice.[30] In fact, the governor or his representatives merely endorsed the election of a leader, but only if the individual in question was the preferred choice of the other chiefs. Daniel Claus again noted in his journal on June 9, 1773, the complaints of the Iroquois chiefs of Kahnawake, who denounced the poor procedure surrounding the naming of a chief and the meddling of Governor Carleton in the election of said chief. The Iroquois declared that the governor had created a precedent by presenting a chief's medal to an Indian—a foreigner, to boot, and that "there was no such thing as appointing a Chief among them without the Concurrence of the other Chiefs of the place he belonged to."[31] On August 28, 1853, the chiefs of Kahnawake sent a letter to the chiefs and warriors of the Abenaki of Saint-François in which they reminded them that "It is to you in your Village and not to another that falls the right to choose your Chiefs."[32]

The Indigenous people didn't have the right to dismiss a leader without discussing the matter with the representatives of the British government who, by the same token, could revoke the individual's duties and responsibilities. The colonial authorities therefore played a role as mediator, as the domiciled nations could not act without their approval. On August 28, 1767, Daniel

Claus noted in the *Journal of Indian Affairs* that the Nipissing of Lake of Two Mountains had dismissed their leader on their own initiative, and relieved him of his duties as a result of some internal division. The deputy agent of Indian Affairs described the situation as "irregular."[33] According to established customs and rules, no individual could become chief without the approval of the village council and the governor or his official representatives. In December 1824, Bernard Saint-Germain, an interpreter for the Abenaki of Saint-François, received orders from Sir John Johnson regarding the initiative of the village's missionary, who had issued power of attorney to two Abenaki, emphasizing that the missionary had no business meddling in the nation's political affairs. The superintendent then asked the Abenaki council to appoint two other chiefs "in the location and in place of those dismissed" and to "name others to fill the vacant positions and to replace those who had died."[34] On February 3, 1842, Édouard-Narcisse Delorimier, an interpreter for the Iroquois, wrote to Duncan C. Napier, Secretary of Indian Affairs, informing him that the chiefs of Sault-Saint-Louis were very angry because a certain political party in the village of Kahnawake had

> extended an invitation to various Villages, namely to the people of Lake of Two Mountains, to the Algonquin Abenaki & St Régis, to hold a Council against our Chiefs, to remove their titles of Chief from them and to elect other Chiefs in their stead, which is the greatest of obscenities, since only the Government and their Bands have the right to do so.[35]

James Hughes, the superintendent in Montreal, explained to Secretary Napier on February 10, 1842, that no chief could be "broken" or "relieved of his rights" without the sanction of the band to which he belonged, and that, likewise, the chiefs and council could not create chiefs without the consent of the "majority of the tribe" and the sanction of the governor.[6]

Indeed, on April 3, 1845, in a petition from the domiciled Huron addressed to Governor Metcalf and presented by their missionary, François Boucher, the Council of Lorette affirmed that the government they represented was "legitimate," in other words, the members of the council submitting the petition were duly mandated by the entire village and approved by the Executive Council of Canada. The missionary explained that "the government of the village where said 'Savages' reside has always been in the hands of their chiefs, named by the Executive and tasked by it to maintain order and good morals."[37] It was also the custom for the governor to assist his Indigenous allies in the ceremony. It was his duty and his role as provider in the alliance. Around 1807, the council chiefs of the domiciled Huron recalled the custom:

> According to custom among all the Indian nations, it is the chief who keeps the Great Fire who shall lead the Rising the Dead ceremony marking the death of the predecessor approved by the nation that suffered the loss of that chief. Consequently, My Father, the chiefs of the village of Sault St Louis, as those who must approve this appointment shall arrive tomorrow or the day after to do so. In this circumstance, it has always been customary for the Children to address their father for some assistance. We therefore venture to turn to you, Father, so you can grant us some victuals for this occasion.[38]

The Indigenous councils of the members of the Seven Fires were also tasked with presenting the individuals selected to become chiefs to the villages of the Great Fire of the Confederacy. Since the Great Fire was a source of legitimacy, it could ratify political appointments in the villages of the alliance. Daniel Claus reported to Sir William Johnson on August 7, 1771, that the "Caneghsadageys" went to the council in Kahnawake to "name" their new chiefs. The following day, the chiefs of the Great Fire approved the appointments.[39] On January 29, 1819, Nicolas Vincent Tsaouenhohoui, Grand Chief of the domiciled Huron, responded to questions from the members of the Assembly of Lower Canada about the political appointments of the chiefs of the Lorette Council. Tsaouenhohoui explained the inauguration process for the chiefs and grand chief, noting that upon the death of the latter, messengers would be dispatched to the Seven Nations of Canada in Kahnawake. On the same matter, an 1829 brief on the Indigenous people of Sault-Saint-Louis includes an analysis of the expenses incurred by the domiciled Iroquois in the management of their political affairs. The document also mentions that electing a chief is costly, given that the chiefs of the other villages must be present at the ceremony, and that they are accompanied by their wives and children.[40] Tsaouenhohoui added that, after presenting the selected individual in Kahnawake, a delegation of members of the Confederacy would gather in Lorette and "rise the dead," which is to say, they replace the dead chief with another chosen in advance by the village. To the question "How is the Council named?" Tsaouenhohoui replied:

> This is the manner, my Brothers: When a Chief dies, the Council names another and announces it to the assembled nation, but when the Captain or Grand Chief dies, Messengers are sent to the Seven Nations or Villages of the Christian Indians in Lower Canada, with orders to announce that the flagpole has fallen and that they must come to help erect it again. A delegation from each then assembles in the Village. The Grand Chief is named by the Council of the nation and presented to the Deputies of the other Villages.[41]

Traditionally, representatives of the Grand Council of the Seven Nations would be present. On November 13, 1844, the chiefs of the domiciled Huron requested that Secretary Duncan C. Napier be present at the Grand Chief's inauguration ceremony, as this was the custom among the Indigenous people of Quebec and all the superintendents and officials at the Department of Indian Affairs. The Huron mentioned that their Iroquois brothers of the Great Fire of the Seven Nations would also take part in the ceremony:

> We have written to our brothers, the Iroquois of Sault St Louis, inviting them to come join in naming another Grand Chief, to replace the one we lost, and we urged them to let you know when they will come so that you can (if it so suits you) join in this ceremony. With regard to the naming of the Grand Chief, Sir, the

superintendent has always been present, as is the old custom. We invite you to continue this custom, and to give us this pleasure and honour. You shall be much obliged to settle on a time with our brothers, the Iroquois.[42]

Consensus and Unanimity

All of the procedures surrounding decisions by the Council or the Great Fire had one common aim: to achieve consensus and complete unanimity. What is meant by "unanimity" in this context? In the literature, the concept can be deduced through such metaphors as "one spirit," "one voice," "one heart," "one body," "one nation," etc. All of these images emphasize unity. A unity that must be reached with the delegates taking part in the political process and who all have a veto over each and every proposal put forth before the councils or the Great Council Fire. All must be in agreement, and as a result, the majority does not have the power to decide for the others. In reality, this was a principle that determined the political rules of most of the Indigenous nations in the Northeast.[43]

Once a consensus was reached, this notion was expressed in the literature in such terms as "rolling our words into a single bundle" or "with the consent of all." This metaphorical language suggests strength through unity. The metaphor "rolling our words into a single bundle," which stems from the Iroquois tradition, is highly significant in this regard: Every nation is like an arrow, and every arrow can be easily broken. But if several arrows are tied together in a single bundle, the whole becomes stronger, and each arrow is protected by the others. The bundle's collective strength is greater than the sum of its individual parts.[44] If no consensus could be reached, then the matter would be set aside, in which case "the fire was covered" and the Council adjourned. In the interest of the majority, decisions had to be unanimous, which is to say, they had to reflect the wishes of all the protagonists.[45] When the councils of the villages who were members of the Confederacy of the Seven Fires were unable to settle their internal problems, i.e., when they couldn't reach a consensus, the discussion could be taken before the Grand Council of the Confederacy, which constituted a moral authority that could suggest how to resolve the problem, without obliging the parties to follow its recommendations. There were therefore no obligations attached to the decisions aside from a moral obligation.

On July 7, 1773, some delegates from the council of the Abenaki of Saint-François went to Kahnawake to present a problem they were having that stemmed from the theft of a wampum belt by some warriors. The complaint was presented to the Grand Council of the Seven Nations, which would pass it on to the colonial authorities.[46] Affairs that were of federal importance were reported to the chiefs of the Seven Nations gathered at the Grand Council. Daniel Claus noted in the *Journal of Indian Affairs* on August 10, 1773, the response from a domiciled Iroquois to a message from the Mohawk of the League of Six Nations, who were complaining that the domiciled nations were encroaching on their hunting grounds. Aquirandonquas, the Iroquois spokesman of the Grand Council of the Seven Fires, replied to the League's ambassadors that "the Belt was of too much Import to give an Answer upon without the concurrence of the whole Confederacy which, by the first Opportunity, they would assemble & consider upon."[47] On March 17, 1851, in response to an inquiry led by the Department of Indian Affairs into the domiciled Iroquois, Joseph Marcoux, a missionary from Sault-Saint-Louis, wrote that when the chiefs of Saint-Régis, Lake of Two Mountains, Saint-François, or Lorette encountered difficulties in their respective villages, they would always solicit the Sault chiefs because they respected their opinions and often followed their decisions.[48]

As with their political relations, the domiciled nations' decision to engage in armed battle rested solely on the decision of each individual nation. Such military matters, where they concerned the alliance between members of the Confederacy, could be debated at the Grand Council of the Confederacy.

In 1775, during the American Revolution, the following events were documented: A delegation of Abenaki from Saint-François travelled to Kahnawake to take part in political debates. The delegation went there with the aim of "jointly" discussing with the other domiciled nations their military participation in the war between the king and his colonies, and all the chiefs of the member nations of the Confederacy were expected there.[49] Each nation was free to agree or refuse to participate in a conflict or war party.[50] The discussions would continue, seeking to satisfy all sides until a fair compromise was reached. This was true not only for the Grand Council of the Confederacy but also for the village councils. On March 1, 1833, the chiefs of the Abenaki of Saint-François submitted a petition to the government of Lower Canada in which they stressed that all government affairs must be debated and resolved following the unanimous consent of the entire nation, as that was the political rule respected by the people in the village.[51]

These lengthy deliberations can be explained by the desire to reach a consensus, and the fact that not only must each person be heard, they must also be brought on board with decisions. On January 30, 1762, Kaghneghtago, an Iroquois chief from Kahnawake, described to Thomas Gage the "unanimous decisions" of the Iroquois council after "mature deliberations." Those long discussions concerned the ceding of their lands into lots by the Jesuits, and deserved to be conducted appropriately, as they would have consequences for the future of their children.[52]

On May 6, 1776, Benjamin Franklin and the American commissioners wrote to the Continental Congress, advising them of a conference that was to be held at Fort George, New York, with a group of representatives of the Seven Nations of Canada. The commissioners noted that the decision they were awaiting from the members of the Confederacy had been postponed due to the fact that all of the member nations of the Confederacy had to first meet to discuss the proposal of neutrality submitted by the commissioners to the domiciled nations. The delays caused by this situation could in no way justify the repeal of the consultation process.[33] For the Confederacy's decisions to take effect, each member had to give their opinion, and the Confederacy had to solemnly reach a consensus among all its members.[34] In this particular case, the response of the Confederacy could be put off until a later time and the discussions postponed, because all the parties concerned had to first be heard and eventually rallied around a shared decision. A speech given by a war chief of the domiciled Iroquois of Kahnawake is very telling: On May 3, 1792, Atiatoharongwen explained to the American government the reason for the slow progress of the Grand Council of the Seven Fires talks, noting that the members of the Great Fire had had to meet on three occasions before reaching an agreement on the American proposal regarding their hunting grounds in the State of New York. So long as unanimity had not been reached, they would keep discussing; there would be no final agreement without a consensus.[35] The talks on the matter of the hunting grounds of the domiciled nations in the United States began after 1784 and didn't wrap up until 1796. Over the course of those years of negotiations, the representatives of the Seven Fires could not make any unilateral final decisions since they were not specifically mandated to do so. However, on May 23, 1796, at a meeting in Manhattan, the ambassadors of the Seven Nations confirmed to the New York commissioners that they now had the authority to conclude the negotiations conducted on behalf of the Seven Nations. The decisions they made would be based on the directives they had received and the guidelines set by the Great Fire of the Confederacy. Consequently, the ambassadors were able to conclude a treaty with New York to extinguish their land claims.[36] Once a consensus was reached, it was then publicly expressed on behalf of the alliance of the domiciled nations. In 1775, the words of the Seven Fires ambassadors to the Americans in the colonies were reported, and the statement used to express the unanimity of their decision was that "there are seven brothers of us (meaning seven tribes); we are all agreed in this."[37]

The political process was the same when ambassadors of other political organizations met at an international conference. Several pre-council gatherings sought separately to reach a consensus, as the diplomatic delegations would retire to discuss in private a specific matter. An observation to this effect was recorded in the proceedings of the German Flats conference in July-August 1770 that included the British, the Iroquois Six Nations, the Seven Nations of Canada, the Cherokee, as well as Indigenous representatives of the Great Lakes. On July 19, the proceedings noted that the delegates of the Six Nations, after deliberating amongst themselves in private, returned to the conference council, and it was only then that they addressed the nations of Canada and responded to their speeches.[58] Once again, it was the political rule of consensus that was applied. On July 20, it was noted that the Indigenous ambassadors had spent the entire day discussing the words spoken by Superintendent Johnson, "without, nonetheless, being able to achieve a result."[59]

Sachems, War Chiefs, and Women Chiefs

Any matter of diplomacy, politics, or war that concerned the Confederacy of the Seven Fires was discussed before the Great Fire. The chiefs of Kahnawake assumed the dual role as representatives of the Iroquois on the council of Kahnawake, and also as representatives of the Grand Council of the Seven Nations. It appears that this was also determined by a law enacted in 1763 by King George III of England, as pointed out in 1854 by four Iroquois grand chiefs of Sault-Saint-Louis in a petition to Governor General Sir Edmund Walker Head:

> His late Majesty George III passed a law whereby our ancestors had the right to choose seven Grand Chiefs who, once elected, would maintain their positions for their lifetime, and who would be invested with all the powers to establish rules and regulations that would serve as law, and to administer and oversee all the affairs of our Seigneurie and those of our village.[60]

In fact, the Iroquois Council of Kahnawake had always been made up of "Seven Grand Chiefs, Seven Subaltern Chiefs, and several chiefs of lower grade."[61] It appears that the chiefs of the Seven Nations therefore served in the village of the Great Fire. The following document dating from 1842, while posing a problem of legitimacy, notes that it was in Kahnawake that the Algonquin and Nipissing of Lake of Two Mountains gathered to meet the chiefs of the Seven Nations:

> We, the principal Algonquin and Nipissing Chiefs, wish to inform our Father that, having been summoned by a certain group of young people who dare to call themselves Chiefs of the Village of Sault St Louis, we traveled to the Village of the Great Fire, believing that it was the Chiefs who had called for us on some matter of great importance. We were very surprised upon our arrival to see that the true chiefs of the Seven Nations had no idea what we were doing there, and neither did we know why we had been summoned [...] my Father, as we declare ourselves fully in favour of our brothers, the Chiefs of the Great Fire of the Seven Nations, and wholly disapprove of those who oppose them.[62]

On February 12, 1842, the missionary at Sault-Saint-Louis noted an extraordinary political situation prevailing in the village: "some letters were sent from the Office of the Superintendent to the Seven Nations in Saint Regis, Lake of Two Mountains, and Sᵗ François, summoning them to Sault Sᵗ Louis for some important business, entirely unbeknownst of the Chiefs of the Sault, who have the sole right to summon the nations to their villages,"[63] as the Sault chiefs are the chiefs of the Seven Fires.

Meetings between the chiefs of the different councils of the alliance were held in Kahnawake on a seasonal basis. On September 25, 1817, the Iroquois of Kahnawake responded to an inquiry by the Department of Indian Affairs about their income and expenses. The Iroquois chiefs replied that as the "Main Village" of the domiciled nations, it was their obligation to host the different allied Indigenous nations, and that these receptions were costly.[64] On February 21, 1828, the Kahnawake chiefs asked Governor Dalhousie to provide them with financial assistance to cover the expenses surrounding the Confederacy's Grand Councils since, every summer, their brothers from the other villages would frequently travel to Kahnawake to take part in the Grand Councils of the Confederacy: "Every summer we hold several Grand Councils in this village, and for the whole time our brothers are gathered, we are obliged to feed them, and as such, all the people in this Village have nothing, because the incomes are insufficient for all these expenses."[65] On March 31, 1845, in a report on the lands of the Indigenous people of Quebec, it was noted that certain revenues collected by the Iroquois of Kahnawake were strictly earmarked for hosting the chiefs of the other villages because that was the Grand Council of the Seven Nations.[66] On November 5, 1846, the missionary at Sault-Saint-Louis informed the civil secretary of the Canadian government that a Grand Council of the domiciled nations was held in July of that year in Kahnawake.[67] On December 28, 1847, the chiefs of Kahnawake once again submitted a request for financial aid, noting that they needed money because hosting the chiefs of the other villages "for the affairs of the Government" generated expenses.[68]

This Grand Council included two main types of representatives: sachems (also known as council chiefs, political chiefs, or peace chiefs) and war chiefs (who were also referred to as military chiefs or warrior chiefs). Each had their own distinct mandates. The sachems wielded civil authority. They were in charge of external affairs like trade, alliances, and treaties.[69] In the Iroquois tradition, sachems were perceived as "trees" rising up from among the nations, visible, recognized, and respected by all.[70] It was these representatives who handled political matters relating to peace, as Adyadarony, an Iroquois chef of the domiciled warriors, pointed out to Sir William Johnson at a peace conference held September 15 and 16, 1760, in Kahnawake. The spokesperson for the Iroquois warriors only spoke after the sachems had finished negotiating peace with the new occupants of Canada.[71] This political role of the sachems was recognized by the colonial authorities, who referred to these chiefs as "Officers of the Peace, Men of wisdom and experience."[72] In addition to their mandate of maintaining peace and civil order, the sachems were also tasked with preserving the collective memory, with being the guardians of the oral tradition of their forefathers.[73]

The war chiefs held military power: they organized war-related activities and distinguished themselves in battle. William Tryon, the governor of New York, explained the role of these leaders quite succinctly in a July 29, 1772, tirade against the Mohawk of the Iroquois League of Six Nations, in which he threw down an ultimatum: "When at war, I shall deal with the Warriors, but during times of deep peace, as is now the case, you shall handle your civil affairs with the Sachems."[74] The governor thereby confirmed what the Indigenous nations freely admitted: in peacetime, one deals with the representatives of the civil government, and in wartime, with the representatives of the military government.[75]

Women also held political power within the alliance. They would accompany their husbands as part of the diplomatic delegations, as the men wished them to be present. A domiciled Iroquois spokesman confirmed this before Jonathan Belcher, Governor of the Province of Massachusetts-Bay, at a diplomatic meeting in Deerfield on August 27, 1735.[76] Women had a political voice and were listened to especially when the government's decisions concerned war, in which case the women would advise the warriors. In his *Journal of Indian Affairs* entry from February 7, 1764, Sir William Johnson expressed his great appreciation for the initiative of the Indigenous women of the Susquehannah River who "gave Wise advice and Admonition to your Warriors as it is a Proof of their Sagacity."[77] On August 20, 1779, he described to Daniel Claus the request by the women of the Iroquois Six Nations to their sisters in Canada who implored them, as descendants and allies, to allow their warriors to go to war to defend their Iroquoia brothers.[78]

In a speech dated October 20, 1779, a sachem from the "Seven Villages" explained to Superintendent Campbell that his words were the voice of the "Ancients," the "Young Warriors," and the "Women Chiefs."[79] The expression "Women Chiefs" could refer to one of two things: that either the women sat on the councils and were part of the chiefdom, or that they were the chiefs among the women, i.e., Clan Mothers.[80] Either way, the women chiefs were called on to take part in political debates. In 1780, the Abenaki women of Saint-François addressed the clan mothers of the "Seven Catholic Villages," and presented them with wampum necklaces. Their message provides insight into the role women played in their relationships within the Confederacy. In this instance, they encouraged their youth to take part in military activities because "if there were no women, there would be no warriors."[81]

As part of their maternal duties, during wartime, the women supplied and fed the warriors to "refresh them after their Fatigues" and, as the Cherokee women said, "it is our parts to furnish the Warriors with Provisions whenever they go upon any Exploit, it being our Duty to do so they being our Children & brought forth by us."[82] While the political actions of women were sometimes contested, their words held power, especially in regard to military politics. At councils, they would express their opinions, suggest courses of action, and propose alternatives. However, not all the chiefs approved of the women chiefs' involvement. In his July 7, 1773, entry in the *Journal of Indian Affairs*, Daniel Claus noted that the chiefs of the Council of Kahnawake preferred that the warriors and women not be admitted to the Council.[83] Sir William Johnson agreed with the Iroquois, saying he "disapproved of Women & a few Warriors overruling their Councils & recommended to the Chiefs to maintain their Authority."[84]

The relations between the peace chiefs and the war chiefs adhered to very precise rules. We know that both would attend the Grand Council of Kahnawake and that they hosted the ambassadors. On September 30, 1775, four warriors from the

Iroquois League of Six Nations described to the commissioners mandated by the Continental Congress to oversee relations with the Indigenous people how the conference they attended in Kahnawake was conducted. The Iroquois explained, "when we arrived at the council house, all the chiefs and warriors of the Seven Nations were gathered and wanted to hear our messages,"[85] which they communicated to the Seven Fires on behalf of the Iroquois Six Nations and the commissioners of the "Twelve United Colonies."

The rules established within the Confederacy were based on customs, and were conveyed by means of the members' political traditions. For the chiefdom to operate effectively, it was crucial that the Seven Fires leaders be ready and willing to carry on the traditions of their forefathers. At international meetings, it was important that the protagonists abide by the rules established by those who came before them, in other words, by their customs and diplomacy ground rules. For instance, according to custom, in wartime or periods of conflict, any proposals to form military alliances were relayed to the sachems, who would pass them on to the war chiefs.

In keeping with this custom, on September 7, 1763, Sir William Johnson presented the Iroquois of Kahnawake a war necklace to activate their military alliance. The wampum was given to Sachem Assaragoa, who passed it on to the Seven Fires warriors. In this case, the British were seeking to quell the revolt by the Odawa nation of the Great Lakes and Chief Pontiac by requesting the military assistance of the Seven Fires.[86]

Around 1777, one of the war chiefs of the Seven Fires Confederacy reminded the Seneca of the Iroquois League that their ancestors had established certain precepts that they were obliged to respect with a view to preserving and promoting their political well-being.[87]

Their forefathers had introduced rules like those governing verbal confrontations between political chiefs and war chiefs. At a conference in Ohio, a representative of the Seven Nations warriors took the time to explain to a military gathering of Miami and Shawnee chiefs the customary practices of the Seven Fires in wartime, noting that what the sachems decided, the warriors accepted. Since politics took precedence over military matters, the warriors did not make political decisions, even if they were to do with war.

The warrior-speaker therefore suggested that the following changes be made during debates: When councils were held, the chiefs must be seated in the front rows. Since the Shawnee and Miami had placed the warriors in front and the sachems behind, the speaker suggested rectifying the situation; at the Seven Nations, this was not done—the sachems were always seated in front of the warriors. This practice symbolized that the military chiefs undertook to follow the recommendations of their political and civil leaders. At the Grand Council of the Seven Fires, peace was placed ahead of war, in other words, the decisions of the political chiefs took precedence over those of their military counterparts.[88]

However, on occasion, the balance between political and military power could tip, or threaten to tip. On May 3, 1792, Atiatoharongwen, the Iroquois war chief of Kahnawake, travelled to Philadelphia to answer questions from an American government committee in charge of Indian Affairs. The speaker representing the domiciled Iroquois informed the committee that a war proposal must be submitted to the Seven Fires warriors, who would then pass it on to their sachems.[89] Yet, the sachems always insisted in their speeches on the priority of the political chiefs over the warriors. It is worth explaining the context here: Certain Indigenous nations of the northwest United States—Miami, Shawnee, and Wyandot—under pressure from American colonial expansion on their lands, initiated a political consultation process with other Indigenous Peoples of the northeast before they would engage in any military action against the Americans. In his address to a group of representatives of the Shawnee and Miami of Ohio on October 4, 1792, the political spokesperson for the

Seven Fires requested that "the warriors take into consideration and recall what their Sachems had established for the well-being of their women and children and country."[90]

On the Diplomatic Paths of the Northeast

The spokespersons for the Confederacy, i.e., the ambassadors of the Grand Council of the Seven Fires, would make the rounds of all the diplomatic circuits in northeastern North America. These delegations, which usually consisted of orators and interpreters, were identified in documents as the Confederacy's official representatives. They would deliver their speeches in accordance with the mandates assigned by the Grand Council of Kahnawake and in keeping with the recommendations of the sachems and the war chiefs. In this way, the diplomatic representation of the Seven Fires ambassadors was subject to a certain degree of control.[91] While not a systematic practice, if one of the Seven Fires villages was more concerned by a particular negotiation, it would sometimes have a greater representation in the delegation. It might also be the case that the embassy of a single village would also be the spokesperson for the Seven Fires. This was true for the delegation of 11 Iroquois sachems from Akwesasne which made up the embassy that travelled to New York City on March 6, 1795, to meet the representatives of that American state with a view to negotiating a land extinguishment agreement.[92] The reason they appeared before the commissioners on behalf of the Seven Nations of Canada was that these sachems from Akwesasne would have deliberated in advance about the embassy before the Grand Council of the Confederacy, which would have mandated them to negotiate on behalf of their alliance. In this case, it would have been up to the Iroquois of Akwesasne to lead the negotiations because they were the ones with the most at stake.[93]

Key to this practice was the fact that none of the fires represented by the delegation were opposed to an ambassador speaking on their behalf. On July 9, 1773, Daniel Claus noted that the sachems of Kahnawake had officially designated a spokesperson to represent their nation and the Iroquois of Akwesasne. After reaching a decision together, Chief Saghtaghroana, who was known for his oratory skills, was appointed to speak on behalf of the two nations. Saghtaghroana would represent the domiciled Iroquois of Kahnawake and Akwesasne in their negotiations with the British.[94] The presence of all the members concerned by a specific problem was a fundamental principle. However, on some occasions, ambassadors might be delegated for a shared problem without any prior consultation. This might indicate an internal conflict like the one that opposed the domiciled Iroquois and Abenaki. Eleven years after the village of Saint-François was sacked by the British troops of Colonel Robert Rogers, a group of Abenaki went to Johnson Hall to demand that the superintendent intervene in their dispute with the Iroquois of Akwesasne, with whom some of them sought refuge after 1759.[95] On July 31, 1770, an Iroquois chief who was, by all indications, from the village of Akwesasne, denounced the unilateral diplomatic initiatives of the Abenaki at a meeting with Daniel Claus at the Great Fire of Kahnawake: "We see plainly that, according to their usual practice they want to take advantage of our not being present in order to misrepresent matters."[96]

One particular detail concerning the diplomatic delegation caught our attention. On September 30, 1775, a number of representatives of the Iroquois League of Six Nations described to the American commissioners of Indian Affairs the conversation that took place in Île-aux-Noix between the Seven Fires ambassadors and Richard Montgomery, chief of the "Long Knives," referring to the leader of the American soldiers. At the end of the talks, Montgomery thanked the Seven Nations ambassadors and made a ceremonial offering of gifts, which was described as the American general offering a gift for the seven nations of the "Canada Indians" as well as a gift for the seven ambassadors,[97] the latter being the representatives of the Seven Fires who, by their number, symbolized the union of the Confederacy members and the unanimity and consensus obtained from the other members of their alliance. In another report from the same period, the event is described as follows: "the Caughnawaga retired to a house nearby and then, seven of their principal men waited for General Montgomery."[98] In other words, it was usually the Iroquois of Kahnawake who represented the Seven Nations of Canada.

The archival documents also reveal other details about the status and role of the Algonquin and Nipissing ambassadors within the Confederacy and about the special relationship these domiciled peoples of Lake of Two Mountains had with the Indigenous nations of the Great Lakes. In his correspondence with Sir William Johnson, Daniel Claus noted that the domiciled people of Lake of Two Mountains spoke a language similar to that of some of the Great Lakes nations, and there existed a close relationship between the domiciled Algonquin and Nipissing and these American Indians, as they are "connected" with all the "nations up above."[99] In fact, this special relationship dates back to the French Regime in Canada, when the Odawa allowed the Nipissing and Algonquin to speak on their behalf to the other diplomatic partners of the governor of New France, since they were the older members of the alliance system at the time. The importance of precedence in the protocol hierarchy points to the role of the different parties in their political relations: When diplomatic relations concerned the nations of the Great Lakes, the Algonquin and Nipissing spoke first. This privilege was granted to them as elders in the alliance. French officer Bougainville explained in his journal that the Nipissing "were the oldest of all the Indians," and that this position gave them "the right of precedence" by virtue of their "seniority"[100] as one of the first nations to be allied with the French. That position gave them precedence over the other nations and the authorization to speak first when it came to relations with the nations of the Great Lakes. The same was true for the Algonquin.[101] And the British, in turn, carried on the same practice.

In some instances, the Confederacy of the Seven Fires' diplomatic relations with political organizations further up the Ottawa River were conducted with official spokespersons from Kanehsatake, meaning the Seven Nations could play a diplomatic role in the Great Lakes. The 1770 conference at German Flats is a good example of this, and is significant in that it clearly demonstrates how diplomatic representation functioned in the Great Lakes area. In a speech he gave on July 22, Saghtaghroana, the spokesperson for the domiciled Iroquois, speaking on behalf of the Seven Fires, clearly set out the role of the people of Kanehsatake within the Confederacy: "our Brethren at Canasadaga [Kanehsatake] should have their eyes upon all the Nations up the Ottawa or great River. [...] We resolve in order to promote the work, which you have begun, and so successfully conducted, to send proper Deputies to the Indians to the Westward, taking that part of the negotiation entirely upon ourselves..."[102] The Kanehsatake allies therefore had their eyes turned towards the Great Lakes. It was their diplomats who would represent the Seven Fires and speak on their behalf; they would be the official messengers and would be tasked with carrying the information about the decisions made at the conference to the Indigenous people of the Great Lakes. Their mission would also include sending messengers with the information to Michigan and Pennsylvania, by way of Detroit and Pittsburgh.[103]

The Seven Nations had assumed this diplomatic role since the early days of the British Regime in Canada. The colonial government would organize its relations with the Indigenous people of the Great Lakes, with the help of their allies in the Seven Fires Confederacy. It was for this reason that, in the summer of 1763, a group of domiciled people was chosen to travel to Detroit and Makinaw via the St. Lawrence and Ottawa rivers to carry a message from the British to the insurgent nations in the Great Lakes area.[104]

Likewise, in August 1763, several Mississauga went to Kanehsatake to inform the people there that the nation they represented would not take up arms against the English and would have no part in the plot against the British Crown, unlike the Odawa.[105] On May 30, 1764, Daniel Claus informed Sir William Johnson that some messengers from "different nations" at Kanehsatake had been dispatched to Makinaw among the Odawa.[106] On July 16, Thomas Gage wrote that the Odawa had travelled first to the village of Lake of Two Mountains, before attempting to land on the Island of Montreal.[107] The location of the village of Kanehsatake offered easy access to the Great Lakes via the hydrographic network formed by the Ottawa and St. Lawrence rivers, and in fact, from Montreal, two major waterways lead to the Great Lakes. The first consisted of navigating up the St. Lawrence from Montreal to Kingston, close to the outlet of Lake Ontario, while the second route connected Montreal to Lake Huron via the Ottawa River, the Mattawa River, Lake Nipissing, the French River, and Georgian Bay.

As for the diplomatic relations of the Seven Fires in the Maritimes, they were occasionally entrusted to the domiciled Abenaki from the village of Saint-François. One significant reference to this appears in a brief dated February 10, 1797, written by Jean-Baptiste Destimauville, an interpreter for the Abenaki. In the document, Destimauville reports on the political situation of the day, of the imminent danger of war with the United States and Spain, which were attempting, by every means possible, to rally the Indigenous nations to their side. Destimauville suggested a "remedy," a solution based on his knowledge of the Indigenous diplomatic networks so that England could bring as many Indigenous nations on board as possible. He pointed out the very close ties binding the chiefs of the Seven Nations of Canada to the chiefs of the other Indigenous nations, and added that the Abenaki of Saint-François, like the Seven Nations chiefs, were known to have diplomatic relations with 42 villages located between the Saint-François River and the Maritimes. Those relations could help provide the British Crown with nearly 5,500 warriors. Destimauville went on to suggest that the Indigenous people could play an influential political role, so long as they were treated fairly and that their land claims were addressed.[108] The

Abenaki of Saint-François would therefore play a diplomatic role similar to the one the Algonquin and Nipissing played with the Indigenous nations of the Great Lakes, meaning the domiciled Abenaki could act as intermediaries between the British and the Indigenous Peoples of eastern Canada and the United States, likely the peoples of the Wabanaki Confederacy.

The Diplomatic Family: Related Individuals and Nations

All diplomatic relations rested on the status of the member nations of the alliance networks. The cornerstone was the diplomatic family: in northeastern America, social and political relations were never expressed outside of references to the system of kinship, the basis for all Indigenous societies. Historian Francis Jennings emphasized the importance of kinship metaphors to express political relations, noting that it would be a mistake for the modern reader to perceive this system as an insignificant or childish mode of expression. He noted the high degree of importance that Indigenous orators placed on these metaphors, and how they were in no way interchangeable. Jennings also highlighted the interpretation challenges these terms posed for negotiators from two cultures for whom the role of kinship—and the significance of the terms related to it—could be diametrically opposed. Lastly, he underscored the Indigenous peoples' refusal to accept the interpretation that the colonial authorities sought to impose on them.[109]

In Indigenous societies, each individual was named in accordance with the place they occupied in the bloodline and the alliance, i.e., in the kinship networks. When foreigners were adopted, they were automatically given a new name, otherwise they were not considered to exist. In many such cases, the adoptees were representatives of the colonial power.[110] This was one aspect of the unique and special relationship they had with the Indigenous people. The French governor, for example, was given the name "Onontio," which translates as "Great Mountain." This name, given originally by the Huron of the Great Lakes to the first governor of New France, Charles-Huault de Montmagny, was subsequently applied to all the French governors who followed. According to some sources, the name Montmagny came from the Latin *Monte Magnus*, or Great Mountain which, in the Huron language, translates as "Onontio."[111] The title "Grand Onontio" was strictly reserved for the kings of France.[112] The Algonquin and the other Indigenous peoples whose languages were similar to theirs referred to the governors as "Kitchi Okima," "Grand Captain."[113] Under the British Regime, the governor in Quebec City was known as "Hatiyathaque."[114]

In the British colonies, the Dutch representative in Albany was named "Corlaer" by the Iroquois of the League, the actual patronym of a representative of the Treaty of Fort Orange (Albany). The name stuck, and was subsequently used in reference to all the governors of the New York colony. The Iroquois used the same name for the first British governor, Edmund Andros.[115] In Pennsylvania, the Iroquois of the League named the governors "Onas," which means "feather" or "pen," since it was the name originally given to Governor William Penn.[116] Louis-Antoine de Bougainville was named "Garoniatsigoa" (Thunderous Sky) by the Iroquois.[117] This new name was likely in reference to de Bougainville's military duties, although he was also known as "brother" and perhaps even as "father." Pierre Pouchot, another French soldier, was renamed "Sategayogen," (the Centre of Good Transactions).[118] In 1784, the Americans, in their speeches to the domiciled nations, referred to General Lafayette by the name "Kayenlaa," a word that can express three things: "Great Man Among the French," "Great Chief of the Great Onontio," or "Great Chief of the Army."[119] In short, if you weren't part of the kinship, you didn't exist.

Any individual who had a close relationship with the Indigenous peoples was therefore adopted and brought into the kinship system. Sir William Johnson, the first superintendent of Indian Affairs, received an honorary title of wisdom and

knowledge from the Iroquois of the League—"Warraghiyagey"—
which meant "the Man Who Undertakes Great Things."[120] This
title was often prefaced by "Gorah," which "implied a person
in authority under His Majesty."[121] Daniel Claus, Sir William's
representative in Montreal, was renamed "Sotsitsyowane,"[122]
and Superintendent Guy Johnson was "Uraghqudirha," which
translated as "Rays of the Sun enlightening the Earth."[123] His
successor, John Johnson, received the name "Owanoghsishon."[124]
As for Secretary Duncan C. Napier, he was given the name
"Sakoienteris," or "He Who Knows Us."[125]

The decision to adopt and rename an individual was a sign of
distinction and honour for that person, and the gesture was one
of the ways of perpetuating the memory of a chief. In the 19th
century, Charles Canawato, an Iroquois chief from Lake of Two
Mountains, renamed governors Lord Aylmer "Generous Heart"
and Sir James Kempt "Master of Artillery" in honour, respectively,
of their generosity and role as provider in their relations with the
domiciled Iroquois. The chief also renamed two Iroquois from
the village "Lord Aylmer" and "Sir James Kempt" in memory of
the two British governors.[126] "Assaragoa" or "Cimeterre" was the
name given by the Iroquois to the governor of Virginia.[127] We
know that in the 18th century, there was a domiciled Iroquois
chief and orator who went by the name "Assaragoa."[128] All of these
names, most of them from the Iroquoian language, tended to be
preceded by the title "Brother" or "Father."

The father-child paradigm stems from French-Indigenous
relations, and when the French were present at diplomatic meetings, this "father and child" metaphor would resurface, as it did
in 1778 when General Lafayette met with the children of the
King-Father of France. Despite the fact the French-Indigenous
alliance no longer existed after 1760, that relation was still evoked
eighteen years later, as if the familial bond could never be erased.[129]
In 1784, it was the Seven Nations ambassadors who, in turn,
reminded Lafayette that "the Nations of the North had long been
the Children of the Great Onontio."[130] This relation harkened back

to the Huron-Odawa tradition, which had been characterized since approximately 1650 by a paternal and filial relationship between father and sons.[131] In 1700, at a council between Officer Paul-Joseph Le Moyne de Longueuil and several ambassadors from four Indigenous nations near Detroit, the commander of the French royal troops reminded the Great Lakes Indigenous representatives that the nature of their father-child relationship clearly obligated them to join the military alliance. In addressing these Indigenous spokespersons on behalf of Onontio, the officer said, "Children, I have an enemy. I am your father; you are my children. Could it be that this enemy would not be yours also?"[132] This Huron-Odawa tradition was adhered to by all the members of the French-Indigenous alliance. On August 2, 1709, a gathering that included domiciled Abenaki, Iroquois of Sault-Saint-Louis, as well as Iroquois, Algonquin, Nipissing, Odawa, and Mississauga from Sault-au-Récollet met near Crown Point, New York. All of their speeches were addressed to their French father, Officer Ramezay.[133] The French also used father and children metaphors with the Iroquois of the League.[134] And this practice continued after 1760, when the King of Great Britain became the father of the Indigenous Peoples of the Seven Nations, replacing the King of France in that role. His representatives in North America were also addressed as "father." For the domiciled nations, the term referred to the paternal function in their own societies, to the functions associated with the roles of provider, protector, and non-coercive moral authority as father and advisor or as father and one who renders justice. This father figure was therefore not exclusively reserved for kings; it also applied to the governors and any other civil or military official. This role is expressed in a petition the Iroquois of Sault-Saint-Louis addressed to Governor Dalhousie on February 21, 1828: "My Father, since it is you who is the greatest in this Province and that all the important affairs are decided by you; since it is you whom God has chosen to decide our affairs since we have been together; Because we have always been very content with the way you act."[135]

Provider, protector, unifier... this was exactly what the Indigenous people recognized in their chiefs, and therefore in authority figures, and this is how they perceived the colonial authorities. While coercion and subjugation were not intrinsic to their culture, they accepted the government's authority as they perceived it in the same way they would, on an individual basis, that of their own Grand Chiefs. To the minds of the Indigenous people, it was not a simple relationship of equal allies; rather, there was a very real form of subordination, although it was not a resigned subservience, because every Indigenous person considered himself or herself to be free.

Father-Provider

On November 13, 1760, Pierre Roubaud, a Jesuit missionary with the Abenaki of Saint-François, wrote to Superintendent Johnson to advise him of the expectations of these new Abenaki allies: They requested that their father assist some 20 elderly Abenaki women by providing them with clothing. This gesture would "at the same time that they Love & Cherish the present Government, confirm them more & more in the Sentiments of fidelity that animates them."[136] On July 28, 1770, at a meeting at Johnson Hall, the domiciled Abenaki expressed all the joy they felt at belonging to the same diplomatic family as the superintendent. As father-provider, the colonial official would be bound to meet, insofar as possible, all the demands of his allies.

The domiciled Abenaki, who were in urgent need of interpreters, petitioned the father of the Indigenous Peoples of Canada, Sir William Johnson: His children implored him to cover the financial burden of this service, as only a father would be able to fulfill their request.[137] On August 5, 1810, the Department of Indian Affairs in Quebec City received a petition from the Abenaki of Batiscan and Missisquoi calling for their father to give them some lands belonging to the Crown. They requested that the British governor, as a good father and the only one in a position to provide for them, give them a "dish" in which they could eat, i.e., lands on which the Abenaki could hunt and fish.[138] On December 16, 1822, in his correspondence with London, Governor Dalhousie wrote that the Indigenous people expected their father, the King, to give them gifts, as they were his children. According to Dalhousie, breaking with this tradition would constitute a serious offense and would be perceived by their counterparts as a violation of the rules of the alliance. To no longer give gifts would be akin to no longer being a father, to no longer caring for one's children. And that was why his children were defending his interests in North America.[139]

Father-Protector

As father-protector, the king and his representatives had a duty to protect the interests of their children. On July 26, 1773, the chiefs of the Council of the Huron of Lorette asked their father to decide in their favour in the dispute that pitted them against the Catholic clergy in the matter of seigneurial lands. The paternal protection of the colonial authorities must ensure the Hurons' security, failing which, they said, they would be driven out of house and home. The Huron addressed their brother, Daniel Claus, representative of their father, the superintendent of Indian Affairs.[140] In January 1775, Superintendent Guy Johnson reassured the Seven Fires ambassadors that they would always find in the King a person disposed to protect them and promote their interests "like a Tender Father would towards his children."[141] This relationship was, in fact, identical to the one between the Seven Nations and the King of France, as the members of the Grand Council of the Seven Fires pointed out, on October 5, 1827, to the superintendent of Indian Affairs. They promised to "obey the commands" of the governor as they had in the time of the King of France, in other words, to remain faithful to the decisions and directives of the British Crown, as they had always done since 1760,"[142] when the King of Great Britain effectively replaced the King of France as the father of the Seven Fires.[143]

In a speech they addressed to the Odawa of the Great Lakes, in the context of war with the Pontiac, the Seven Nations specified the role and behaviours of a father within the alliance. They explained to the Odawa that they should consider the King of England as their father, because he only sought to have with his children a relationship based on "peace and fraternity." The Seven Nations representatives added that the king also sought to establish "fair and equitable" trade with all his children living in his "American Dominions," as the King of France had before him.[144] In the fall of 1784, at a meeting at Fort Stanwix, New York, in the presence of American commissioners and ambassadors from the Six Nations and Seven Fires, a Kahnawake chief reminded General Lafayette of the former alliance with the King of France. The general replied to his former allies that, one day, the alliance would once again take root, and that the "Roots of the Tree" would reappear in North America: "I tell you, also, that in leaving you, I bid you not an eternal farewell, and that the day would come when the Roots of the Tree that bound our Hearts would regain their strength and unite us once again. That Day is not Far." A father's duty is to protect his children and watch over their interests—this is what Lafayette meant when he told the Seven Nations not to fear for their American possessions now in the hands of the Americans of the United States: "Do not be concerned, my Children, for all the Lines you see Drawn on my Former Lands."[145]

Father and children shared the same interests, the same spirit, the same heart, and were united in defending their shared interests; each must watch over the safety of the other. This was a close relationship because both parties saw the world in the same way, shared the same spirit and the same love. This was the message of the Seven Nations of Canada sachems to an assembly of Indigenous representatives from the Great Lakes on October 4, 1792.[146] On December 22, 1803, Thomas Martin, a chief of the Huron nation of Lorette, petitioned the governor of Lower Canada, Robert Shore Milnes, as "father and protector of the

Huron" to provide the members of his council with two medals that would serve to differentiate them from the other representatives of the nation, since his role in the alliance was to protect his children and acknowledge their value. In this case, the father was both protector and provider, and the Huron pointed out that the governor had always promised to "protect and assist them in all their needs."[147] The chiefs of the Algonquin and Nipissing of Lake of Two Mountains explained the importance of these medals in the context of the alliance with the British: "My father, if your orders so require, and especially if the war were to begin, these marks of distinction that you give to your children would give us, the chiefs, the strength to carry out your orders."[148]

The British Army generals also played a paternal role in the alliance: On February 26, 1811, the Iroquois chiefs of the "Great Fire of the Seven Villages" and the chiefs of the Huron of Lorette reminded their father, Francis, Baron of Rottenburg, of the promises he made them to obtain from the Crown two medals for the Huron war chiefs.[149] They also petitioned their father-governor for assistance under the military alliance during the American Revolution, requesting that the general of Rottenburg play a role as mediator and speak to the governor on their behalf to remind him of the services that the Huron of Lorette had provided to the British Crown. The General of Rottenburg and his wife, mother of the Huron, were considered members of the Huron family. "You are too just to refuse Your Mediation," said the Huron, adding "May the Master of life award you Long and happy days and to Our Mother, Your Wife."[150]

Father-Mediator

The father-advisor was also father-mediator, the man who exercised his moral authority, and all the colonial power's representatives were duty-bound to exercise the same functions within the alliance. As father-advisor, the governor exerted considerable influence, because his opinions had to be followed and respected as the law. One domiciled Nipissing from Lake of Two Mountains, on behalf of the Algonquin and Nipissing, strongly recommended to a gathering of Iroquois of the League in Montreal in the winter of 1756 that they follow the "good advice" of the Governor of New France, Pierre de Rigaud De Vaudreuil-Cavagnal, as he was the alliance's guide, and he inspired their conduct and stimulated his children.[151] On March 28, 1762, several domiciled Abenaki brought their grievances against the Iroquois of Akwesasne, who wanted to expel them from their village, after having taken them in in 1759. They complained to the father-superintendent, as they felt that, as father of the alliance, he was authorized and duly mandated to intervene. The superintendent would play the role of mediator in their dispute with the Iroquois, and the Abenaki expected him to advise them and that, as he saw fit, to reprimand them if they had been lacking in their relations with the English or their allies.[152]

On August 30, 1765, Daniel Claus advised Sir William Johnson of a land dispute between the Seven Fires and the Iroquois League. The members of the Confederacy petitioned the superintendent to intervene and force the Iroquois to respect the agreements binding the Confederacy and the League.[153] In this instance, the father-advisor was also father-protector. On August 14, 1778, a group of Iroquois from the League of Six Nations evoked the notion of consensus with the alliance, reminding Superintendent John Campbell that the wampum necklace they were offering him was presented to them by Sir William Johnson to keep them united in the interests of their father, the King of England.[154]

The king and his representatives were therefore fathers and forefathers who held ancestral positions within the alliance, and the British looked to it as a moral authority. In 1779, in the context of the American Revolution, Frederick Haldimand reminded the "Seven Villages of Canada" that their father of England wished that his domiciled children, by virtue of the alliance, defend the lands of his kingdom in North America, as such were the formal commitments made by his children, the members of the Seven Fires Confederacy.[155]

A father must ensure peace among all his children, and on October 5, 1827, at a Grand Council of the Seven Nations, the Superintendent of Indian Affairs expressed the wishes of the governor general of Lower Canada regarding the good neighbourly relations that should govern the relationship between the domiciled nations and the *Canadiens*. The Department officials thus placed the king-father above all his children, affirming both the father's obligation to ensure the happiness of his children and his obligation to consider all his children, whether white or Indigenous, on the same footing. Both the advice of a father to his children and the father's obligations to those children were expressed here, failing which the children would lose the father's support and alienate themselves from his protection: the father demanded that his children obey him, as every good child should.[156] The father protects and sees to the security of the rights of all his children; he must listen and foster equitable relationships between all partners of the alliance, Indigenous and non-Indigenous alike; the father renders justice.[157]

On October 26, 1829, Superintendent Louis-Juchereau Duchesnay met with the Huron of Lorette, the Algonquin of Pointe-du-Lac, and the Abenaki of Saint-François and Bécancour in Trois-Rivières and informed them that Governor General Sir James Kempt wished to obtain as much information as possible on the dispute that divided them over their hunting grounds, so that he could render justice as fairly as possible. The governor was the father and therefore the one to render justice; it was up to him to decide.[158] As the representative of their father, the King of England, the father-governor must reassure his children, in other words, refrain from alienating the trust they placed in him. The Grand Chief of the Huron, Michel Scioui, supported by the other chiefs present at the Trois-Rivières gathering, expressed that belief at the conference: "We always place the greatest confidence in the ordinary justice of our good father the King, well represented by our good and worthy governor, and trust that he will maintain for us these rights."[159]

The father is thus differentiated from the other alliance partners by his ability to render justice. The council chiefs of the Algonquin and Nipissing of Lake of Two Mountains also affirmed this notion in a petition dated July 8, 1830, that they addressed to Sir James Kempt. The father-governor must be fair and impartial to all his political partners, for only he appears able to remedy the problems of his children. The chiefs noted that they were counting "on the paternal kindness of Your Excellency and on his acknowledged desire to render justice to all and to allow all his children to enjoy the same advantages. We dare to hope that you will be touched at the sight of the misery that awaits us and that you will hasten to provide relief from it."[160] The father must also exercise his moral authority as a guarantor of honour, and it was on this principle that the Iroquois of the Seven Fires relied in 1840 to exonerate themselves from having collaborated in the 1837-1838 rebellions of the French-Canadian Patriots.[161]

The Brother Paradigm

The role of father was not exclusive; it did not prevent one from being a brother at the same time. The relationship could change depending on the alliance's political relations. On May 10, 1765, at a convention in Pittsburgh between colonial officials and a group from the Great Lakes nations, Lawoughqua, a spokesman for the Shawnee, clarified the role of father and brother within the alliance, even if they were the same individual. The Shawnee chief mentioned that within an alliance, the father was an influential figure and that his paternal function made him duty-bound to his children. His duties also distinguished him from the brother, who occupied other functions in the kinship system. Lawoughqua explained that while a father has authority over his children, a brother has no authority over another brother.[162] The brother metaphor is rooted in the Iroquois tradition that prevailed for a long time in Albany in the relations between the British, the Iroquois of the League, and the domiciled nations in Canada who travelled to that city to negotiate with the commissioners of Indian Affairs.

On August 2, 1684, the sachems of the Onondaga and the Cayuga of the Iroquois League reminded Governor Dongan of the first contacts between the Iroquois and the English, and of the welcome that the latter received from the Indigenous people. The brother metaphor here is indicative of the alliance between the English and the Iroquois. The Iroquois determined the roles of a brother as well as his obligations in the alliance, i.e., to protect the Iroquois from attacks by the French and thereby ensure the continuity of trade relations between the two partners.[163] On February 25, 1693, Benjamin Fletcher, then-general of the British Army and governor-in-chief of the province of New York, met with his Iroquois allies of the League at the Albany town hall, following a military victory over the French troops. In his speech, the governor recalled why he had been given a mandate in the region. If he addressed the Iroquois as his brother, it was because they were his military allies and they were united against a common enemy, the French and their Indigenous allies. Sadekanaktie, an Onondaga sachem of the League, replied using the same figure of speech.[164]

The domiciled nations of Canada also followed this tradition when they addressed the authorities of the British colonies. On June 28, 1700, the sachems of the Catholic nations of Canada, on behalf of the alliance of "Canada praying Indians," expressed themselves this way in keeping with the fraternal trade relations that bound them to the government authorities and to the merchants of Albany.[165] On August 1, 1735, in the context of the renewal of the pact between the domiciled nations and the New York authorities of Albany, the ambassadors from Canada reminded the attendees of the customs for meetings of this kind: regarding matters of peace, trade, and friendship, they would follow the usual customs of those between brothers.[166] This tradition was also respected in relations between the governors of the other New England colonies and the domiciled people. In August 1735, a group of Iroquois delegates from Sault-Saint-Louis and Abenaki from Saint-François travelled to Deerfield in New Hampshire to meet with Jonathan Belcher, governor-in-chief of the Province of Massachusetts-Bay. Iroquois Chief Ountaussokoe spoke with his brother, the English governor, on behalf of the ambassadors from Canada.

As we mentioned, this practice was rooted in Iroquois tradition. And the governor drew a parallel between the Iroquois origins of the ambassadors from Sault-Saint-Louis and the fraternal relation that bound them to the English, a relation that was made official by means of a formal agreement between the Government of Massachusetts and the "Caghnawaga Indians" in Albany, in 1724.[167] Indeed, on March 13 and June 26, 1724, several Iroquois, Algonquin, and Nipissing sachems from Lake of Two Mountains, as well as some Iroquois ambassadors from Sault-Saint-Louis were in Albany as brothers of the British.[168] As mentioned above, while the governor was addressed as "father," that did not mean he was no longer a brother, as it was entirely possible for the relation to be simultaneously fraternal and paternal. And so, after discussing with the brother-governor of Massachusetts at the Deerfield conference in 1735, the ambassadors of the domiciled Iroquois asked the governor to be the father-provider of their well-being.[169]

Until 1759, the members of the Seven Nations of Canada adhered exclusively to Iroquois tradition in their discussions with the English. And then the dialogue changed. The English father had replaced the French father. The English assumed the figure of Father Onontio, of the paternal figure of the governors of New France, but these new relations within their alliance were just as fraternal. In 1760, Sir William Johnson who, on behalf of General Jeffery Amherst and the King of England, negotiated the treaty of neutrality and non-aggression with the Seven Nations at Oswegatchie, became the brother of the domiciled nations of Canada. In 1828, a chief of the Iroquois of Lake of

Two Mountains recalled the words of the superintendent in 1760: "My Brothers, all that you ask of me shall be granted to you," in reference to their lands, their religion, and their missionaries.[170] On September 16,1760, two weeks after the meeting at Oswegatchie, the British, represented by Sir William Johnson, met with the members of the Seven Nations Confederacy in Kahnawake to renew the Oswegatchie agreements and conclude others. The discussion surrounding the different aspects of the treaty were conducted according to very precise rules: All of the words pronounced by the sachems and the Seven Nations war chiefs were articulated around the "brother" metaphor, marking the equality of the relations between the Confederacy and the English, a sense of belonging to a new community of allies, to the same family. In so doing, the Seven Fires carried on their pre-1760 policy of designating the British governors as brothers. This new alliance relation was characterized by several keywords—equality, reciprocity, hospitality, friendship, peace, satisfaction, respect, joy, kindness, love—indicative of an alliance between brothers. These terms also determined how the allies would behave with each other.[171] On September 11, 1763, during military talks between the Seven Fires, the Six Nations, and the British in the context of war in the Great Lakes area, Sir William Johnson expressed all the joy he felt knowing that his allies in Canada—his brothers—were firmly upholding the agreements surrounding the 1760 Peace and Friendship Treaty since, when maintaining a fraternal relation with one's political partners, one must, out of principle, respect the ties that bind them both.[172]

When negotiating an alliance treaty or its renewal, or when reminding those in attendance of the historical conditions surrounding the negotiation of a pact, the protagonists used the metaphor of brother because the brother was an ally, an ally with the same status and to whom authority, even moral authority, would not be conceded. They would present the problems afflicting them to their brother because allies share the same blood and the same sorrows. On July 22, 1770, in German Flats, the Seven Nations of Canada sachems and war chiefs informed Sir William Johnson of the difficulties that were driving them apart and reminded him of his solemn promises underlying their 1760 alliance: that the Seven Fires would continue to enjoy their rights and possessions, and that they would maintain their religious customs. The superintendent, in his role as brother, had a duty to reassure his allies. In an alliance relationship like the one binding the Seven Nations to the British Crown, the brothers shared the same interests.[173] This fraternal relationship between the authorities of the Department of Indian Affairs and the members of the Seven Nations of Canada was carried over to all the official representatives of the British Crown. On July 15, 1771, Sir William reminded the Iroquois of Kahnawake that their brother Daniel Claus was mandated to look after their affairs; he had the same status as the superintendent since he was a member of the same community of allies.[174]

On July 28, 1773, Daniel Claus responded to petitions from the Huron chiefs of Lorette concerning their legal disputes with the Jesuits. Claus addressed his Huron brothers by sharing with them the opinion of the British authorities concerning their settlement in the St. Lawrence Valley and their legal claim to the seigneurial lands of the St. Lawrence. In this regard, the Indian Affairs official had a relationship with the Indigenous people of Canada that was similar to the one his superior had with them.[175] During a congress held in Montreal in the summer of 1778, the domiciled Iroquois explained to an assembly of Iroquois of the League and to colonial representatives that the Seven Fires were linked to the King of England by virtue of the alliance. Their speeches referred to the family unit, to the alliance between English brother and Indigenous brother. These allies shared the same blood and, therefore, the same interests.[176] The allies were born of the same father and so were equal in the alliance because, at the time of the Conquest of Canada, the Seven Nations and the British had become members of the same family, forming "one and the same person."[177]

However, the fraternal relation was not systematically mentioned when evoking old alliances. On February 8, 1788, Aghnneetha, an Iroquois chief from Lake of Two Mountains, recalled, for the benefit of Sir John Johnson, the agreements reached with Sir William, in 1760, in the name of their father, the King of England. If Aghnneetha addressed the superintendent as father, it was because the domiciled nations and the British were allied brothers, being both from the same family stock since they were both children of kings. In fact, the use of "father" in these cases referred to the King of England and, as mentioned earlier, to his proxy, his representatives in North America,[178] and when seeking justice from the king, one would address the allied brother in his role as father-judge. It was this logic underpinning the alliance that was expressed by a Seven Fires ambassador in 1795, when he mentioned for the benefit of Superintendent McKee the 1760 Treaty of Oswegatchie: "My father, would you be the only one who would ignore our rights? Ask all of the Savage nations if it be not the truth."[179]

This fraternal relationship would be extended to the Americans of the independent colonies after 1776. In 1784, at a meeting at Fort Stanwix with several commissioners mandated by the Continental Congress, the governor of New York State informed the ambassadors of the Seven Nations of Canada that the peace concluded between the King of Great Britain and the representatives of the United States concerned them:

> My brothers, We shall not cease to thank the Master of life for Giving us the Pleasure of seeing you on our lands without having asked, and that we have no quarrel with You. You are not unaware, my brothers, that when we made Peace with the King Cora, Your Father, that you were considered to be his Subjects, & that we have always considered you as Such.

The governor went on to explain the reason for the congress at Fort Stanwix, and demanded of the "7 Villages of Canada" that they do not interfere with the negotiations, and that they take part only as witnesses: "You shall Be witnesses to a Council that the commissioners of the 13 Provinces shall hold with the Six Nations, to conclude a treaty with Them, in which we ask that you not interfere, as we have been warned of their ill intentions, and that they have already made every effort to indispose the nations against us, though they have not succeeded in doing so."[180]

All of the meetings and negotiations conducted between the Seven Fires Confederacy and the U.S. Government after 1784 revolved around the figure of the brother. On March 11, 1795, the Americans met with the Kahnawake and Akwesasne Iroquois to discuss the extinguishment of their hunting grounds in the State of New York. The Seven Nations ambassadors used the opportunity to remind their audience of the atmosphere that must reign when brothers meet: that the sentiment of justice alone must inspire talks between two allied brothers. The commissioners consented, thereby putting their word on the line.[181] On August 10, 1795, John Jay, then-governor of New York State, sent a message to his domiciled Iroquois brothers in Akwesasne in which he, too, acknowledged a kinship relation like the one uniting the Americans and the domiciled nations, in which each brother must hold up their promises, in this case, the promise to hold discussions to find a diplomatic solution to the problem that was dividing them, i.e., the recognition of Seven Fires hunting grounds in the State of New York.[182] On October 2, 1795, while at Lake George, the chiefs of the Seven Nations of Canada addressed a message to President George Washington in which they described to their brother-president the events surrounding negotiations with their New York brothers.[183] To differentiate the place and role occupied by each party in the relationship, and their attendant behaviors, they employed other figures of speech related to the fraternal relation.

At a treaty meeting held May 23, 1796, the Seven Nations delegates declared to the New York commissioners that their elder brother Washington possessed a declaration confirming the legitimacy of their diplomatic embassy. The president could therefore be confident that his Seven Fires brothers were honest in their actions, while the Confederacy ambassadors knew they could count on him and, if it came down to it, all the brothers could call on his wisdom as an elder.[184] This fraternal relation also bound the Seven Nations to the governors of the other American states, like Vermont, with which the Confederacy, then the domiciled Iroquois, had attempted in vain to negotiate for annuity payments for the lands they held in that state, and that had been occupied by the Americans since their independence.[185] By addressing Governor Isaac Tichenor as "elder brother," the domiciled nations were demonstrating their willingness to find a compromise to the problem pitting them against the governor. This could be considered a form of obedience. While there were discussions of shared interests, the big brother's decisions would prevail over those of the younger brother. In the context of these negotiations with Vermont, the elder brother-governor could exert pressure regarding the choices to be made. This form of seniority would have been deemed unacceptable by a mere brother.[186] At diplomatic meetings, the younger brothers could only address the gathering after having consulted with their older brothers, as they were obliged to follow their elders' advice at all times. He who occupied top spot in the alliance was the elder brother. The nation or person who held this title was therefore considered the main reference. One could compare this to the father-child relationship, although the relationship of authority was less apparent.[187]

Metaphorical kinship also marked the relations between the Seven Nations of Canada and the other Indigenous nations. The relation among the members of the Seven Fires Confederacy was fraternal, dating back to the first alliance under the French Regime and continuing on through the British Regime. It was a relationship valued highly by the King of France at the time of New France, and continued to be so under the King of England.[188] "My children! You are all Brothers," exclaimed the governor around 1670, referring to the domiciled Iroquois,

Huron, Algonquin and Nipissing.[189] The Iroquois laid the ground-work for this fraternal relationship in 1791 in a speech on the history of the relations that led to the creation of the Seven Fires Confederacy. The Iroquois orator reminded Superintendent Campbell of the nature of those relations that bound them at that time to their Algonquin and Nipissing brothers from Lake of Two Mountains: two allied brothers must provide each other with mutual assistance and support, and when one was threatened, the other would come to their aid. Describing a war plan that the Iroquois of the League intended to enact against the domiciled Algonquin and Nipissing, and that had been presented to the domiciled Iroquois, the latter apparently replied to the League's representatives,

> [t]hat we could not consent to abandon our Algonquin and Nipissing brothers after having sworn eternal fidelity; that we held them beneath our wing, and our hands on their heads; that they could not strike them without spilling our blood. With that response, our Six Nations brothers set the affair aside, wholly convinced that we were determined to support the Algonquin and Nipissing.[190]

Problems between brothers could only be resolved by diplomatic means. For example, when tensions arose in 1829 among the domiciled nations about their hunting grounds, negotiations were conducted in accordance with the rules governing relations between allies, which is to say, without one conceding his rights to the other or obliging the other by force to submit to his demands.[191] Just as the Seven Fire Nations were brothers, so were the chiefs of the Confederacy village councils and the Seven Nations chiefs.[192] On January 28, 1848, the interpreter of the Iroquois of the Great Fire of Sault-Saint-Louis wrote to the Secretary of Indian Affairs to inform him of a request from the chiefs of the Seven Nations: "I have been instructed on behalf of the chiefs of this village to inform you that they are bringing their Brothers from Lake of Two Mountains, that is to say, two or three Algonquin & other Iroquois, as well as their brothers from St. Regis."[193]

Throughout history, not all the domiciled nations were viewed the same way. On May 6, 1762, Sir William Johnson wrote to Daniel Claus that he was satisfied with the reprimands made by his "brothers and friends," the nations of Canada, to their cousins, the domiciled Abenaki, namely the suggestion that the Abenaki negotiate peace with the New England Stockbridge with whom they were about to go to war over a dispute about prisoners. These Abenaki cousins of the Seven Fires, who belonged to the same family as their domiciled brothers, should, in principle, respect the directives of their other relatives, and they, in turn, should ensure that their Abenaki cousins remain faithful to the pledges and promises of their brothers to the Superintendent. In the event of difficulties, it fell to the members of the same family, to the members of a group from the same lineage, to come to the aid of other members with whom they shared the same interests.[194]

Throughout their diplomatic history, the chiefs of the Seven Fires Confederacy and the chiefs of the Iroquois Six Nations Confederacy sought to maintain their fraternal relations. Whether it was under the French Regime or the British Regime of Canada,[195] the members of these two organizations would attempt to maintain regular diplomatic relations, even when problems arose, in which case they would attempt to reach a solution through political consensus rather than military confrontation.

On May 9, 1780, Chief John Deserontyon of the Ontario Iroquois replied to a letter from Daniel Claus, reminding the Indian Affairs official that it was the political rule of consensus that underpinned relations among brothers, since no single person had authority over another, and among allies, they sought instead to build a consensus rather than to impose their choice.[196] On April 6, 1798, the Kahnawake chiefs addressed Sir John Johnson, denouncing the defamation and slander of certain chiefs from the League of Iroquois from Grand River: "My

Father, we cannot help but express our surprise at the Petitions our brothers, the Six Nations, have made to you; claiming that we are predisposed against them."[197] It is because they are allies that the Seven Fires and the Six Nations held discussions before endorsing any proposal. In July 1799, the chiefs of the Seven Nations expressed their pleasure at seeing their brothers from the Iroquois Six Nations of Ontario gathered around the Great Fire of Kahnawake. They had come to rekindle the old alliance disrupted by recent political unrest between the two organizations and to re-establish the diplomacy that had been neglected between their great political councils.[198] The Iroquois of the League and those of the Seven Fires were allies, and as such, were bound by fraternal ties of kinship; these ties authorized each to speak on the other's behalf. On July 12, the Seven Fires chiefs emphasized to Sir John Johnson: "Father and Brothers, As we now speak in conjunction with our Brothers of the Five Nations."[199]

As previously pointed out, in order to understand the kinship system, one must consider not only the role played in the alliance, but also the diplomatic partners. Kinship relations between nations were not set in stone, and that is why, throughout history, a given nation did not always have the same status. For the same group, the kinship terms used to designate diplomatic partners and allies, and their place in the alliance, varied depending on the period. For example, under the French Regime, the Odawa, in relation to the Algonquin and Nipissing, were the younger brothers, and at the same time the nephews of their Algonquin and Nipissing uncles; this meant that, in some instances, the domiciled people of Lake of Two Mountains were mandated by their Odawa nephews to speak on their behalf to the governor or to the other Indigenous people. The qualifier "young," which, it is worth clarifying, had nothing to do with age, implied that the Odawa must defer to the authority of their elders.[200] The Odawa of the Great Lakes were also "grandfathers." They received this honorary title from the Wabanaki and Seven Nations Iroquois in recognition of their role as mediator in the triple Wabanaki-

Odawa-Iroquois alliance.[201] In other words, the Odawa could be grandfather, brother, or nephew, depending on the role they played and the partners with whom they had diplomatic relations. They were "grandfathers" in the sense of mediators, "brothers" in their capacity as allies, and "nephews" as subordinates.

The uncle-nephew system was unusual, as it implied a relationship of obedience. On January 1, 1797, the interpreter Jean-Baptiste Destimauville, in his report to the Department of Indian Affairs, wrote that the Abenaki of Saint-François were the uncles of the Shawnee and the Wolves, and that this status gave them a certain authority in their diplomatic relations. Destimauville added that one word from the Abenaki to the Shawnee and the Wolves would "summon them to order."[202] Within the uncle-nephew relationship, nephews were expected to respect their uncles and, as such, the uncles wielded authority, which meant that, in this case, the Abenaki ambassadors could voice their opinions and use their wisdom and moral authority that their position within the alliance granted them to exert a degree of persuasive power over their kin. In May 1757, Bougainville noted in his journal that "the Wolves view the Abenaki as their brothers; they speak the same language. But in regard to the Iroquois, whom they refer to as 'uncles,' they fear them more than they love them."[203] The relations therefore varied depending on the time and partners.

A final point worth exploring is the metaphor of "woman" attributed to certain nations. Among the Iroquoian, this term referred to both the sexual division of labour and to political relations: men filled the offices of traditional chiefs and spoke at meetings with the Europeans, while the women spoke at the village councils and at the Confederacy's grand councils, but never addressed international gatherings. As such, women-nations were not granted the privilege of dealing with the Europeans.[204]

Inter-nation relationships were designated in terms of kinship, and all of the allied nations belonged, metaphorically, to the same related group. As in any kinship system, it was the relationship that determined the role or status. Each party was therefore designated by as many kinship terms as they had diplomatic relations. The kinship system governed social relations within a nation and played the same role in the alliance relations between nations. It is therefore crucial to decode the metaphorical kinship that structured the discourse of the Indigenous peoples. In fact, it is key to understanding the logic behind their political relationships.

CHAPTER THREE

Forest Diplomacy: Indigenous Rituals and Protocols

International councils and conferences followed strict protocols and practices: Matters regarding the village were discussed at village councils, whereas international affairs were addressed at conferences. These two events followed similar rules, the exception being that councils were on a smaller scale, while certain rites were reserved exclusively for international events. International conferences would bring together protagonists from different nations and other alliance networks, which implied the presence of two or more parties, be they Indigenous or European.

One observation worth noting about these congresses is the duration of the events. They tended to stretch over a long period, due to the large number of attendees. Given that underlying all debate was a desire to reach a consensus, conferences could span several days, weeks, or even months. A message would be presented on one day, and the reply would generally be formulated the following day. This was a formula adopted by all the protagonists. In principle, in order to organize a major international conference, the Europeans would have to obtain approval from the authorities in place, i.e., the governor or superintendent.[1] When an official called a conference, in other words, when he kindled a fire at a specific location to debate and negotiate, his representatives would be the first to speak. This was the custom established between the Indigenous people and the Europeans, and it was a custom mentioned by an Iroquois of the League of Six Nations at a conference on March 24, 1764, before the superintendent of Indian Affairs. On that occasion, the orator explained to Sir William Johnson that the Mohawk nation would speak before the other Iroquois of the League because they were the ones who had called the meeting, and this was in keeping with the unanimous agreement of all those in attendance at the conference.[2]

Conferences between Europeans and Indigenous nations were conducted according to the traditional protocol of Indigenous culture. The Indigenous people imposed their figures of speech and rhetoric—which the Europeans borrowed and used[3]—as well as their ceremonies and rituals. Sir William Johnson received a letter from Philadelphia dated April 24, 1756, in which the author observed the pains to which the superintendent went to conclude a treaty with the Iroquois Six Nations, the Delaware, and the Shawnee, considering how "the Indians adhere so closely to their Tedious Ceremonies." He goes on to say that "I am sensible you must have had a most fatiguing time of it," but the superintendent notes that it is important to adhere to them.[4] In fact, if Sir William consented to comply with the ceremonies, it was because he believed that the success of the British in their colonial endeavours with the Indigenous people hinged on their ability to understand their customs, practices, and habits. On May 31, 1764, Sir William met with some Seven Nations warriors in Niagara, regarding the military alliance against the Odawa chief, Pontiac. The superintendent and other British civil and military representatives, wampum in hand, took part in the Indigenous people's war songs and dances. The British, aware that these rituals occupied an important symbolic place in the military alliance, and that they gave courage to their warrior allies from the Seven Fires, understood that, in the interest of the Crown, they must become accustomed to and take part with all the solemnity required of these rituals.[5] All of these international conferences followed a strict diplomatic process. They would begin with condolence and pipe-smoking ceremonies, then gifts would be exchanged and there would be a feast. Throughout the ceremonies, wampum strings and necklaces would be exchanged on both sides. Conferences between the Europeans and the Indigenous nations followed the same protocol, the only difference being that they would sometimes wrap up with the ratification of a written treaty.

Political Nature of Wampum Necklaces

All the initiatives surrounding the alliance would be marked by a material exchange of beaded shell strings or necklaces called "wampum." These beads were made by perforating clamshells (*Venus mercenaria*) found in large numbers along the shores of the Atlantic Ocean. The beads would be threaded together to form a wampum. As an object of exchange, wampum, for the Indigenous people, held a mystical value and quality that was often poorly understood by the Europeans.[6] In English and French documents, wampums are described using the terms "word" (*parole*), "voice" (*voix*), "string" (*cordon*), "necklace" (*collier*), or "belt" (*ceinture*). The French referred to them as *porcelaine*, and the English as "wampum." The term "necklace" rather than "belt" is the one we will use here, as these objects were worn most often around the neck. This is reflected in the British proceedings of a July 1764 conference held in Niagara between Indian Affairs officials and the Odawa. In describing the gesture made by one of the Odawa spokespersons, the transcriber noted that the Odawa chief "Gave two Belts from about his Neck."[7]

Wampum strings were of lesser importance than wampum necklaces, as suggested by Sir William Johnson in a letter addressed to the New York interpreter, Arent Stevens, in May 1755. After sending a string of wampum to certain Great Lakes nations, the superintendent corrected himself, noting "At my first arrival I sent a String of Wampum, but lest that not be sufficient, I now send this belt," implying that strings were used to send less important messages.[8] On March 24, 1766, Sir William gave Louis Pertuis, an interpreter with the domiciled Iroquois, some letters and a bunch of six wampum strings to inform the Iroquois of Kahnawake that the superintendent had written to Governor James Murray about their complaints about some of the English.[9] Wampum strings were also used as invitations or to introduce ambassadors who came to speak. At a meeting at the home of Sir William Johnson in July 1768, a messenger arrived at Johnson Hall to inform the superintendent of the arrival of a delegation of Abenaki from Saint-François. The messenger was carrying wampum strings from the Abenaki.[10] The following exchange is highly telling about the significance of wampum "bunches" as an object presented when inviting a party to speak: Jean-Baptiste Destimauville noted, on April 6, 1811, that the Iroquois of Kahnawake had invited the Huron of Lorette and the Abenaki of Saint-François to the Great Fire of the Seven Nations, and that, from there, the Confederacy members would continue on to Niagara. The Indian Affairs official in Quebec City subsequently wrote to Superintendent Salaberry that the Iroquois ambassadors told him they had been "tasked by the Iroquois of Sault St Louis to beat three bunches of *porcelaine* to invite the Huron to their village, and to have their brothers, the Abenaki, join them along the way, so as to all go together at the invitation of the brothers from the *Pays d'En haut* to Niagara."[11]

All of the material characteristics of wampum—colour, pattern, shape, length—were symbolic of its content. Generally speaking, pale colours like white symbolized peace, whereas dark colours like black or purple represented war. In the instructions concerning a speech that the American Continental Congress commissioners were to make before the Seven Fires, an explanation was given as to which colour wampum to offer, noting that if a peace proposal was to be made to the Seven Fires, then a white wampum should be made.[12] On July 4, 1770, a group of Ontario Mississauga met with Sir William Johnson at Johnson

Hall, where they presented the superintendent with a large, white wampum necklace commemorating an alliance between their nation and the British.

The white colour indicated that the message proposed was one of peace, and the figures depicted on the wampum symbolized the alliance which, in this particular case, included the Mississauga Nation, Sir William Johnson, and Providence (represented by a cross). All of the figures were holding hands.[13]

When they were primarily black or purple, or combined with red, the necklaces symbolized war or death. This was the case of the wampum offered by the British to the Great Lakes nations in 1777 in the context of the American Revolution. Black signified hostilities, and was an invitation to engage in war.[14] On March 17, 1814, George Provost, Governor and Commander of the British Armed Forces, met with the Great Lakes council and war chiefs in Quebec City to urge them to maintain a climate of war with the American colonists who had settled on their lands. After admonishing them to consider the advantages of a military alliance with the British, the leader of the British Army ended his speech by presenting two wampums to members of the delegation, one black and the other blood-red, which he referred to as a "bloody belt."[15] The designation and description of these wampums characterized their content, meaning they could be "bad," "ominous," "threatening," or even have "a dangerous tendency."[16] On April 19, 1774, Sayenquaraghta, an Iroquois war chief from the League of Six Nations, reported to Superintendent Johnson that there were "bad necklaces" circulating in the American Southwest; these necklaces signified enmity, antagonism, and conflict between certain nations of the Southwest and the Iroquois League.[17] When these wampums symbolized a coalition or common front, they were referred to as "belts of Alliance."[18]

Black wampums were associated with sadness, grief, affliction, death, or war. In this context, by offering a white wampum, one would be expressing the grief they felt over a shared sorrow. White wampums were used this way to avoid such sentiments and the actions that caused them. On August 20, 1767, Sir William Johnson received a letter from Quebec City informing him that a military officer had presented the governor with a broad, white belt from the people of Kanehsatake so he could intervene and prevent the European settlers from selling alcohol in their village.[19] Inversely, on August 5, 1768, an Oswegatchie sachem presented to Superintendent Johnson a black necklace to urge Sir William to step in and prohibit the sale of alcohol, which had been resulting in bloody violence in the village.[20]

In some cases, wampums would combine black and white beads. On April 21, 1759, Sir William Johnson replied to the messages of some domiciled warriors from Oswegatchie and presented an Iroquois delegation from the League of Six Nations with a number of wampum necklaces destined for the Indigenous people in Canada. One of the necklaces, which expressed Johnson's ultimatum to the domiciled nations to leave the French-Indigenous alliance, was two-toned. This combination of colours reflected sentiments of life and death, peace and war.[21] In the context of Pontiac's Revolt, Sir William Johnson handed a message to the Seven Fires representatives on July 24, 1763, so they could pass it on to Daniel Claus. Johnson's message was accompanied by a white and black wampum necklace that the Seven Fires ambassadors presented to the other Confederacy members in the hopes they would not join the Great Lakes insurgents. It was a message of peace and neutrality in a context of war: white vs black.[22] On March 4, 1768, Sir William repeated the same gesture, presenting a two-tone necklace to the Iroquois Six Nations and Seven Fires ambassadors gathered at a conference at Johnson Hall, to signify to the delegates that he desired their political collaboration in peace negotiations with the Cherokee of North Carolina, who were in conflict with the British.[23]

Wampum, as a keeper of memory, was a record of oral proceedings and bore witness to actions and speeches. The Iroquois of Akwesasne spokesperson in attendance at the Seven Nations Great Fire on August 21, 1769, reminded the British of the clauses in the treaty concluded in Oswegatchie nine years earlier between the Crown and the Confederacy. The wampum presented by the orator from Akwesasne was like an archival object that is exhibited to remember the terms of the past: "By this String of Wampum we beg to remind you of what you Transacted with the Department of the Seven confederate Nations of Canada in August 1760, near Swegachy."[24] On October 20, 1779, some delegates from the Seven Nations of Canada presented Superintendent Campbell with a wampum commemorating the agreements reached between the Confederacy and the British in Oswegatchie, as they appeared on the necklace: "Here is a Necklace that represents the King, who is the Tree that holds the Seven Branches that are the Seven Villages, and you, Colonel Campbell, are the eighth."[25] Seven branches for seven nations. The eighth represented much more than just the official; it symbolized all of the British who had been allied with the Confederacy since 1760.

It was the symbols inscribed on these objects that served as mnemonic devices. The symbols took on different forms: human, animal, plant, geometrical, or material. They included representations of figures, diamonds, hexagons, lines, diagonal shapes, hatchets, trees, branches, roads... However, a wampum could sometimes metaphorically represent an object that was not depicted in its design. In such cases, the wampum was like a "flask of liquor" or a "pouch of tobacco."[26] Objects other than wampum could also be exchanged, although they didn't carry the same political weight. On February 25, 1756, at a meeting between Sir William Johnson and some Six Nations allies, the warriors' spokesperson, delighted with the superintendent's words, expressed his satisfaction by offering him a pack of animal skins.[27] A Chippewa sachem did the same thing at a meeting with Sir William in Niagara, on July 14, 1764. With his first entreaty, the Chippewa chief presented the superintendent with skins, with the second, a beaver blanket.[28] Indeed, as demonstrated in the literature, this connection between the oral and the tangible meant that words were always accompanied by a material offering.

The patterns that appear on wampums are indicative of the prevailing situation at the time they were in circulation. Where there were hatchets, the wampums signified war. In English documents, these were known as "ax belts," war axes," or "hatchet belts." This was the metaphorical hatchet, emblematic of hostilities between the groups. At a conference in Canajoharie on April 16, 1759, the Iroquois of the League of Six Nations presented Sir William Johnson with a proposal for a military alliance from the governor of New France, who had given them an "Ax," that is, a wampum necklace bearing the form of an ax.[29] A Seven Nations of Canada spokesperson, who was in Albany on June 28, 1761, to meet with George Croghan, Sir William Johnson's representative, lamented in his speech the fact that the ambassadors had encountered "all sorts of hurdles" on the road between Kahnawake and Albany, making their journey very risky. To remedy this situation, the domiciled nations presented a "Road belt" so that Sir William would not forget that they were entitled to journey freely on the roads connecting Canada to New England.[30] On July 29, 1764, some Chippewa from Lake Ontario met with Sir Johnson in Niagara, where the superintendent presented one of their sachems with a necklace that he was to carefully preserve. That wampum was his way of recommending to the Chippewa chiefs that they keep an eye on the fort and village of Niagara, which were symbolically represented on the object. It depicted two men holding the fort fast on each side, and a road running through it.[31]

Those who received a necklace generally agreed to discuss the proposals put forth, without necessarily endorsing them. A rejected wampum could signify that the message or suggestions had been put off. On June 10, 1776, Benedict Arnold wrote to Peter Schuyler to report on the proceedings of a Grand Council of the Seven Fires and a conference attended by Kahnawake representatives in Montreal. He wrote that the Confederacy had refused the military alliance proposed in 1775 by Governor Carleton, in the context of the American colonies' revolution against the king. Then, at the Montreal conference that followed the one in Kahnawake, the members of the Confederacy, represented at that time by the Abenaki of Saint-François, the Iroquois of Kahnawake, and the Iroquois of Kanehsatake, decided to give back the wampum necklace to the governor, having chosen instead to remain neutral in the conflict and thereby turning down his proposal for a military alliance.[32] On June 19, 1777, Théorgointé, an Iroquois chief of the League of Six Nations, asked John Campbell why Commander Haldimand did not come to the aid of the Iroquois of the League, who were being struck down by the troops of the American Continental Army. Frustrated by the failure of the British to fulfill their military promises and commitments, the spokesperson for the Iroquois of the League ended his speech by saying, "Shall we be at last escorted, or must we fear People of Your Colour [...] as now it is only we Iroquois to wage war on them."[33] And with that he is said to have "thrown the Necklace on the Table in Anger."[34]

Offering wampum was a political obligation that the Europeans complied with. On July 28, 1770, following negotiations that had taken place a few days earlier at German Flats, Superintendent Johnson presented the deputies of the Seven Nations of Canada, who were gathered at his residence, with a necklace of wampum so that they would remember his advice to "remain united" and "behave properly" in their alliance with the British, as this could only contribute to the "Happiness" of the "Indian People."[35] On June 26, 1774, Superintendent Johnson wrote to Daniel Claus with a request: "If You have any Belts of Wampum I shall want them much, especially black ones, as I have none but what came from the Indians, & would be known by them which would not looks so well."[36] Clearly, the superintendent had no desire to try and fool his allies by undoing his previously received wampums to make new ones. From a price list detailing the articles required to conduct negotiations with the Mississauga in 1808, we learned that wampums were stored in the Montreal area (Lachine), at the Department of Indian Affairs general storehouse.[37]

Some of the wampums made by the Europeans bore the initials of the negotiators, as well as the official seals of the colonial administrators. On October 17, 1763, Sir William Johnson presented to the Oneida and Tuscarora of the Iroquois League of Six Nations a necklace on which there appeared his initials and the year 1756. This was the year Johnson was commissioned as British Superintendent of Indian Affairs, giving him exclusive control over relations between the British, the Six Nations, and their allies.[38] The necklace is described as "A Black Belt marked WJ 1756."[39]

During the American Revolution, the members of the Continental Congress presented some Great Lakes Indigenous nations with a "four foot long" necklace illustrating the alliance of "fifteen American colonies," an alliance known as that of the "fifteen united Sachems."[40] A document dated March 28, 1780, includes a description of another necklace, this one offered by Colonel Guy Johnson before a gathering of Six Nations members and their allies. The secretary recording the proceedings of the conference noted: "Gave a long black Belt of 9 Rows with the sign G.J. and his Seal at one End."[41] In his correspondence with Thomas Gage dated February 19, 1764, Sir William Johnson emphasized the importance attributed to wampum by the Indigenous Peoples and the British, who recognized the political value of these objects. The superintendent suggested to the military governor how to deal with the Great Lakes nations who refused to side with the English: "... we should tye them down [in the peace] according to their own forms of which they take the most notice, for Example by Exchanging a very large belt with some remarkable & intelligible figures thereon. Expressive of the occasion which always be shewn at public Meetings, to remind them of their promises."[42]

Wampums were a communication tool and also a way to formalize discussions. Every important message had to be accompanied by a wampum, otherwise it would not be taken into consideration. The Mohawk of Canajoharie emphasized this notion at a meeting with Sir William Johnson at Fort Johnson on February 13, 1757. The superintendent was lamenting the fact that certain Mohawk of the League were threatening to break off their political agreements with the British, in response to which the Mohawk representatives replied "you may know our words are of no weight unless accompanyd with Wampum."[43] In October 1759, Sir William reminded the Iroquois of the League of Six Nations of the promises of the domiciled people of Oswegatchie, Kahnawake, and Kanehsatake to remain neutral in the conflict between Great Britain and France. Referring to the wampum necklaces sent to Canada, the superintendent let them know "that I have hitherto befriended them; that they have it in their power now, by quitting the French, to become once more a happy people."[44] Johnson then described the response from the domiciled nations that was transmitted to him by way of the "many and solemn professions made to me and the Six Nations, and the assurances they lately, by belts and strings of wampum, gave me of their fixed resolutions to abandon the French."[45]

In other words, wampums served to underscore speeches and confirm commitments. On January 30, 1762, a spokesperson for the Iroquois of Kahnawake offered Thomas Gage one such necklace after a long speech on the rights of the Iroquois to the lands of Sault-Saint-Louis.[46] On August 5, 1810, the council chiefs of the Abenaki of Bécancour complained to the governor, Sir James Henry Craig, about what the Abenaki Council considered to be the dishonest dealings of an individual from Trois-Rivières who, they claimed, was attempting to dispossess them of part of their seigneurial lands in Bécancour. To "prove" the veracity of their argument, the Abenaki presented their petition along with some "branches de porcelaine" (porcelain branches).[47] Accompanying documents with wampums was a guarantee that the written discourse was truthful, and that it was in keeping with the words of the speakers.

Kahnawake, Keeper of the Wampum

Wampums had to be carefully preserved because they were the guardians of historical agreements. They served as documentary references or archival objects that could always be re-read when needed. On September 21, 1741, the governor of New France wrote that Vincent, a chief of the domiciled Huron, had gone to Lake of Two Mountains to inquire about "their treasure," that is, their collection of wampums, which had to be carefully stored since they had been offered by the Huron of Lorette at the time of the founding of the village, and served as a "constitution" for establishing a political council.[48] On February 8, 1788, the Iroquois of Kanehsatake presented to Sir John Johnson the ancestral necklace that confirmed their right to reside at Lake of Two Mountains. The Iroquois orator stressed the risk of losing the wampums or having them stolen. To prevent this, the wampums used to be buried in the ground, as if their sacred power acted as a sort of talisman to protect the land. The domiciled Iroquois reminded the superintendent that the necklace had been made in the traditional manner of their ancestors.[49] Each village in the Confederacy would safeguard its own wampum strings and necklaces.

The validity of the transmission of history through the use of wampums was endorsed by the Department of Indian Affairs officials. On July 28, 1765, the Seven Nations representatives showed Sir William Johnson all the wampum necklaces he had given the Confederacy on the occasion of their earlier meetings. The Confederacy chiefs, who had come to "refresh" the terms of the alliance between the Seven Fires and the British, took special pains to exhibit a necklace with 10 rows of wampum featuring white squares, which they considered of the highest importance. It confirmed all the past agreements and showed the superintendent that the Seven Nations had not forgotten his advice. Sir William replied that he was pleased that the Confederacy members had kept his necklaces, and hoped that the substance of his words that accompanied them would not be forgotten.[50] On October 10, 1838, Secretary Napier suggested to the superintendent of Upper Canada, Samuel P. Jarvis, that he consult the "Porcelain Necklaces" received from the Indigenous nations because they were archival objects that were every bit as valuable as written documents. Napier and Jarvis subsequently attempted to ease the tensions between the Algonquin and the Nipissing, who were accusing the Ontario Mississauga of having illegally taken part of their hunting grounds.[51] Wampums would be regularly "re-read" in order to preserve their message and hand down their content for posterity. In other words, if the words were lost, and if the oral discourse became separated from the object, then its reading would become virtually impossible. Wampums were a way to support the oral tradition; they were not a form of writing.[52]

The wampums offered by the Seven Fires Confederacy usually took the form of necklaces with seven rows of beads (when placed horizontally). The seven rows symbolized the union of all the Confederacy councils. Take, for instance, the wampum presented by the "Caugnawagas" to Sir William Johnson on July 22, 1770, at the conference in German Flats. The purpose of the necklace was to remind the superintendent of the pledges set out in the 1760 Treaty of Oswegatchie binding the Confederacy and the British Crown.[53] When necklaces were offered on behalf of the Confederacy, it signified that a unanimous agreement had been reached among all the Confederacy fires. To commemorate that unanimity, the Confederacy members could offer seven different necklaces, each accompanied by a speech given on behalf of each of the member nations, which is what one of the Seven Fires sachems did on October 4, 1792, during a conference in Ohio, at the Auglaize River: "He gave Separate Necklaces for each of the 7 Nations, with a brief speech for each one, indicating the Nation to which the belt belonged."[54] These messages from the Seven Fires, which conveyed their desire to maintain the political peace, were backed by a "very wide" necklace of white wampums.[55]

These wampums were the material representation of the discussions held at the Great Fire and of the consensus reached during negotiations in Kahnawake. When the documents mentioned an eighth necklace, this could symbolize the unity within the Confederacy, to which other partners could be added, such as with the alliance with the colonial authorities. When eight necklaces were laid down, it meant that the message stemmed from a consensus among each of the Seven Fires, on one hand, and the colonial authorities, on the other.[56]

The Iroquois of Kahnawake, guardians of the Grand Council of the Seven Fires, were invested with diplomatic initiative. Consequently, Kahnawake was the main depository for the wampums exchanged with the Confederacy, and it was to the "Coghnawageys" that the wampums for the Seven Nations were given.[57] The necklaces were laid out before the Grand Council of the Confederacy, which transmitted their content to the Confederacy members. The Huron of Lorette described this practice at a conference held in Québec City in the presence of Frederick Haldimand on July 18, 1779:

> When you left here for England, you gave us a Necklace that was to be presented to all the Nations to keep them firmly tied to the Engagements during your absence, which we brought with great attention to Cachnawaga, and from there, we are certain that it was transmitted to all the Nations.[58]

On October 26, 1829, the Algonquin of Pointe-du-Lac, who were attending a conference in Trois-Rivières with Louis-Juchereau Duchesnay, referred to the Grand Council as the guardian of the archival objects concerning the Confederacy. The Algonquin orator suggested that the British official go to Kahnawake to consult some of the documentary pieces there, including wampums and written documents regarding the hunting grounds of the member nations of the Seven Fires Confederacy.[59] Kahnawake was the depository of all the Confederacy's transactions.

The oral tradition of the Wabanaki provides other details on the wampums kept in Kahnawake. At diplomatic meetings between the Wabanaki and the Iroquois, the wampums were displayed in the middle of the Kahnawake parliament, where they were hung from a wooden hoop, a metaphor for the central council fire around which the Confederacy members sat and where they re-read the necklaces. The wampums hanging on the hoop would symbolically "nourish" the fire.[60] Studies on the Iroquois have shown that the necklaces were often guarded by an individual who bore the title of "guardian of the wampum." He would be chosen based on his ability to recite the words associated with the necklaces. The presence of a "guardian of the wampum" therefore signified that the agreement wampums and the memory associated with them were preserved in a village.[61] The same was true for paper documents. On July 28, 1834, the Iroquois of Kahnawake reminded the Indian Affairs officials that the Grand Council Chief was in charge of the chest containing the archives of the Seigneurie of Sault-Saint-Louis as well as other documents relating to the history of the village, and that this mandate was only given to a member of the council.[62]

"You Who Depend on Ink and Paper"

The Indigenous people deemed their oral tradition to be just as valid—and their memory just as reliable—as the literature or memories of the Europeans. There is a mention to this effect in the *Journal of Indian Affairs* dated June 4, 1765, regarding a meeting that was held at Johnson Hall in the presence of delegates from the Great Lakes Mississauga and Six Nations Iroquois. Wabbicommicott, the spokesperson for the Mississauga, reminded Sir William of the content of the 1759, 1761, and 1764 negotiations between the British and his nation. Holding the necklace that the superintendent had given them in Niagara in 1764, the speaker went on to recount the discussions that had taken place since the fort was seized in 1759. As the secretary noted in the proceedings: "Here he repeated all that had been said to him in 1759, 1761, & 1764."[63] In 1818, the Iroquois of Kahnawake reminded Governor Charles, Duke of Richmond, of the "ruses and tactics employed by the Jesuits" to dispossess them of their seigneurial lands. In their petition, they recounted the words of the missionaries at the time:

> We require part of your land to build a flour mill, to support our subsistence. You must abandon it to us, and from the moment we cease to be Your missionaries, you will take back this piece of land with the mill. If you consent to our request, you shall surely go to Heaven, as surely as if you had a ladder before you to climb there, &, on the contrary, is you should refuse it, we shall abandon you and God will be angry. He will bring down upon you disease, and evil Spirits will take hold of you, you shall no longer be able to kill the bear and other animals, and your Children shall starve to death.[64]

Nevertheless, the Europeans considered the written word as an element demonstrating the superiority of their culture. For example, in response to the wampum offered him by the Iroquois of the League in Detroit in July 1761, the superintendent told them that the necklace that lay before him and that was supposed to remind him of his promises was needless: "I have it on record, as well as your promises and conduct never to be forgotten."[65]

The superintendent expressed the same sentiment, in March 1762, to the Seven Fires delegates, referring to the content of the peace and alliance treaties between the Crown and the Confederacy, claiming, "You have not the advantage of Records like us."[66] The written archives of the Indian Affairs Department were therefore considered by the British officials to be the primary reference source. On July 28, 1765, Sir William reminded the Seven Fires, papers in hand, of the content of all the messages he had sent them between 1755 and 1760 concerning the alliance between the domiciled nations and the French, as well as the proposals of neutrality offered by the British during the Seven Years' War: "I have every thing that passed between us fresh in my memory, I have it down in Writing so that it cannot be forgotten."[67] Indeed, the signed and sealed document was considered by the Europeans in North America as concrete proof of a treaty. In March 1768, Sir William addressed the ambassadors of the Seven Nations of Canada, the Iroquois Six Nations, and several Cherokee who were gathered at Johnson Hall, in the hopes of getting them to sign a peace and friendship treaty. On March 9, following a week of discussions, the negotiations were concluded. Johnson declared he had "heard and committed in writing everything that transpired during the present Congress."[68] For the Europeans, the signing of a treaty was a finality, while for the Indigenous people, the words that accompanied the act were also part of the agreement. For the Indigenous people, no agreement was definitive; rather, it must always be reactivated, like a friendship. In other words, it must be maintained and kindled. Moreover, for the oral tradition to remain alive, such agreements must be regularly renewed.[69] On September 28, 1742, a group of representatives of the domiciled nations of Canada travelled to Albany to renew a peace and friendship treaty that contained clauses about military neutrality and trade. The secretary in charge of submitting the report wrote that their embassy's goal was to "refresh their memory and renew this Agreement."[70]

Oral communication was the primary point of reference for the Indigenous people, while for the Europeans, it was writing. For the Indigenous people, it was important that words be backed up by wampum, as when they were transmitted on paper, they felt they could lose their effect; it was said they were "reduced by writing."[71] On May 23, 1796, during negotiations between the Seven Nations of Canada and the State of New York regarding hunting grounds, the Seven Nations orator scorned the changing nature of the supposedly superior written tradition: "You, who depend on ink and paper, which ought never to fade, must recollect better than we, who cannot write, and who only depend on memory; yet your promises are fresh in our minds."[72]

Nevertheless, the Indigenous people were keenly aware of the importance of the written word, since, from the early days of the colonial period, wampum had no longer been the sole repository for memory. And while the Indigenous people relied on the memory of witnesses, peers, or elders, and they believed that wampum had symbolic power, they were aware that the interpretation attributed to it could be based on a memory that could, in some cases, be quite selective. The domiciled Abenaki said as much when they denigrated the words associated with the wampum the Algonquin of Pointe-du-Lac presented to them in 1829 as part of their land negotiations. They pointed to the written word, in this instance, the Royal Proclamation issued by George III of England, rather than wampum, as the symbolic and moral power, demonstrating the respect they felt for the written word. Indeed, did not the domiciled people refer frequently to the Royal Proclamation in the oral traditions?[73]

On March 19, 1761, Daniel Claus mentioned to Sir William Johnson that the Seven Fires representatives were demanding that the 1760 Oswegatchie and Kahnawake agreements between the British Crown and the Confederacy be set down on paper for the "Memory of our and their Posterity."[74] In defending their interests, the members of the Confederacy were clearly not averse to using elements of European culture. On January 30, 1762, Kaghneghtago, a sachem from Kahnawake, reminded Thomas Gage of what had become of the letters of concession given by King Louis XIV to the Jesuits for the Iroquois of Sault-Saint-Louis. The document in question had, until that time, been carefully safeguarded in the village by one of the chiefs until, some 50 years prior, the chief had been killed in battle. The document was put in the hands of his wife but, before she died a short time later, she was "prevailed upon by her Confessor to deliver him the parchment, he persuading her that her salvation would be at stake in case she should dye possessed of it."[75] It appears, then, that the Iroquois, throughout their history at Sault-Saint-Louis, attempted to preserve the document as best as possible, as the Jesuits had told them at the time that only "the paper from the King of France spoke" and was valid.[76]

On June 29, 1795, Jean-Baptiste Destimauville wrote to Alexander McKee at the Department of Indian Affairs, noting that the domiciled Abenaki of Saint-François and Bécancour were calling for "several papers of importance both for These Villages and for those of Missisk8i," that were presently being held at the superintendent's office in Montreal.[77] On May 25, 1796, the Seven Fires ambassadors requested that the State of New York provide them with handwritten proof of their legal claims on the Seven Fires hunting grounds south of the St. Lawrence River. For the domiciled ambassadors negotiating with New York, in order for the commissioners' veto to be admissible, they were required to present written proof of their claim showing that the reclaimed lands had been ceded by contract or treaty.[78] On November 7, 1801, the Abenaki of Saint-François submitted a petition to the governor in which they laid out their doubts and concerns about certain land surveys that had been carried out on their lands. In it they asked the governor to provide them with the survey they deemed "to be the most correct."[79]

On January 15, 1830, two Iroquois deputies from Kahnawake who were headed to London to meet with Sir George Murray asked the Secretary of State for Colonial Affairs to write down the result of their negotiations with the Crown about their rights to the seigneurial lands, so they could report back to their members on their return to Canada. The Iroquois ambassadors had, in fact, taken with them all the relevant documentation regarding their claim.[80]

On August 18, 1830, the Iroquois of Lake of Two Mountains made the same request to the government of Lower Canada: that if the governor would grant them what they were asking, that he "write it on a good paper."[81] In 1836, the Indian Affairs agent posted in Saint-Régis conducted an inquiry into the land titles of the domiciled Iroquois. The chiefs of the Iroquois council of Akwesasne confirmed to the agent that there existed a hand-written copy of the agreements reached with the British between 1760 and 1776, that this document was conserved in the public archives in Quebec City, and that, sadly, the copy they once had had burned along with the church in which the village archives had been kept. The Iroquois chiefs then provided the agent with additional information on how to proceed: if they were still unable to track down the document, they would have to pursue their search either in the archives of the provincial secretary, those of the governor general, or the archives of the Department of Indian Affairs.[82]

In 1854, the Iroquois of the Seven Fires reminded the governor of Vermont that his predecessor had, in 1798, required that the nations of Canada provide the documents proving that the lands they were claiming in that state actually belonged to them. They added that the Indigenous people relied only on the oral tradition of their ancestors, who safeguarded the memory of public affairs.[83] And yet, on June 21, 1855, the Iroquois of Kahnawake pointed out to the Vermont State commissioners that they had in their possession "volumes of treaties published by the general government, and other official documents" about past land negotiations.[84] From then on, references to history were no longer solely oral; written or printed documents could also confirm historic agreements.[85]

Tears, Tobacco, Gifts, and Feasts

Wampums were the polarizing focus of protocolary rituals, playing a central role in the condolence ceremony and the "blood blanket" essential to the diplomatic process. The ritual would involve two groups: On one side were the Indigenous political and military leaders, sachems, and war chiefs, and on the other were the representatives of the colonial power, governors, and officials. On July 18, 1770, at a conference in German Flats, the Oneida sachem, Conoghquieson, stressed the importance of the ceremonial rituals when two groups gathered. The sachem reminded Sir William Johnson that, in keeping with the rituals established by the ancestors, it was customary, before every public discussion, for both parties to offer their condolences.[86] This ceremony would follow very strict rules, as described in the 1767 *Journal of Indian Affairs* in which Daniel Claus's visits to the Indigenous villages in the St. Lawrence Valley were detailed. At many of his stops, he would proceed with the condolence ceremony, following all the stages of the ritual. On August 27, he travelled to Kanehsatake, where he was welcomed by the chiefs of the three nations gathered there. The domiciled nations presented him with a string of wampum, explaining to him that one of the village's Iroquois chiefs had died at the hands of a gang of drunken individuals.

Daniel Claus asked that a meeting be held. He was then welcomed by the Iroquois, Algonquin, and Nipissing sachems, and war chiefs. After the customary salutations, they informed him of the death of eight other people as a result of excessive alcohol consumption. The ceremony in which he was to take part consisted of seven stages, in specific order, to mark the death of an Iroquois chief:[87]

1. Daniel Claus offered three strings of wampum, to "wipe the Tears, Clear the Throat, and Open the Ears." These metaphorical, sensory purifications were required to prevent any distortion of the messages that were to follow.

2. He then offered a black wampum to cover the grave of the dead, in tribute to the deceased. In so doing he was expressing the fact he shared the community's pain and presented his condolences.

3. With another necklace, he would "raise" the deceased sachem so that he could be replaced by another. Thus, the dead man's powers were transferred.

4. Then, he proceeded with the "covering" of the bones, a gesture that signified placing the deceased's remains out of sight. He offered a necklace, and the deceased was covered.

5. A wampum string was given to exhort the warriors to obey the ancients. This conveyed on the new chief a power that took immediate effect.

6. Another string was offered to "cleanse" the council room so that the fire around which they were gathered would not in the future bear the sad memory of the deceased.

7. Lastly, Daniel Claus offered a necklace to "purify the Sky" and "Make the Sun Shine bright." This gesture marked the duality between light and darkness, between life and death. Now, the focus was on life. And so ended the ritual.

On behalf of the Confederacy, the colonial officials sanctioned the election of an individual to the position of chief by "raising" a political or military leader and "replacing" him with another. The Albany Conference of June 1761 marked an important diplomatic event: The Seven Nations delegates asked George Croghan to "raise" one of their men, as per the tradition between allies. According to custom, it was the colonial partners who formally appointed the individual to the council, as per the role of the father in the alliance. The Seven Nations ambassadors went on to point out that, due to the large number of deaths during the Seven Years' War, all the deceased must be covered. The fighters who, yesterday, were enemies and who lost their lives during the last war between the French and the English had to be covered. Shedding tears together over the dead was a sign that they now all belonged to the same family.[88] The British, too, "cried" for the dead, in keeping with the Indigenous tradition.

In December 1764, Sir William Johnson conducted a ceremony at Johnson Hall in honour of a sachem from the Huron of Lorette who fell in battle in the Ohio region during the war with the Great Lakes nations. By virtue of their established alliance traditions, the other Seven Fires ambassadors present at Johnson Hall expected the superintendent to perform the ceremony, since he was formally bound to his political and military partners. If one was fighting a common enemy together, it was important to mourn together because allies are metaphorically related.[89] Among certain Indigenous peoples of the Northeast, when a death was covered for a nation, it was the other members of the alliance who would speak on their behalf.[90] This practice was also common among the Seven Fires. The condolences offered by Sir William Johnson to the domiciled Huron were received not by the Huron of Lorette but by the other Confederacy members present at the ceremony, who would speak on behalf of the grieving community.[91] In March 1768, prior to peace talks between the British, the Seven Nations of Canada, the Iroquois Six Nations, and the Cherokee, Sir William Johnson knew that he must perform a condolence ceremony on behalf of the King of England and his British subjects, to erase any painful memories from the minds of the Indigenous people present at the conference.[92]

Generally speaking, at these ceremonies, wampum strings were exchanged, but there could also be necklaces exchanged as well. The object that was exchanged marked the degree of human loss and the intensity of the emotion it created. On May 6, 1762, at a meeting he held at Johnson Hall with the Seven Fires ambassadors, Sir William paid tribute to the domiciled people who had been struck down by disease. Offering three long necklaces of wampum, the superintendent sought to "wipe away the Tears from your Eyes so that you may look up to the Divine being & crave his blessing, and a Continuance of health to those who have Survived" and to remind them of the sadness that their British brethren shared with them.[93]

In an entry in the Johnson Hall journal dated March 23, 1764, there is a note to the effect that an Onondaga chief from the League chose to perform the usual ceremony of condolence "with two Belts of Wampum, instead of Strings as formerly, which was to shew in a stronger light their Concern for our losses" during the war with the Great Lakes nations.[94] All of the symbols associated with these ceremonies reflected the content and scope of the speeches made at the gatherings. At a meeting in Montreal in 1756, the sachem Chinoniata of the Onondaga of the Iroquois League performed the ceremony with wampum and other specific objects, including "a flask of liquor," which was part of the metaphorical language surrounding the ceremony of condolence, where the attendees would cleanse the throat so as to speak more clearly, and clean the ears to hear better. The precious liquid was, in the same vein, a sort of medicine to purify the heart.[95] The Europeans would also sometimes offer manufactured goods in addition to wampum at the ceremony. On September 12, 1761, Sir William Johnson offered a number of British-made products to compensate for the death of a Seneca thief killed by the British. The details of that particular condolence ceremony are described in the journal: "they condoled the Seneca who was killed by our troops stealing horses with two black strouds, two shirts, and two pair of stockings; gave them their liquor."[96] The obligation to compensate or pay tribute to the dead was always a moral one, and was part of the alliance relations between the parties.

The death of an Indigenous or British leader would always give rise to such official ceremonies where condolences were offered to the grieving community; it was the tradition. The melancholic ceremony would commemorate the grieving community's membership in the alliance. The obligation to pay tribute to the dead stemmed from a conception of social relations expressed exclusively in terms of kinship. To grieve and share sadness was to share the same blood. Tagawara, an Oneida sachem of the Iroquois League, performed this ceremony on behalf of the English king at a conference in German Flats. On July 18, 1770, he addressed his brothers of the Seven Nations of Canada: "Brothers. As a proof of my regard for the wise institution of your Ancestors, and from the information I have received of the losses you have sustained since our last meeting, I do now on behalf of His Majesty the King of Great Britain sincerely Condole with you on this melancholy occasion.[97] The following day it was the Seven Fires sachems' turn to "cover" the dead.[98]

Sir William Johnson died on July 11, 1774. The following day, Guy Johnson wrote to Thomas Gage, informing him that crowds of Indigenous people had gathered at Johnson Hall, and that they wished to offer a wampum necklace to all the other nations, to advise them of the superintendent's death.[99] On September 29, 1774, he wrote to Gage again, explaining the particular manner in which the Six Nations Iroquois leaders conducted the condolence ceremony in honour of his father: The Iroquois orator described all that had passed between William Johnson and his nation regarding himself, and expressed the "strongest assurances of affection" stemming from the alliance between the League and the British.[100]

The pipe ceremony also occupied an important place in the rituals performed by certain nations in the Northeast. It would be performed when two allied groups gathered to meet, and was a diplomatic ritual that was conducted before any public discussion. Tobacco and ceremonial pipes—the long-stemmed pipes that were officially smoked during solemn discussions—were two elements of exchange that were essential in diplomacy, and it was customary to offer them. In a letter dated November 2, 1684, Baron de Lahontan explained the origin and meaning of the ceremonial pipe (*calumet*):

> Essentially, it is a pipe. It is a Norman-French word that comes from "chalumeau" (torch). The Indians did not know the word "calumet" because it was introduced in Canada by the Normans in the first settlements the people of that Nation made in the country, and it was maintained in use there by the French. The Iroquois called the "calumet," or pipe, Ganondaoué in their language, while other Indian nations called it Poagan.[101]

Tobacco was thought to possess magical properties that would spur good thoughts, as expressed by a Wyandot chief from Sandusky in June 1761 at a diplomatic conference held near Detroit. The chief was addressing the Iroquois League of Six Nations ambassadors: "With two pouches of Tobacco that I offer you on behalf of our Chiefs, who pray you will come to this fire on your Route [council of the Huron of Sandusky in Ohio] that I told you I had lit, smoking the tobacco to bring good Thoughts."[102] To offer—and accept—tobacco was to show the willingness of those taking part in discussions. As such, when the superintendent of Indian Affairs offered the leaders of the Great Fire of the Seven Nations a pipe full of tobacco after one of their discussions in October 1827, he did so on behalf of the governor, to show the friendship and kindness he felt toward his allies.[103]

The pipe ceremony was performed at every diplomatic gathering because it symbolized conciliation. Smoking a pipe together was an important diplomatic gesture that was part of Indigenous protocolary rituals, and that was also common among the Europeans. On August 1, 1735, a delegation of sachems from Kahnawake travelled to Albany to meet with the Indian Affairs commissioners. There they smoked a ceremonial pipe "in all solemnity." Each protagonist who took a puff would symbolically occupy an active place in the council. Pipe smoking was also a way to rekindle friendships. The secretary who noted the proceedings of the Albany conference described the beginning of the talks, mentioning that the ambassadors started by offering to all of the commissioners a ceremonial, or peace, pipe, then, according to Indigenous tradition, they each took a puff. After this solemn ritual, the spokesperson for the domiciled nations of Canada opened the conference.[104]

In 1775, the Seven Fires representatives performed this ceremony in the company of some Stockbridge representatives at a meeting in Kahnawake. These representatives from New England were gathering around the Great Fire of the Seven Nations because they had come to renew an old friendship pact, and to reinforce that pact, the long-time allies would smoke the ceremonial pipe together. The pipe ceremony was a way to seal agreements and rally the different groups. Offering tobacco was part of smoking together and by sharing the smoke, they would share the same spirit. The speaker representing the Iroquois of Kahnawake suggested that the ambassadors "sit beneath the great tree" to "smoke their pipes" and "pray to the great God." [105] Politics and smoking together went hand in hand. In November 1776, the British invited the Mohawk of the Six Nations to come to Kahnawake for discussions. The colonial authorities sent them a message signifying that they wished to smoke a pipe with them in the village. They would meet there to talk about politics and, in the context of the American Revolution, of military politics, in particular.[106] On September 30, 1792, at a conference in the Auglaize River region of Ohio, the pipe ceremony was performed by all the parties. The political and military delegates from all the nations in attendance, including the Seven Nations of Canada, would each take their turn smoking the ceremonial pipe that the Shawnee and Miami chiefs offered them.[107]

All of the metaphors associated with the ceremonial pipe expressed diplomatic proposals. A speech given on July 23, 1788, that is attributed to a Wyandot ambassador from Sandusky reveals some of the meanings of the symbols surrounding the ceremonial pipe. The Wyandot orator, speaking at a council near Detroit before a group of Kickapoo, Chippewa, Potawatomi, Mohawk, and Seneca dignitaries from the Iroquois League, addressed the Kickapoo specifically, stressing that the pipe he offered them was "good," meaning the proposed alliance was honourable. The pipe was also shared by the Wyandot with their English father. The smoking of the ceremonial pipe marked this alliance and the one uniting the British and the Seven Nations of Canada, because the flame of the pipe "reached" the Great Fire of Kahnawake. The reference to the long stem of the pipe was analogous to the "roots" of the "Great Tree of Peace" according to Iroquois tradition.[108] In this instance, the Wyandot were seeking to graft the Kickapoo of the Wabush and Illinois rivers onto the alliance and, in turn, they could "branch out" the agreement to their allies."[109]

The pipe was often a symbol of friendship; a guarantee of the good will and sincerity of the parties. Smoking the pipe was a solemn prelude to the speeches that would be made, and was an important element of protocol. On July 28, 1770, Sir William Johnson, anxious to ensure that these messages would be transmitted appropriately, offered the Seven Nations ambassadors a wampum necklace and a pipe. In this way, the Seven Nations, as Britain's allies, were tasked with representing the superintendent with the Great Lakes nations and passing on these objects. Sir William entrusted this task to the domiciled ambassadors because he recognized their diplomatic tact and knew they were adept at negotiating on his behalf.[110] The ceremonial pipe joined the nations in the same spirit, serving to ratify their unions and honour past promises, which is why it had to be safeguarded. The Seven Nations domiciled people stressed this point to the Odawa of Makinaw at a conference at the Great Fire at Kahnawake, in February 1786. The ceremonial pipe that was presented to the Odawa would have to stay in their village and be protected.[111] A pipe that was conserved this way could be presented again as a sign of commemoration or reconciliation. The pipe that was presented in Niagara in July 1764 by the Potowatomi of Wisconsin ambassadors was one of friendship, upholding the alliance between the British and their nation. Because it endorsed the pledges of the Potowatomi to the British Crown, the pipe would have to be carefully guarded. The oral tradition required a material object to support the spoken words and, in this case, it was the pipe that commodified the alliance.[112]

The Europeans introduced a number of new elements into diplomatic rituals, including harquebus and cannon firing, and the distribution of rum, food, and other manufactured goods. The Indigenous people, in turn, incorporated these elements of European material culture into their diplomatic exchanges with the French and the British. On July 9, 1757, Bougainville described how the Iroquois, Algonquin, and Nipissing of Lake of Two Mountains welcomed the French military authorities: "Upon our arrival, we were saluted with a triple firing of two swivel guns and musketry by the Indians lined up on the shore, a missionary at their head."[113]

In a petition dated May 31, 1831, the Algonquin and Nipissing of Kanehsatake requested that Governor Colborne procure them a cannon:

My Father, over time, we have possessed a Cannon in our village; we still have one that was given to our ancestors by the French when they were masters of this land, but it is so worn from use and rust that it is a danger to use. Nine years ago, our then-father told us "My children you shall have another Cannon; yours is too old." Every year since then, we have been told, wait a bit; the King will give you the gift of a Cannon. We have always believed in these words; we have always spoken French "from the mouth of our Cannon" and now we would like you to have us speak English by giving us one of the many Cannons that belong to the King, our father. We shall cry "thank you, thank you" from the mouth of our Cannon on the day of birth of the King, our father, upon the arrival of the annual gifts, when you come to visit us, or when we are visited by someone on your behalf. We shall cry "thank you" from the mouth of our Cannon.[114]

Material gifts also occupied a fundamental place in the alliance's diplomatic processes. On February 13, 1757, superintendent Johnson met with the Mohawk of the Iroquois League at Fort Johnson for the purpose of sealing some political agreements. According to the proceedings, at the end of the meeting, Sir William gave them "6 Barrels of Pork & flour, a Barrel of Powder, one of Lead, 3 Casks of Rum, a Chest of Pipes & a Bag of Cut Tobacco etc."[115] An entry in the *Journal of Indian Affairs* dated February 21, 1765, noted that Sir William received at his home at Johnson Hall a Seven Nations embassy and that he offered them all manner of provisions, pipes, etc.[116] On July 31, 1767, Sir William travelled to Kahnawake where he met with the domiciled Mohawk. The Department's journal notes that he gave "nine barrels of Flour, one of Salt, and 30 skipples of Corn"[117] to each of the village bands. On January 3, 1768, a messenger from the Seven Fires Confederacy arrived at Johnson Hall to advise Sir William that the sachems "would reach this place, provided they were assisted with Sleds and Provisions."[118] At a meeting at Johnson Hall in March 1768 with a group of Seven Fires, Iroquois Six Nations, and Cherokee of Carolina ambassadors, Sir William offered each delegate pipes, tobacco and a drop of alcohol.[119]

During diplomatic exchanges, gift-giving was fundamental. In October 1827, the superintendent of Indian Affairs drew up a list of additional gifts he would give to the political and military leaders of the Great Council of the Seven Nations at the next congress in Kahnawake. It included cloth, sheets, blankets, munitions, knives, gunpowder, rifles, and tobacco.[120] In the written proceedings of that conference in 1827, it was noted that, after the deliberations, "a small gift consisting of some stockings, blankets, and munitions was left with the Interpreters, to be divided up among the Chiefs, under the direction of an Officer of the Department."[121]

The officials had to fulfill the material needs of their allies, as that was one of the mechanisms of the alliance. On August 11, 1770, in the proceedings of a meeting that took place at Johnson Hall between the Abenaki and Iroquois of Akwesasne, it is mentioned that Sir William presented the domiciled speaker with "a Handsome Present" and "provided Everything for his long Journey."[122] Daniel Claus wrote in the *Journal of Indian Affairs* that on September 12, 1770, he offered all the members of the Kahnawake Council "a Meal of Victuals, pipes & Tobacco, & Dram."[123] In another entry dated July 26, 1773, he noted a request by the Huron of Lorette: A council chief asked the Indian Affairs official for clothes on behalf of the women and children, while the warriors begged for ammunition and axes for hunting. Was this not how Indigenous warriors were to be treated in times of war? With the "Necessities of Life?"[124]

Indeed, during wartime, gifts took on strategic significance. The *Journal of Indian Affairs* entry from June 5, 1764, notes that Sir William Johnson had clothed and armed most of the 62 "Cognawageys" warriors, who were allied with the British against the Odawa. On June 6, the "Cognawageys" complained that they didn't have enough powder to hunt, or even "to shoot Pidgeons with."[125] On March 31, 1783, during the American Revolution, Robert Matthews, a military officer, described why it was important to offer gifts to the Huron of Lorette, noting that, where there was a military alliance with the Indigenous people, the colonial authorities must equip their allies and fulfill their material needs, as per the orders and pledges of the general of the British Army, Sir Frederick Haldimand. In this particular case, since the Huron had showed little interest in playing a military role in the conflict between the colonies and the British Crown, the authorities had been dragging their feet.[126]

On February 1, 1815, François Deschambault, the military agent posted in Saint-François, wrote to Sir John Johnson about the complaints of the domiciled Abenaki regarding the British military officials. Deschambault noted that it was difficult to satisfy the Abenaki, who were constantly demanding more gifts, adding "It is my honour to warn you that they are determined to go to Quebec, doubtless to grasp more presents."[127] In the wake of this extraordinary request, Sir John wrote to the Secretary of Indian Affairs on February 3, 1815, explaining that the British had a duty to offer gifts to the domiciled Abenaki by virtue of the military services they provided during the War of 1812 against the United States.[128] In a document dating from the early 19th century, the war chiefs from the village of the Huron of Lorette asked Governor Craig to procure them a cannon so they could salute British dignitaries when they came to their village, as they had "always done for the Representatives of our father, the King." That was also the recommendation of Officer Louis de Salaberry, who had seen the cannon and recommended they not use it, for "fear an accident should occur."[129]

On June 18, 1831, Charles Kana8ato and some other chiefs from the council of the Iroquois of Lake of Two Mountains addressed a petition to the commander of the British Armed Forces, Lord Aylmer, in which they requested that he replace the rusty old cannon that the village used during celebrations and on solemn occasions, like saluting the governor when he came to visit. The Iroquois chiefs backed up their demand with the promise of a future military alliance: "Give us one, my father, whose noise is capable of exciting [...] our warriors in battle, if the time should come to wage war against the enemies of the king, our father. The one we have would scarcely waken our warriors if they should fall asleep."[130] The long-desired object was delivered on November 23 by the Hudson's Bay Company, and was accompanied by other gifts offered by the governor. At the end of the meeting, a salvo was fired in acknowledgment of the gift.[131]

Despite the fact that, after 1815, the warrior activity of the domiciled nations dropped sharply, the British Crown continued to offer gifts, as it ensured the safety of the country and helped the Indigenous people to survive. On October 8, 1828, the council chiefs of Kanehsatake, Akwesasne, Saint-François, Bécancour, and Lorette explained to Governor Kempt that the King of England had given them, every year, "very considerable gifts" in exchange for their earlier military services, but also "to maintain their good dispositions." The chiefs reminded the governor that, in the beginning, when they were "rich," those gifts served only to "maintain the union," but now that the hunting and fishing were no longer sufficient, those gifts took on a whole new meaning. They insisted "that the gifts be the same as before with regard to their quantity and quality."[132] On May 16, 1829, Sir James Kempt wrote to London that any reforms of the tradition of giving gifts to the Indigenous people of Canada should be considered with great prudence, as such gifts were guaranteed under the treaties: "As their issue is generally guaranteed by treaty, it would be alike impolitic and unjust to discontinue them at present, though I have no doubt that object may be hereafter gradually attained."[133] In a memorandum dated March 29, 1832, on the departments of Indian Affairs of Upper and Lower Canada, it is noted that some of these gifts took the form of a "pension" offered to the Indigenous warriors who were allied with the King of England during the American Revolution.[134] But again, this was a European logic being expressed in regard to the alliance. To the Indigenous way of thinking, the gifts were an obligation, not a reward.

On February 3, 1837, the Seven Fires nations reminded Governor Gosford of the scope of this ancient system of redistribution. The chiefs explained that gift giving was a policy of exchange, and that these gifts represented compensation for their lands. They therefore considered them an obligation, or their due. The Seven Fires Confederacy felt that the governor was bound to and must support the Indigenous members. The way the signatory chiefs understood the role of the governor in the alliance, he was the father and must provide for his children. The governor must pay his debts and compensate the Confederacy with presents:

> My Father, these presents (as we have been taught to call them) are not gifts as such; rather they are part of the Government's sacred debt promised to our fathers by the Kings of France to indemnify the lands they abandoned for them, and confirmed by the Kings of England since the country was ceded, and until today, regularly paid and acquitted.[135]

There was an imperative nature attached to the act of gift giving. To maintain his credibility, every chief must be able to redistribute gifts. As Bougainville said in 1757, to "keep the pot uncovered" was to have the means to give, and giving allowed one to acquire authority and power. The French officer observed that among the Indigenous people,

> there is a voluntary subordination; each individual is free to do as he pleases. The village and war chiefs may have credit, but they don't have authority. And, even so, their credit with the young people varies depending on whether they give more or less, and whether they are careful to keep the pot uncovered, so to speak.[136]

The governor and his official representatives were duty-bound to be providers because the king's policy of gift giving in the alliance with the Seven Fires was fundamental. It stemmed from the obligation of the father to feed his children as prescribed under the kinship system. The British authorities recognized and understood the diplomatic importance of offering gifts. In his journal entry on May 20, 1761, Sir William Johnson expressed his full agreement with Daniel Claus's decision to provide his

Canadian allies with ammunition so they could hunt and sub-sist. The superintendent added that, what's more, "keeping it from them would doubtless make them, & all other Nations harbour bad thoughts of us."[137] No presents would mean no alliance; offering presents was an obligation, not a reward. On June 28, 1761, the Seven Nations ambassadors reminded George Croghan, who represented the superintendent in Albany, that in an alliance, there were rules to be followed, and one of them was to offer gifts, as was customary.[138] On July 28, 1770, Sir William received the Seven Nations of Canada ambassadors at his home; he wanted to give them some more presents as he had run short at the conference that had just wrapped up in German Flats. The gifts he would give would symbolize the role of the King of England in the alliance, that of a father-king to his children.[139] Offering gifts was a way to cultivate friendships with and among the allied groups. And in politics, that was essential, as noted in a report dated November 10, 1770, that Thomas Gage dispatched to London.[140]

On another note, although still on the matter of the political interest of relations between the British and the Indigenous people, Sir William Johnson sent Thomas Gage a list, on August 27, 1768, of the employees he considered crucial not only to the operations of the Department but, more importantly, to good Anglo-Indigenous relations. The superintendent justified the positions and salaries he deemed "indispensably necessary" and that were established "after the reduction of Canada extended our Interests & encreased our Connections & Alliances." His list included the superintendent, his three deputies, five inter-preters, as well as one gunsmith and blacksmith with assistants.[141]

Feasts also occupied an important role in diplomacy. After every major international meeting between Europeans and Indigenous parties, the attendees would take part in these fes-tivities, which were highly popular with the Indigenous partici-pants. Following their discussions, they would eat and drink until all the guests were satisfied.[142] These festivities generated considerable expenses for the colonial power.[143] As part of the Confederacy's Grand Councils, the Iroquois would organize feasts for their guests, and it was the colonial government that would have to provide its Indigenous allies with the necessary supplies to maintain their diplomatic relations. On February 12, 1845, Joseph Marcoux, a missionary at Sault-Saint-Louis, wrote to the Secretary of Indian Affairs to remind him of this policy: "You are surely not unaware that, until recently, the government always gave the Indians a certain amount of rum on New Year's Day, then whenever there was a grand council of foreign chiefs, which would occur quite regularly."[144] On January 28, 1848, Édouard-Narcisse Delorimier also wrote to the Secretary of Indian Affairs, informing him that the leaders of the Seven Nations had summoned the domiciled Iroquois, Algonquin, and Nipissing of Lake of Two Mountains, as well as the Iroquois of Akwesasne, to the village to discuss the new British policy concerning the exchange of gifts with the Indigenous people and the decision by the colonial power to no longer provide them the "annual equipment" they were used to receiving. The Iroquois Sault chiefs petitioned the Department secretary to ask their father-governor to "make a charitable gesture" by giving them the provisions to receive their brothers with honour.[145]

Feasts were a symbol of the alliance between groups. But, more than simply an occasion to celebrate, feasts were also a way to connect nations and individuals. As Bougainville wrote in his journal, on August 6, 1756, "Nipissing, Abenaki, Algonquin, Iroquois, Menominee, bound together by a feast, sang war songs."[146] On July 10, 1757, the French officer described the ceremony where he was adopted by the Iroquois of Sault-Saint-Louis: "I was shown to all the nation, presented the first morsel of the feast, and I sang my war song together with the first war chief. Then the others dedicated their war songs to me."[147] The "first morsel" was given to the officer, this courtesy and sign of hospitality confirming and cementing the relation between the domiciled Iroquois and the French officer. Since the exchange was reciprocal, each party made their contribution. Bougainville added: "I visited my whole family and presented the supplies to hold a feast to each *cabane.*"[148]

Indigenous diplomatic protocol dictated that a banquet be held after every major meeting or negotiation. On February 10, 1764, Sir William Johnson sent special instructions in this regard to Daniel Claus. Under the military alliance with the Seven Fires, and in the context of the war with the Odawa of Pontiac, the superintendent's representative must "make a War Feast, and that properly."[149] Holding a feast was part of the protocol. In his entry in the *Journal of Indian Affairs* dated June 8, 1764, Sir William noted that, for the 64 domiciled warriors encamped for their first night at "Cognawagey," he ordered an Ox and some liquor for their war feast, where they were joined by a few Mohawk warriors from the Iroquois League.[150]

CHAPTER FOUR

Diplomatic Relations Stretching from the Atlantic to the Great Lakes

The Seven Fires Confederacy did not operate in a vacuum. On the contrary, it maintained diplomatic relations with a host of other political organizations, and its network of alliances and relations was far reaching. The Confederacy was part of the geopolitical world of the northeastern part of the American continent and was a key political player. It developed and maintained political and diplomatic relations with the Wabanaki Confederacy, the Iroquois League of Six Nations, the Great Lakes confederacies, the French, and the British.

Metaphorical Fires of the Political Sphere

We will begin by analyzing the many meanings of the word "fire," in order to gain a better understanding of its different symbolic significance in the political context. "Fire" could be used as a geographical as well as a sociopolitical term; as a place of dwelling; as a council of a nation; and as an indicator of the state of alliances. In some instances, "fire" referred to a specific house. In his description of an encampment in Oswegatchie, Bougainville noted in his 1756 journal that "next to the fort is the village inhabited by 100 fires or Iroquois chiefs of the 5 nations, warriors all."[1] These fires referred to the homes, longhouses, or colonial homes where Iroquois warriors and chiefs lived, likely identifiable by the smoke emanating from them. In other words, the term was used in the sense of "home." The word "fire" took on a different connotation when it referred to a community, nation, or council of a nation. For example, the United States of America were referred to as the "Thirteen United Fires," likely an allusion to the 13 allied colonies during the American Revolution.[2]

A fire would be lit in any of the northeastern villages that was an important site of diplomacy and exchange.[3] The Seven Nations ambassadors would often go to the Albany Fire under the French Regime since, in the early days, the Iroquois of Kahnawake were tasked with maintaining diplomatic relations with this colonial town, and in fact, Kahnawake had a long tradition as a hub for trade. The correspondence between the governors of New France and the ministers of the Crown is telling in this regard. For instance, on September 21, 1741, Governor Beauharnois wrote to the Minister of the Marine, describing the business dealings of the domiciled Iroquois of Sault-Saint-Louis: "Sault S^t. Louis has become, Mister Minister, a Sort of Republic, and nowadays, it is the only Place where Foreign Trade is conducted. Here is the proof that I hold, and that I must bring to your attention."[4] The governor denounced the trade organization the Iroquois of Sault had with the British of Albany, relations that were made official in 1735 when formal treaties were signed with the English colonies.[5] On October 17, 1751, Governor La Jonquière wrote to the minister with much the same message as one of his predecessors: that trade between the people of Sault and Lake of Two Mountains and the British was still just as active, and was in fact even encouraged by the example of the French.[6]

The fire established at the home of Superintendent Johnson at Johnson Hall, New York, would, for a long time, be the meeting place for Indigenous speakers from across northeastern America. Certain rules were put in place in this regard in 1755, when Sir William was commissioned by General Edward Braddock to manage relations with the Iroquois Six Nations.[7] On July 10, 1755,

Daniel Claus, who was attending a congress at this new council site, paraphrased Sir William's speech, noting that "The Council Fire was lighted with such Wood as never wou'd burn out, and the Embers removed from Albany and brought to Mount Johnson [Johnson Hall] to burn there forever."[8] From that moment on, the "Great Fire" of Johnson Hall would be the new gathering and diplomacy site, replacing the former Albany fire, and it was there that the British officials would meet and negotiate with the Iroquois of the League of Six Nations.[9]

The central role of the Johnson Hall Fire would continue after 1760, following the British conquest of Canada. On January 27, 1762, Canaghquieson, the speaker and chief of the Oneida of the Iroquois League of Six Nations, reminded Superintendent Johnson that, during the Seven Years' War between France and England in North America, it had been decided, of a common accord, to extinguish the Albany fire and light another at Johnson Hall.[10] The choice of Johnson Hall over Albany suggested that the British authorities were taking charge of Indian Affairs. Albany was a small colonial town, and the political authorities of the New York colony would appear there. From then on, British Superintendent Sir William Johnson was the only person officially mandated and authorized to oversee all relations with the Indigenous people. The fire at his home therefore became a place of choice for councils, negotiations, and treaties, and the decision was unanimously supported by the British-allied Indigenous people.[11] On March 29, 1762, the superintendent welcomed the domiciled Abenaki to his home, saying "I bid you hearty Wellcome to my House, where there is a Council fire always burning clear for the benefit & reception of all Indians who are Friends to the English."[12]

The Johnson Hall Fire would retain its importance up until the death of the superintendent, in 1774. After that time, the great fire of the Anglo-Indigenous alliance would be relocated to the residence of Superintendent Guy Johnson in Guy Park, in the colony of New York, where it remained until 1776.[13] The

Americans rekindled the Albany fire in 1775, where representatives of the Continental Congress and various Indigenous delegations would come to gather. On August 15, 1775, the "Twelve United Colonies" asked the Iroquois ambassadors of the League of Six Nations to invite their Seven Nations of Canada allies to come join in discussions in the town.[14] In 1765, George Croghan, in accordance with Sir William Johnson's directives, lit the fire at Fort Pitt, in Pennsylvania.[15] This council gathering place would be reclaimed after 1776 by the Americans, and it was there that the Seven Nations of Canada ambassadors would meet with General Lafayette when France allied herself with America's Continental Congress.[16]

After 1776, following the American Declaration of Independence and the British withdrawal to Canada, the English lit or rekindled fires, in other words, they established new sites for treaty negotiations and signings. Detroit, Niagara, Montreal, and Quebec City all became key places for diplomatic meetings between the British and the Indigenous people. Sir William Johnson had lit the Detroit fire in 1761 as part of a meeting with the Huron of the Great Lakes. The Detroit Council became an important venue for diplomatic meetings between the western nations, the British, and their Indigenous allies,[17] which at the time caused an uproar among the Iroquois authorities of the League, who denounced the initiative of Sir William, with whom they had agreed that they would only negotiate with the Indigenous nations at the great fires of the British at Johnson Hall and at the Amerindian fire at Onondaga (near Syracuse, New York).[18] The American Revolution forced the British to rekindle the fire at Fort Niagara that had been officially lit by the English during the Seven Years' War.[19]

Montreal and Quebec City were also key sites for diplomatic gatherings, and numerous international conferences were held there. Château Saint-Louis in Quebec City was an important venue, as it was there that the Indigenous delegations generally met with the governor of Canada, and where he would transmit his messages to them.[20] For instance, in February 1794, the Seven Nations of Canada ambassadors travelled there to hear Governor Dorchester's reply to a message the Seven Fires had sent him on their behalf and on that of certain Great Lakes nations: "My Children, You have told me that you are the Deputies, the seven Villages of Lower Canada, in the name of all the Nations of the *pays d'en haut*, who sent Deputies to the General Council of the Miami, with the exception of the Shawnee, Miami, and Wolves.[21] Indigenous delegations also went to Quebec City to meet with the British chiefs of staff, especially during wartime, for instance, during the American Revolution[22] and the War of 1812-1814 with the United States.[23] Quebec City was the site of several major international diplomatic meetings, notably when the presence of the Governor of Canada or the Commander of the British Army was required.

As for Montreal, throughout the French Regime, it had been the meeting point for representatives of New France, members of the Seven Nations of Canada, and all the other Indigenous delegations. Whether they came from the Great Lakes, New England, or the Maritimes, the Indigenous ambassadors could meet the King of France's representatives there at any time. In July and August 1701, Montreal was a venue for important peace negotiations between the Iroquois of the League and the government of New France and its Indigenous allies.[24] Under the French Regime, the colony's governors used to transport the government's affairs to Montreal, then return to Quebec City for the winter.[25] Montreal's importance continued after the British Conquest of Canada. In fact, a number of conferences that were once held in Albany at Johnson Hall or elsewhere in New England now took place in Montreal, where the Department of Indian Affairs was based, and where Daniel Claus, Sir William Johnson's representative in Canada, resided. It was only after 1776, that is, with the American Revolution and the British withdrawal to Canada, that the Montreal fire became central, replacing the large, traditional centres for Anglo-Indigenous diplomacy.

The discourse surrounding the fire is telling of the nature, intensity, and quality of alliances and international relations. Since the fire played an important centralizing role, all the members who gathered around it would have to participate in one way or another to keep it alive, whether by their presence in the council or by presenting wampum. The warmth that emanated from the fire symbolized the enthusiasm and fraternity of those gathered there, and the act of feeding the fire demonstrated the willingness of the protagonists and the official proxies to continue to respect the agreements. All of the descriptions of the fire in the literature further our understanding of the political and diplomatic relations between nations.

In a report on French-Indigenous relations that the governor of New France sent to the Minister of the Marine in Versailles on September 21, 1741, Beauharnois mentioned the importance of the fire among the Indigenous people. Writing about the people of Lake of Two Mountains, he noted, "The chiefs of the Lake came again this summer to tell me that they no longer had any credit with their young people since their fire had been taken away, and they begged me to mend the situation as quickly as possible without which they could not guarantee anything."[26] The metaphorical extinguishment of that fire also removed the political authority of its keepers over the other people in the village, especially the warriors. In order for power to be restored, the fire must be rekindled, thereby re-establishing political authority, failing which, the village leaders insisted they could not be held responsible for any disorder caused by its extinction. The fire was therefore of capital importance because it was the focal point around which discussions were held and debates conducted.

When a fire was extinguished, as it was at Lake of Two Mountains when Beauharnois was governor, it meant that the council was no longer invested with political authority and that it no longer belonged to the alliance. To avoid this situation, the fire had to be symbolically preserved, nourished, and protected as best as possible from being extinguished. It was nourished by all the members gathered at the council with the leaders and parties inclined to join the discussion. The exchange of wampum around the fire, and the discussions and debates generated by their reading was a way to keep the fire burning, i.e., the wampum kindled the fire by symbolically feeding it.

And it was precisely because the domiciled people of the Lake had lost their wampum that, in 1740, Vincent, a chief of the domiciled Huron of Lorette, declared their fire extinguished: 10 of the 12 necklaces offered by the Huron at the time the village of Lake of Two Mountains was founded had disappeared. What happened to them? The sachem who was in charge of them apparently had no satisfactory answer for the Huron chief, who considered their disappearance a sign of the irresponsibility of the chiefs of the domiciled people of the village. Thereafter, they were no longer able to perform their government duties; they were excluded.[27]

If a fire died out through negligence, it could be rekindled. The Seneca of the League of Six Nations provided an interesting testimonial to that effect in June 1761. While they were gathered in Detroit, they invited the "four Nations of Detroit," Huron, Odawa, Chippewa, and Potowatomi to come talk in Sandusky, Ohio. Needless to say, the following language is metaphorical:

> I arrived in Sandusky, I expected to find there a burning fire, but there was nothing. I only found dead fires. I combed through the ashes and found some coals, where there were the remains of a fire. I gathered up these coals with the embers, and I lit a good fire. It is there we invite you to come talk of important affairs; it is there our chiefs are assembled, at the fire I told you I rekindled.[28]

While the speaker did not physically search the ashes for charcoal, he did clearly recall that, in the past, meetings had been held there. By "combing" the ashes, he found "the remains of a fire" and, indeed, council meetings had once been held in Sandusky, a Wyandot community; so, it was there that these people proposed to meet. In other words, lighting a fire meant choosing a place to meet, discuss, and negotiate. So it was that in the fall of 1768, the British and the Iroquois Six Nations, the Seven Fires, and other Indigenous representatives from New England and the Great Lakes gathered at Fort Stanwix to negotiate the surrender of lands in Ohio. The Indigenous representatives praised the initiative of Superintendent Johnson, who had "kindled a fire at Fort Stanwix in order to hold a Congress of great importance."[29]

Every Indigenous coalition had a place where the central fire would burn, in other words, a place where the grand councils were held and where all diplomatic delegations were received. The Great Fire of the Seven Nations of Canada burned at Kahnawake. Until 1776, the Great Fire of the League of Iroquois Six Nations burned at Onondaga. In 1758, an orator from the League of Six Nations reminded Sir William Johnson that the great fire at Onondaga was "only for the Iroquois Confederacy's private consultations," adding that when decisions were made in Onondaga, the Confederacy would delegate representatives to go to Johnson Hall to inform the superintendent of what had come to pass there.[30] In November 1774, some ambassadors from the Seven Nations of Canada went to the Grand Council of Onondaga to meet with delegates from the Great Lakes Shawnee. The speaker for the Iroquois of the League reminded the assembly of the ancestral origins of the great fire of their Confederacy, and that it was the result of deliberations among their ancestors, who unanimously chose that site for debate by instituting rules so that political affairs could be conducted "in the appropriate manner."[31]

However, around 1777, during the American Revolution, the Iroquois Six Nations chiefs, unable to reach a consensus on the Confederacy's commitments in the conflict between the King of England and his American colonies, "covered" the Great Fire of Onondaga. The Onondaga, who were the keepers of the fire, told the American commissioners at a meeting in Albany that they had been unable to gather around the fire the members of their alliance, and that since they could not hold discussions together and reach a consensus on the matter, the League's ancestral fire had had to be extinguished.[32] It wasn't until 1783 that the Iroquois

League was able to reinstate a grand council. In fact, two separate great fires were lit, one in the United States (in Buffalo Creek, New York) and the other in Canada, at Onondaga, on the Grand River in Ontario.[33] There, the Iroquois re-established all the earlier political rules that had been in place before the first Great Fire of Onondaga was extinguished.[34]

As for the Odawa and the Wyandot of the Great Lakes, an interpreter for the domiciled Iroquois provided an explanation to the commander in chief of Lower Canada on August 26, 1796. Jean-Baptiste Delorimier wrote to him that there was a great fire in Makinaw (Michilimakinac) of which the Odawa were the chiefs, and another among the Huron of Sandusky that served as a discussion place for all the people from southwest of the Great Lakes.[35]

In 1832, the chiefs of the Iroquois Six Nations Confederacy informed the British that the Iroquois of the League and the Wyandot of Detroit had decided to establish at the Wyandot "reservation" near Amherstburg, Ontario, the "Great General Fire" of all the western nations. The chiefs explained that they had reached this decision because the Great Council Fire on the American side of the Detroit River was now extinguished, and that after receiving this news from the Wyandot, they had decided to revive their ancient customs by re-establishing the "Great General Fire" among the Wyandot of Ontario.[36] Meanwhile, on the Atlantic coast, the nations of the Wabanaki Confederacy centralized the councils of their political alliance in the village of Oldtown, Maine.[37]

When East Met West: Wabanaki of the Maritimes, Odawa of the Great Lakes, and Iroquois of the St. Lawrence

The Wabanaki Confederacy was an alliance of the "People of the Rising Sun." At the outset, it consisted of several nomadic and semi-nomadic communities that shared the same language and a similar sociocultural structure and beliefs system,[38] including the following four communities: the Penobscot from the Penobscot River basin; the Maliseet from the St. John River valley; the Passamaquoddy from the Sainte-Croix River and Passamaquoddy Bay area; and the Mi'kmaq from Cape Breton, Nova Scotia, Prince Edward Island, and northeastern New Brunswick. Between 1750 and 1850, the alliance had a population of over 6,000.[39] The oral tradition of the Indigenous peoples of the Maritimes has passed down a considerable amount of information on relations between the Wabanaki, the Odawa of the Great Lakes, and the Iroquois of the St. Lawrence.[40] Each nation occupied its own specific place in the alliance: the Penobscot were considered the first members, as they were the oldest nation. As the primary spokespersons for the alliance, they were responsible for gathering the member nations around the Great Confederacy Fire at Oldtown on the Penobscot River in Maine. The other three nations referred to the Penobscot as their older brothers. In keeping with the order described in the oral tradition, the younger brothers were the Maliseet, the Passamaquoddy, then the Mi'kmaq.[41]

It is interesting to note about the Mi'kmaq that they were allied with the French in the early 17th century and, in 1749, they established a fire on Cape Breton, in northern Nova Scotia.[42] Frank G. Speck wrote that, like the relations between the Iroquois and the Wabanaki, the Mi'kmaq negotiated with the Mohawk (domiciled?) to bring an end to the bloody conflicts that had been pitting the nations against each other, opting to reach a permanent peace.[43] The oral tradition doesn't specify when exactly this agreement was reached. Perhaps in 1701?[44] We do know that in the 19th century, the Mi'kmaq of the Maritimes maintained regular diplomatic relations with the Seven Nations Great Fire and, in 1838, an Englishman who journeyed in the area noted in his journal that it was customary for the Newfoundland nations to dispatch at various times of the year a canoe and several men up the St. Lawrence River to pay tribute to the Mohawk chiefs of Canada.[45] According to Speck, the alliance between the Mi'kmaq and the domiciled Iroquois was more firmly established than that between the Mi'kmaq and the Wabanaki.[46]

The Grand Council of the Iroquois of Kahnawake was also a source of moral legitimacy for endorsing the political choices made by the members of the Wabanaki Confederacy. In January 1776, in the early days of the American Revolution, a number of Penobscot representatives met with George Washington in Cambridge, Massachusetts, where they were surprised to encounter a group of ambassadors from their "friends" in Kahnawake. The Penobscot delegates, having pledged their military support to the American revolutionaries, took the presence of the Seven Nations of Canada representatives as a moral endorsement of their initiative:

> God is on the side of our brothers, and they will fight. There is Providence in our encounter with our Caughnawaga friends at this time, who have come from so far in Canada. We are keen to return home to tell our friends what we have seen here and, next spring, many from our nation shall come and help the people of New England.[47]

On July 17, 1839, the *Royal Gazette* of Fredericton, New Brunswick, contained an article noting that the Maliseet chiefs, before reaching an official political agreement with the Penobscot and the Passamaquoddy, would have to first consult with the "Grand Chief of Caughnawaga."[48]

The Wabanaki joined the diplomatic circuit formed by the Seven Fires Confederacy and the Odawa. Historian Dean R. Snow explains that, in the beginning, the Penobscot strengthened their ties with the Maliseet, the Passamaquoddy, the Mi'kmaq, and the Huron, to counter British colonial expansion on their lands.[49] Speck recalls the historic roots of the alliance, noting that after many long deliberations, these nations put an end to intertribal wars by founding an alliance of four Wabanaki nations headed by the Penobscot.

The "Mohawk of Caughnawaga and Oka" and the "other neighboring tribes"—presumably the member nations of the

Seven Fires Confederacy—were chosen to preside over this alliance.[50] The Great Fire was installed in Kahnawake with the Mohawk, as they had strongly encouraged the peace initiative. According to Wabanaki oral tradition, the members of the Confederacy met every three years at the Great Council of the Iroquois of the St. Lawrence. These gatherings were an occasion to renew the terms of the alliance, settle problems of shared interest, delegate ambassadors, and vote for peace or war.

In the 17th century, a group of representatives from these nations appear to have gone to see the "venerable" Odawa of the Great Lakes to "receive their counsel" because, according to the Mohawk, they were their elders.[51] The Odawa occupied a symbolic position within the alliance: The Odawa Grand Chief was represented as the "master" of the alliance, sitting in his village with a "stick" in hand as if to reinforce the notion of obedience to the pact. The descriptions provided by the oral tradition are somewhat surprising, referring to a coercive power symbolized by the whip and the death penalty which, in our opinion, is expressed here in a caricatured and exaggerated manner. Nevertheless, the preeminent position of the Odawa was clear and, indeed, the physical arrangement of the allies in the Kahnawake parliament was significant: The delegates of the Seven Nations and the Wabanaki sat on either side of the fire while the Odawa ambassadors would stand at the far end of the parliament, in the centre, symbolizing their role as mediators. As arbitrators and mediators, the Great Lakes Odawa therefore bore the diplomatic title of "grandfather," which conferred on them a definite moral influence. Up until 1875, i.e., until the last Wabanaki delegates were dispatched to Kahnawake, the Odawa presided over this alliance system.[52]

The Wabanaki Confederacy maintained diplomatic ties with the Seven Fires Confederacy until the late 19th century, after which time the Penobscot no longer attended the conferences in the village of the Iroquois of the St. Lawrence. According to traditionalist historian Joseph Nicolar, the last time the Penobscot sent their delegates to Kahnawake was in 1840. In August 1862, Chief Nick Sockabesin refused a necklace from the Seven Fires: the "dishonored" necklace lay in the dust and "no one moved to raise it up again," signifying that the connections with the confederacy were severed. The Passamaquoddy and the Mi'kmaq of the Maritimes, meanwhile, maintained their relations with the Great Fire of Kahnawake until around 1870. According to Speck's research, the oral tradition of the Odawa retains no memories of the alliance between the Seven Fires and the Wabanaki. The wampum that were to have been preserved were lost, and the alliance was over.[53]

The Iroquois of the Six Nations and the Iroquois of the Seven Fires: Multiple Fraternal Agreements

The French and British referred to the alliance formed by the Iroquois of New York as the "Confederacy" or "League of the "Five" or "Six Nations." The Iroquois, meanwhile, used the Iroquoian term "Haudenosaunee" to designate their alliance, or "People of the Longhouse," in reference to the traditional dwellings built by the Iroquois where their grand councils took place. The name meant that the nations allied with the Iroquois League shared the same longhouse, the same great fire. Historians, anthropologists, and archeologists do not all agree on the exact moment the league was founded—some peg the founding in the 14th century, while others believe it to have been in the 17th century. Iroquois "traditionalists" place its founding several hundreds of years earlier, well before the "White man" encountered the "Indians."[54]

The Iroquois Six Nations comprised the Mohawk, Oneida, Onondaga, Cayuga, Seneca, and Tuscarora. They occupied a territory stretching from Schoharie Creek to the western shore of the Genesee River, near Rochester, New York. The Mohawk, Seneca, and Onondaga had specific tasks within the Iroquois Confederacy, owing to their seniority and their participation in the signing of the Great Peace, i.e., the constitution of their Confederacy. These nations were the symbolic guardians of the entrances to the longhouse: the Mohawk guarded the eastern door, while the Seneca Nation guarded the western door. The Onondaga were the keepers of the wampum, and were also the keepers of the "sacred fire" of the Grand Council of the Confederacy which, until the American Revolution, had been in Onondaga.[55] Around 1777, some Iroquois sympathetic to the American cause lit a fire in Buffalo Creek and, around 1783, other "loyalist" Iroquois built another fire at Grand River. Nowadays, the Haudenosaunee consists of seventeen communities. In the United States, they are spread across the states of New York, Wisconsin, and Oklahoma, and in Canada, in the provinces of Quebec and Ontario. Some of these communities are headed by traditionalists allied with the Grand Council of the Onondaga of Ontario, while others are run by band councils disaffiliated from the Confederacy. Their members are religious traditionalists, but also Christians.[56]

The ties between the Iroquois Six Nations and the Iroquois of the Seven Nations date back a long way, as they shared the same roots. On March 31, 1755, an Iroquois of the League reported to the governor of Pennsylvania a discourse by the domiciled Iroquois evoking the close ties that united them. He described how, in a speech advocating for peace and military neutrality addressed to the Six Nations ambassadors, the chief speaker for the Seven Fires had raised these ancient relations in the hopes they would help prevent any form of hostility against one another: "We hope—said the domiciled Iroquois—that the Six Nations will consider us as their own flesh and blood. We know that we do not come from the land of this country, but from that of the Six Nations. We have suckled at the same breast as they have, and we wish them to take that into consideration and to join us in our resolution of neutrality."[57]

Two brothers cannot wage war against one another and, consequently, they could not take part in conflicts between the

French and the English. Therefore, in the name of this familial bond, discord must be avoided, and consensus encouraged. On April 21, 1759, the secretary of Indian Affairs noted that, given that they considered themselves "of the same flesh and blood" as the Iroquois of the League, the Iroquois of the Seven Nations—specifically those of Oswegatchie, Kahnawake, and Kanehsatake—will refuse to return to Iroquoia, as proposed. This is war, and for the moment, they shall remain neutral.[58]

Throughout the 18th century, the Iroquois of the Seven Fires and those of the Six Nations would maintain their diplomatic ties, despite their respective alliances with the French and the British. In February 1760, all of the member nations of the Seven Fires Confederacy re-established diplomatic ties with the League of Six Nations. On February 13, a spokesman for the domiciled people of Pointe-du-Lac, on behalf of the 22 nations of the French-Indigenous alliance, announced that he and his deputies had "come to take you by the hand, and Lead you to Caughnawaga, where a Council Fire is Lighted, and awaits Your Arrival." He also reminded the Iroquois that since the beginning of the hostilities, "the English and French having blocked up the Road between us and You, We Come now to remove Everything in the way, that might hinder our Mutual Correspondence, and Signify our hearty Inclination to make the Road of Peace open as before, and to Light up the Council fire here at Onondaga."[59]

Relations between the Seven Fires and the Six Nations took a new turn after the British conquest of Canada. Now that they were officially allied with the English, the Indigenous chiefs agreed to submit to the colonial authorities any joint political resolutions reached by consensus. In order to "preserve the peace and tranquility," this was the political rule that would henceforth govern talks between the League and Confederacy chiefs. The state of war was officially over, and a broad, 30-row necklace of wampum was presented to the British authorities.[60]

This alliance of the Seven Fires and the Six Nations would be regularly renewed and kept up with the exchange of numerous wampum necklaces. In 1762, Daniel Claus wrote to Sir William Johnson that the Seven Fires had received from the Iroquois Six Nations a number of necklaces inviting them to join together in a "Confederacy of Friendship."[61] On September 8, 1763, the spokesmen of the Iroquois League gathered at Johnson Hall in the presence of deputies from the Seven Nations of Canada and advised Superintendent Johnson of their unanimous resolutions to remain united and allied with the English. By offering the superintendent a wide necklace of 13 rows of wampum, the chiefs wanted Sir William to make their resolutions public and share them with the General of the British Army and the Governor of Montreal.[62] On July 22, 1770, the Seven Nations of Canada ambassadors reminded Sir William Johnson of their resolutions during the British conquest of Canada. Holding up the wampums exchanged in 1760, the Seven Fires spokesman declared that, at that time, they had pledged to comport themselves "as men," in other words, to remain faithful to the alliance they had forged with the British. They also promised to "scorn lies," that is, to always seek out the counsel of the British when they had a concern of international importance. It was decided that the Grand Council of the Six Nations in Onondaga would be the venue for meeting with the League, while the Johnson Hall fire would be for meeting with the British.[63] Under the "Covenant Chain," the Anglo-Iroquois agreement that we will discuss in greater detail below, the British were allied first with the Iroquois League, and later with the other Indigenous nations.

The Seven Nations of Canada, like all the other Indigenous nations of northeastern North America, therefore did not enter into direct relations with the British; rather, they had to go through Onondaga, in other words, through the Iroquois League, which was responsible for diplomatic relations. On August 15, 1775, the Iroquois League of Six Nations delegated a number of representatives to German Flats to meet the American commissioners tasked with negotiating the neutrality of the Indigenous people in their conflict with the British Crown. The Continental

Congress commissioners subsequently asked the Iroquois of the League to go to the Seven Nations Great Fire to transmit their joint political decisions. The League spokespersons corrected the Americans, explaining that discussions between the Seven Fires and Six Nations were usually held at the house of the central council in Onondaga.[64]

Up until the American Revolution, diplomatic initiatives among the Indigenous people were conducted by way of the Iroquois of the League, in Onondaga. The Iroquois Confederacy was top of the list among the Indigenous nations for diplomacy with the British, then with the Americans, but only for a time.[65] After the Iroquois dispersed during the American Revolution, it was Kahnawake that became the primary site for such diplomacy, and that thereafter oversaw most relations with the Indigenous nations of the northeast. As a result, these nations would go through the Seven Fires Confederacy in order to meet with the dispersed Iroquois of the League. After the Great Fire of Onondaga was extinguished and the British had withdrawn to Canada, the Grand Council of the Seven Nations in Kahnawake became the intermediary, the central meeting place. Rather than simply one stage, the way it was before, Kahnawake became the key site for diplomacy with the British. The fires of Detroit and Niagara continued to serve as a liaison between the "loyalist" Iroquois and the British, but Kahnawake surpassed them both in terms of importance.

On August 14, 1778, at a gathering in Montreal in the presence of British military officers and members of the Seven Fires Confederacy, Tiawhanroté, a Six Nations Iroquois spokesman, declared that the nations loyal to England deferred to the representatives of the village of Kahnawake, the "main village of Canada"[66] and the main Iroquois village now that Iroquoia was no more. On August 10, 1779, a group of Seneca travelled to the Seven Nations of Canada Great Fire to present wampum necklaces on behalf of the five Iroquois nations. There, they officially declared war on the Americans. Their initiative reflected their formal pledge to go through the Seven Fires, which is to say, through the Grand Council of Kahnawake, to advise the Confederacy members and their British allies of their political decisions: "Since we promised to communicate our sentiments, we consequently assure you that we have been delegated by our villages to tell and convince you that we are declaring the most bloody of wars against the rebels and that we would prefer to die a thousand deaths than to falter in the face of the enemies of the King."[67] On May 9, 1780, John Deserontyon, the political chief of the Iroquois of the League of the Bay of Quinte, in Ontario, wrote to Daniel Claus, reminding him that when the Iroquois of the League representatives went to Kahnawake to discuss any and all matters, the Seven Nations chiefs could speak on their behalf; it was a consensus that reflected the unanimity of their relationship. The chief went on to explain that Sir John Johnson, the Seven Nations, and the Six Nations were of a "single mind" and acted "as one."[68]

With the founding of two separate grand councils among the Iroquois of the Six Nations, relations changed. It is unknown what approach the Iroquois of Buffalo Creek would have had to take when they wished to speak to the British or to the Seven Fires. We do know the Americans would meet them in Niagara, where they would pass on their messages. On March 7, 1784, an orator-chief with the Six Nations, in his response to a speech by Peter Schuyler, a general in the American Continental Army, affirmed that the Six Nations would be sure to transmit the words of the general to the Indigenous people of Detroit and the St. Lawrence River Valley. He added that Thayendanegea alias Joseph Brant, the Mohawk sachem of the Iroquois of Grand River, would be the ambassador tasked with going to the Seven Fires to transmit the Americans' invitation to join them for discussions at Fort Stanwix. Thayendanegea would then have to relay his discussions with the Seven Nations of Canada around the Niagara Fire.[69]

The Seven Nations of Canada also joined a military and trade agreement that was originally established between the Iroquois

Confederacy and the colonial authorities in Albany in 1677, by governors Edmund Andros and Thomas Dongan known as the "Covenant Chain" or "Friendship Chain." This alliance would long exist through the presence of royal and Iroquois ambassadors in Albany. Francis Jennings wrote about this agreement that was founded on consultations and the desire to reach consensus.[70] The "Chain" symbolized relations between the British, the Iroquois, and the allies, and it was said that it must "be protected against corrosion," "polished," and "made to shine" regularly by means of presents, to metaphorically maintain the alliance's relations.[71]

On August 1, 1735, several sachems from Kahnawake travelled to Albany to meet with the commissioners of Indian Affairs in response to a message they had received from the British in May 1735 inviting them to come and renew and consolidate the old trade alliance they referred to as the "Peace Friendship & Intercourse" between their "constituents," the New York Government and the Iroquois of the League. The pact signed at that time between the British, the Iroquois of the League, and the representatives of the "Cacknawaga Canada Indians," who were accompanied by dignitaries from three other "Indian Castles of Canada," was founded on the principles of mutual aid and on their free trade agreements.[72] Secretary Wraxall, who subsequently transcribed the proceedings of the meeting, noted that this treaty was one of the most formal and solemn he had ever come across in his Indian Affairs transcriptions in the Albany archives.[73] The "Treaty of Peace and Friendship" was renewed on September 28, 1742, in Albany, this time in the presence of Iroquois ambassadors from Kahnawake and Kanehsatake, as well as Algonquin ambassadors from Kanehsatake and Pointe-du-Lac "living in & about Canada."[74] On October 30, 1753, virtually all of the Indigenous Peoples of Canada joined this alliance.[75]

Was the agreement that bound the Iroquois of the Six Nations to the British in Albany similar to the one that tied the Seven Fires to the governor of New York? In other words, what was the scope of the British commitments to the Seven Fires under their agreement? Did they enjoy the same advantages as the Iroquois of the League? This is not clear with respect to the period prior to 1760, i.e., before the British took possession of Canada and officially allied themselves with the Seven Nations. On September 10, 1762, a Six Nations orator described the agreement as a trade and military alliance that included a clause on territorial protection. The League's chief and spokesperson added that the governors at the time had intentionally left space in the wampum necklace that was exchanged to mark the occasion so that the Iroquois of the League could "Fill with as many Nations of Indians, as we cou'd bring into their, and our Alliance."[76]

We also know that in Kahnawake, on September 15 and 16, 1760, the Seven Nations of Canada, which actually consisted of eight nations at that time, renewed and strengthened the ancient pact known among the domiciled sachems as the "Covenant Chain" and by the domiciled war chiefs as the "Chain of Friendship." Did that pact include the same trade, military, and territorial clauses regarding the alliance? We cannot say with certainty. We do know that, like the British-Iroquois agreement, the Kahnawake treaty of September 16, 1760, contained certain agreements about military matters, notably that, in the event of a crisis, if the "chain" were threatened, the allies would mutually support one another.[77] On September 7, 1763, in the context of the war with the Odawa of Pontiac, Sir William Johnson reminded the delegates from the League and the Confederacy that they had an obligation to take up arms to defend the alliance of the "Covenant" if it was threatened in any manner whatsoever.[78] Until 1776, the "chain" would be "polished" or "greased," however the American Revolution would once again alter the relations. The agreement "eroded" and was never broached again.[79]

Diplomatic Prestige in the Great Lakes Area

Under both the colonial regime of New France and the British
Government of Canada, several alliance systems operated in
the Great Lakes area, centered around the Huron-Wyandot,
Odawa, Chippewa, Miami, Shawnee, and Potawatomi. Over the
years, they were referred to, in turn, as the Wendat Confederacy,
the Three Fires Confederacy, and the Wabash Confederacy.[80]
Throughout history, these Indigenous nations joined together to
defend their shared interests and, during those historic moments,
they also forged ties with the Seven Nations of Canada. Prior
to 1760, diplomatic and trade activities in the Great Lakes were
focused primarily in Michigan and Ohio, around Niagara, and,
especially, in Makinaw, Detroit, and Sandusky.[81] The Great Lakes
nations were well aware of their crucial role in the political and
diplomatic development of New France and in the intercolonial
competition between France and England over the fur trade, and
they formed coalitions by creating numerous political alliances.
Given that these nations were key stakeholders in the fur trade,
they also formed an alliance with New France and, consequently,
established various contacts with their political and diplomatic
partners in the St. Lawrence River Valley.[82]

In the early 18th century, in 1701 precisely, there was an
alliance of seven nations that negotiated a peace agreement in
Albany with the Iroquois of the League of Five Nations. This
alliance had nothing to do with the one formed by the Seven
Nations of Canada. On July 14, 1701, John Nafan, Governor of
the Province of New York, met with the Iroquois Five Nations
in Albany, where the Iroquois informed him of the treaties the
Iroquois of the League had signed with the "7 Nations." The
Iroquois spokesman referred to the "Dowagenhahes" and the
"Far Indians," i.e., the Indigenous Peoples of the Great Lakes:
the Skighquan Nipissing; the Estjage Chippewa; the Assisagh
Mississauga; and the Arundax, Karhadage, Adgenauwe, and
Karihaet Algonquin.[83] In Daniel Claus' correspondence dated

July 10, 1755, there is a description of the conference that took place at Johnson Hall attended by the Iroquois Six Nations, their Indigenous "dependants" from the Province of New York, as well as the "7 united Nations," the latter apparently allied with the French and hailing from the Great Lakes region. Claus also mentioned that "some of the Diahoga, and a Party of Missisagas" accompanied these "7 united Nations."[84] Prior to 1760, there was an alliance system that united the Huron-Wyandot, Odawa, Chippewa, and Potawatomi, and also grouped together most of the Great Lakes nations. In the Ojibway and Wyandot oral tradition of the 20th century, the memory of this alliance was still alive.[85] The allies were numerous.

In a brief on the state of New France, Bougainville wrote that the Wyandot, Odawa, Mississauga, and Potawatomi were the Indigenous nations that were the most attached to the interests of the French.[86] In a journal entry from July 1757, the French officer also included charts of the origin of the Indigenous warriors fighting in the Marquis de Montcalm's army: Huron of Lorette; Nipissing and Algonquin of Lake of Two Mountains; Algonquin of Pointe-du-Lac; Abenaki of Saint-François, Bécancour, Missisquoi, and Panna8meské; Iroquois of Sault-Saint-Louis, Lake of Two Mountains, and La Présentation; Mi'kmaq of Acadia; Maliseet; and, from the "Pays d'en Haut," Wyandot, Têtes-de-boule or Gens-des-Terres; Odawa; Saulteaux; Mississauga; Potawatomi; Menominee; Miami; Puan; Agouais; Renard; Saki; Wolves; as well as from the nations in regions located north and south of the Great Lakes, all the way to the Mississippi River.[87] All of these nations, "bound together," were allies of the "Grand Onontio" from France and his representatives in Canada. Bougainville described in his journal a ceremony that took place July 13, 1756, at the governor's residence at Château Saint-Louis in Quebec City. In referring to the relations between the Menominee Indigenous nation from Baie des Puants and the French general La Corne Saint-Luc, Bougainville wrote:

Monsieur de St-Luc presented them, on behalf of the Abenaki, Algonquin, and Iroquois of Sault Saint-Louis, a necklace urging them to join them in striking the English at Chouagen [Oswego, New York]. They accepted the necklace and replied that they would go with them to share the meat they had already tested.[88]

Under the French Regime, the village of the Great Fire of Kahnawake served as a meeting place for all the Indigenous nations allied with the governor of New France, as we saw in the context of relations between the Seven Fires Confederacy, the Wabanaki Confederacy, and the Odawa of Makinaw. Indeed, as part of the peace negotiations surrounding the end of the war between the Iroquois of the Five Nations and the French, on July 22, 1701, a group of Odawa ambassadors travelled to Kahnawake, where they met with the other domiciled nations, including Wabanaki ambassadors from the Maritimes.[89] This large gathering at the village of the domiciled Iroquois suggests that the village was the primary meeting venue for all the French-allied Indigenous nations. In other words, when there was cause to meet with the diplomatic partners of the governor of New France, that meeting would be held in Kahnawake.

The central role of the Grand Council of the Seven Nations of Canada continued after 1760, as if the British merely took over where the French had left off. Under the British Regime of Canada, the Seven Nations ambassadors became the main intermediaries between the British and the Indigenous nations of the *"Pays d'en haut et de l'Ouest"* and any Great Lakes nation formerly or newly allied with the Seven Fires could go through the Grand Council of the St. Lawrence to communicate with the representatives of the colonial government of Great Britain. The Seven Fires Confederacy played a key role in organizing these relations. In 1763, in the context of the revolt by the Great Lakes Indigenous nations, the British entrusted the Seven Nations with passing on their messages to the "rebel" nations. The English asked the Seven Fires to approach the Huron-Odawa Confederacy and deliver the superintendent of Indian Affairs' messages to their chiefs. A group of Seven Nations delegates subsequently travelled to Detroit and Makinaw to deliver the British official's news of the Treaty of Paris signed on February 10, 1763, to their Great Lakes brothers, the Huron-Wyandot and Odawa. Condemning the military alliance against the British, the Seven Nations also reminded the Huron-Odawa Confederacy chiefs that they were officially allied with the King of England and his representatives in Canada.[90] Evidently, the British entrusted their messages to the Seven Fires, mandating them to speak on their behalf to the nations of the West.

In the fall of 1764, Colonel Henry Bouquet, who was tasked with quashing the Indigenous revolt, delegated a group of domiciled Indigenous warriors from the Wyandot of Detroit to deliver the terms of the peace negotiated between the British officers and the Shawnee chiefs. The Wyandot were to free the British prisoners being held in their villages.[91] Perhaps there were representatives of the Huron of Lorette who were delegated, as their warriors fought alongside the British in the Great Lakes region[92] and they maintained close diplomatic relations there. It had long been known that they were bound to their ancestors, the Huron-Wyandot of Detroit, with whom they fought under General Montcalm in 1757.[93] The domiciled Huron also later affirmed that they "have been lookd after by all Indian Nations, from Tadousack to Niagara as their Superiors and obeyed as such."[94] The British acknowledged that the close "connection" that tied them to the Great Lakes nations had non-negligible political consequences.[95]

In 1778, in the midst of the American Revolution, it was reported that 250 people from the western nations and from around Makinaw had converged on Kahnawake, at the Grand Council of the Seven Nations, to declare that, with regard to the war between the king and his colonies, they would defer to the political councils of the Seven Fires, declaring by the same occasion that the councils could thereafter represent them before the governor of Canada. The Odawa thereby mandated the Seven

Fires to intercede and speak to the British on their behalf.[96] From that point on, it fell to the Seven Fires Confederacy's representatives to appear before the colonial government of Quebec, and it was to their ambassadors, in February 1794, that Governor Carleton replied regarding the requests of the 28 Indigenous nations of Upper Canada.[97]

Given that the Seven Fires Confederacy was mandated by the Great Lakes nations to represent them, the Confederacy could also exercise this privilege before the Americans in the United States. On August 6, 1796, the Odawa of Makinaw went to Kahnawake to consult the leaders of the Great Fire about certain land transactions made between the Americans, Odawa, Huron, Wolves, Shawnee, Miami, and one other unidentified nation. The Kahnawake chief and orator thanked the Odawa embassy for the trust they placed in Seven Nations diplomacy. A delegation of Seven Nations ambassadors subsequently travelled to the United States to plead the case of their Great Lakes Indigenous allies in their capacity as the "First Indians on the land." This reference to the primacy of nations could mean one of two things: either that the Indigenous Peoples were the first nations to have occupied North America, or that, from a diplomatic standpoint, that the Seven Nations were considered the "First Indians" since they were the first to ally themselves to the British.

Whichever the case, the image of the "First Indians on the land" underscores the special relationship between the Seven Fires and the other North American nations: it was the place they appeared to occupy in the diplomatic hierarchy.[98] Jean-Baptiste Delorimier, in recording the discussions held at the Kahnawake congress, wrote that, with the exception of the Iroquois Six Nations, he was aware of no other nation that did not consider the Great Fire of the Seven Nations as the first.[99]

French, English, and Indigenous: Three Peoples, One Country

The alliance of the domiciled nations took shape at the time of the government of New France, specifically, starting in the second half of the 17th century. Yet, it is through the British colonial archives that we are able to pinpoint its origins. Under the British government of Canada, documentary proof explicitly mentions the founding and organization of a Confederacy grouping together the domiciled nations prior to 1760. From that date on, the Seven Fires Confederacy suddenly became an important actor or, at any rate, an actor that was frequently mentioned. At the time of the conquest of New France by the British, the Seven Fires Confederacy already existed, and it was with the Confederacy that the British negotiated peace and the alliance of August and September 1760. It was then that they became aware of the Confederacy, learned its rules, and sought to understand the way it functioned. But why is there so little mention of it in the French archives? That remains a mystery. While the official correspondence of New France's colonial administrators and the journals of its military officers contain a smattering of clues suggesting the existence of a shared system of political representation among the domiciled nations, there are no explicit allusions to it. However, the fact remains that there is sufficient evidence to trace the Confederacy's origins back to the French Regime.

Indeed, numerous earlier testimonials lend credence to the hypothesis that the origins of the Seven Fires date back to the days of the French Regime. Our arguments are based essentially on the testimonials of domiciled people who, in the 18th, 19th, and 20th centuries, referred back to the tradition of their forefathers and the relations they had with the French. These accounts are recorded in the archives of the Department of Indian Affairs, among others, and contain details on the origins of the organization, on its ancestor-founders, and on the nature of the agreements underlying the political alliance. This information was gathered, in part, from speeches given by Indigenous chiefs at conferences in the presence of British officials who, as a rule, attended the Seven Fires meetings.

The oral tradition of the domiciled nations suggests the alliance originated under the French Regime, an alliance that appears to have been forged in three stages: the first after the arrival of the Huron in the St. Lawrence River Valley in 1651, which would correspond to the political union of the domiciled Algonquin, Nipissing, and Huron. The second stage would have been between 1667 and 1701, corresponding to the integration of the Iroquois, and the third would have been that of the alliance of the Christian Abenaki to the original group. The oral tradition of the Huron of Lorette dates the origins of the organization to the 17th century. This is what can be concluded from the words of the Grand Chief of the Huron, Nicolas Vincent Tsaouenhohoui who, in 1824, spoke before a committee of the House of Assembly of Lower Canada as part of talks on the land claims of the domiciled Huron. The Grand Chief reminded the members of the committee of the ancient origins of the political alliance: "I do not know how to read or write, but according to the tradition of our forefathers, it was nearly two hundred years ago that the seven nations formed an alliance together to live in peace and harmony."[100]

The oral tradition of the Iroquois of Kahnawake is consistent, in part, with that of the Huron of Lorette, establishing the origins of the Seven Fires at the time of the French Regime of Canada. In 1791, in a discussion with Superintendent Campbell, the domiciled Iroquois recalled the origins of the political alliance between the Huron, the Algonquin, and the Nipissing, an alliance later joined by the Iroquois of Montreal. The two traditions are also consistent regarding the following events: After the military defeat of the Huron of the Great Lakes by the Iroquois of the Five Nations, some Christianized Hurons migrated to Quebec, following which, the domiciled Huron, Algonquin, and Nipissing decided to join their political and military forces and unite against their enemies of the Iroquois Confederacy.[101] From that moment on, the three domiciled Indigenous nations acted as one. And it was against that political backdrop that the core of what was to become the Seven Fires Confederacy was formed:

> We will tell you that, before any white man came to Canada, we were the six nations, we made war against the Huron who were north of Lake Ontario, who were forced to abandon their land to us. One group fled to Detroit, and the other below Quebec, while the Huron, Algonquin, and Nipissing were as one. The latter were in part in Trois Rivières, where we chased them still. Some fled to skeg8anett; others to beyond Trois Rivières. A short time later, the French settled on our land and the Priests hastened to spread their religion. Some of our six nations ancestors came to hunt near La Prairie de la magdelène, and seeing the French in Montréal, carried on there. They asked the French general if they could settle at La Prairie, which we renamed Kanawageronon.[102]

The domiciled Iroquois then recounted that, shortly after the founding of the triple alliance of the Huron, Algonquin, and Nipissing, their ancestors, who had been converted to Catholicism by the French missionaries, settled on the outskirts of Montreal, after petitioning the colonial government and receiving its approval. The Iroquois apparently then agreed to join the alliance alongside the other domiciled nations. They added that it was the governor who suggested that the domiciled nations join together to defend their common interests, bring an end to the territorial wars sparked by the fur trade, and focus their future military efforts against their shared enemy—the British and their Iroquois allies.[103]

In 1795, at a council in Kahnawake attended by Superintendent McKee, the Indigenous people of the "Seven Villages of Lower Canada" explained that the relations between the domiciled Iroquois and the French were based on a political and military alliance: "We were never conquered by the French. On the contrary, we have always been protectors of the white skins, and even of the other *nations Sauvages*,"[104] declared the Seven Fires chiefs. That same year, it was also noted that, in accordance with the suggestion of the French missionaries, the domiciled people of Lake of Two Mountains decided to form "three united nations."[105] In 1919, the Iroquois of Oka sent a letter to the Minister of the Interior in Ottawa, reminding him of the French origins of the alliance between the domiciled Iroquois of Lake of Two Mountains, Sault-Saint-Louis, and Saint-Régis. The Iroquois chiefs of the Lake wrote that Onontio, the governor of New France, after the settlement of the domiciled Iroquois in Canada and convinced of the honesty of the political decisions taken by the "federated tribes," exchanged a wampum symbolizing the "easing of the war spirit" and the "opening of new peaceful avenues," noting that it had been resolved to forgo the "war song" for "songs of joy."[106]

As for the domiciled Abenaki, it appears it was the Algonquin who invited them to settle in the St. Lawrence Valley, south of the St. Lawrence River, near the Saint-François River, and to join the alliance alongside the other domiciled nations.[107] This suggestion is corroborated by the Abenaki chiefs who, around 1804, addressed their Algonquin and Nipissing brothers of Lake of Two Mountains: "Our brothers, as We have always had an alliance of kinship, We pray to the Master of Life that this alliance shall continue, as it always has since we have known one another."[108] The Abenaki went on to describe their political relations with the domiciled nations of the Lake: "Our ancestors always told us that the first time they came together with our brothers the Algonquin, we had no place to hunt. So our brothers, the Algonquin, who were the first Indians of Canada, gave us all the part in the south for our hunts, to ensure the subsistence of our wives and our children."[109] From then on, the domiciled Huron, Algonquin, Nipissing, Iroquois, and Abenaki were as one. And it was with those nations, joined together in a confederacy, that the British would negotiate starting in 1759, and with whom they would ally themselves in 1760.

Indeed, during the Seven Years' War, as the English army began to close in on Quebec and Montreal, the British authorities continued their diplomatic efforts aimed at neutralizing and subsequently allying themselves with the Indigenous nations that belonged to the French alliance network. Conversely, as they saw their French partner being pushed back and eventually defeated, the Indigenous nations realized it was in their interest to negotiate with the British. This was the case of the nations of the Confederacy of the Seven Fires.[110] The Oswegatchie Treaty of Neutrality was signed in August 1760 between the British and the Seven Fires, on one side on behalf of the "Great King of England" by his representatives, the Commander-in-Chief of British forces, Jeffery Amherst, and the Superintendent of Indian Affairs, Sir William Johnson, and on the other by the "Seven Confederate Nations of Canada." In other words, the treaty was not signed with only a handful of the domiciled villages, but rather with all those who were members of the Confederacy.[111]

Several days after the Capitulation of Montreal, on September 15 and 16, 1760, a conference was held, attended by Sir William Johnson, the ambassadors of the Iroquois League, and the representatives of the Seven Fires.[112] The resulting treaty, which included pledges of a military nature, led the Seven Fires Indigenous nations, as both allies and dependents, to fight for the British during the American Revolution, the War of 1812, and the Patriots' Rebellion of 1837.[113]

CONCLUSION

Strengths and Weaknesses

The Seven Fires Confederacy was the alliance of the Catholic domiciled nations of Canada. Its members would gather around the Great Fire of Kahnawake, which played a leadership role in political and diplomatic relations with the other governments of northeastern North America. In terms of their internal organization, the Seven Nations established the rules and procedures governing the political functioning of their government, including the founding of a grand council; the position and role of the political chiefs, war chiefs, and woman chiefs; and the function of certain villages in the alliance, particularly Kahnawake, Kanehsatake, and Odanak. All of the member nations of the Confederacy thereby agreed to join forces to safeguard their common interests. We have seen that the Seven Nations of Canada applied all the diplomatic rituals and protocols characteristic of Indigenous political culture, including the exchange of wampum, condolence and pipe-smoking ceremonies, and feasts. We have also observed that the Seven Fires maintained ongoing political and diplomatic relations, first with the French, then with the British, and also with the Wabanaki Confederacy, the Iroquois Six Nations Confederacy, and the different Great Lakes confederacies.

Originating during the time of the French Regime in Canada, the Seven Nations grew considerably in importance after 1776, with the withdrawal of the British to Canada and the dispersal of the nations of the Iroquois League. From that time on, the Confederacy took over diplomatic relations with the British, which had previously been the domain of the Iroquois authorities from the Great Fire of Onandaga. In its role as ally, it became the primary intermediary between the British and all the other Indigenous political organizations in the northeast, with the Grand Council of Kahnawake as its focal point.

Historical studies have often relegated the Indigenous Peoples of Quebec to the background, affirming that they played only a secondary role in North America's political history. However, the archives do not support this affirmation by any means. One has only to observe the movements of their ambassadors: from the Maritimes to the Great Lakes, from the shores of the St. Lawrence to the American seaboard of the Atlantic Ocean, they travelled the length and breadth of northeastern North America on behalf of their political organization.

While we have examined the nature of the Confederacy, the frequency of its meetings, and the scope of its alliances, our research nonetheless remains formal, given the impossibility of determining the actual historical relations that prevailed. We were therefore unable to answer the following fundamental questions: Did the Seven Fires Confederacy serve the Indigenous nations against the colonial power, or was it the other way round? It was certainly an Indigenous political organization, but how independent was it? Was it the seat of anti-imperialist resistance or a puppet of the colonial government? An Indigenous political bastion or the governor's Trojan horse among the Indigenous people? Or perhaps both? And if so, to what extent? And during what timeframe? In that absolutely unique Indigenous world, the colonized people—and in this case, the domiciled nations, those most dependent on the colonial powers—founded a political, seemingly sovereign organization from the earliest days of their colonization. The creation of this alliance can be seen as a stepping stone between the "réductions" of the 17th century and the reserves of the 19th century.

It is worth identifying the weaknesses of the organization. First, like the other Indigenous confederacies, it was based on the political rule of consensus, and consensus was difficult to reach, even more so in those times of upheaval for Indigenous Peoples. This would inevitably often lead to an impasse, which would certainly have been a handicap in relation to the colonial powers, who enjoyed the advantage of statehood. Moreover, consensus did not always mean the same thing to everybody. Some groups or nations would speak on behalf of the Seven Nations of Canada without necessarily having obtained its backing. On occasion, they would express beliefs contrary to those of the alliances, and represent different, or even antagonist, interests. Further study of these factions is required. Second, the Seven Fires Confederacy consisted of Indigenous people who, for the most part, were refugees from elsewhere and who lived in close proximity to the colonists. Third, the Confederacy recognized in the governor they qualified as "father" a moral authority, while the member nations were his children.

As for the organization's strengths, the first is relative, and stems from its ability to play on the struggles between the empires. The French were dependent on Indigenous people for the fur trade, exploration, and, especially, military undertakings against the British. After 1760, this was also true, albeit to a lesser extent, for the British against the Americans. The strength of the Confederacy lay, perhaps above all else, in the determination of the Indigenous societies to survive, and their willingness to defend their interests and negotiate their position.

In the current context of Indigenous political claims, it is worth recalling that the Indigenous Peoples of Quebec once formed a structured alliance that boasted a sophisticated political system with which other political powers—Indigenous and non-Indigenous alike—maintained close diplomatic relations. The historical study of the political functioning of the Seven Fires Confederacy reveals a kind of historical continuity in the discourse of Indigenous Peoples regarding self-government. The

Grand Council of the Seven Nations of Canada is proof of the brilliant and highly organized actions of the Indigenous nations of Quebec.

Notes

Introduction

1. The term "nation" is the one used in most of the literature, and it is the term we use here, as it translates the historical reality of the Indigenous People. As a cultural concept, it signifies that Indigenous societies were sovereign, and that they exercised this sovereignty over specific territories. "Nation" also harkens back to the degree of sophistication and functioning of Indigenous political structures.

2. In 1991, sociologist and historian Denys Delâge briefly touched on this in an article entitled "Les Iroquois chrétiens des réductions," which appeared in *Recherches amérindiennes au Québec*. All of his conclusions were summarized in 1992 by historian Olive Patricia Dickason in *Canada's First Nations*, a general history of the Indigenous people in Canada. In the United States, American anthropologist David S. Blanchard published an article in the *American Indian Culture and Research Journal* in 1983 on the relations between the Iroquois of the Seven Nations and the State of New York.

3. Georges Boiteau, *Les Chasseurs hurons de Lorette*, 1954.

4. The author, however, provides only a very summary analysis of the organization's internal structure and political functioning: Lawrence Ostola, *The Seven Nations of Canada and the American Revolution 1774-1783*, 1989.

5. Jean-Pierre Sawaya, *Les Sept-Nations du Canada: traditions d'alliance dans le Nord-Est, XVIIIe-XIXe siècles*, 1995. The current monograph was inspired by this study.

6. Denys Delâge, Jean-Pierre Sawaya, *Les Sept-Feux et les traités avec les Britanniques*, 1996.

7. The Iroquois League is the subject of a considerable amount of scientific literature. Numerous researchers in the social sciences have examined a range of aspects regarding its functioning and history. The same is true of the Wabanaki Confederacy and the Great Lakes Confederacy, although to a lesser degree.

8. For a complete, detailed list of the manuscripts and printed sources used in this work, please consult the bibliography.

9. The archives of Sir William were originally conserved at his residence, Johnson Hall, in New York State. On the superintendent's death, his successor at Indian Affairs, his nephew Guy Johnson, took possession of the "Books of Indian Records," which contained copies of letters, treaties, and proceedings of dealings with the Indigenous people. In 1782, the superintendent brought all of these documents to Canada: "Statement to the Court of Exchequer," June 7, 1788, *JP*, vol. XIII, p. 733.

10. This extraordinary corpus compiled for the political and diplomatic study of the League of Iroquois Six Nations contains thousands of documents from Dutch, French, English, American, and Canadian archival collections relating to Indigenous history between the 16th and 19th century.

11. William Johnson to Lord Hillsborough, Johnson Hall, August 14, 1770, *DRCHNY*, vol. VIII, p. 225.

12. "Proceedings of a Congress held with the Chiefs and Warriors of the Six Nations at Guy Park," December 1, 1774, *IIADH*, bob. 31.

13. "Captain Brant's Journal of the Proceedings at the General Council held at the Foot of the Rapids of the Miamis," 1793, *RG 10*, vol. 8, p. 8442-8479. For an edited version, see Ernest A. Cruikshank, *The Correspondence of Lieut. Governor John Graves Simcoe*, vol. 2, p. 5-20.

14. William N. Fenton, "Structure, Continuity, and Change," Francis Jennings, ed., *The History and Culture of Iroquois Diplomacy*, 1985, p. 25-26.

15. "At a council held at Philadelphia, Tuesday the 13th of February, 1759," *IIADH*, bob. 23.

16. William Johnson to Thomas Gage, Johnson Hall, November 8, 1764, *JP*, vol. XI, p. 399.

17. Louis-Juchereau Duchesnay to George Couper, Quebec, August 24, 1829, *RG 10*, vol. 6750, file 420-10B.

18. C. Léonard to William Mackay, Lake of Two Mountains, August 18,1830, *RG 10*, vol. 25, p. 26367.

19. "Mémoires du Chevalier De La Pause," *RAPQ*, 1933, p. 327.

20. Fenton, "Structure, Continuity, and Change," *The History and Culture of Iroquois Diplomacy, op. cit.,* p. 26. Mary A. Druke, "Iroquois Treaties: Common Forms, Varying Interpretations," *The History and Culture of Iroquois Diplomacy, op. cit.,* p. 88.

21. François Deschambault to Herman W. Ryland, Montreal, May 24,1809, *RG 10*, vol. 487, p. 4280.

CHAPTER ONE. Peoples of the St. Lawrence River Valley

1. All of this information is from Volume 15 of the *Handbook of North American Indians* edited by Bruce G. Trigger, as well as from various historical and anthropological studies of the sedentary Indigenous communities of the St. Lawrence. See bibliography.

2. In the words of Thomas Gage to William Johnson, New York, March 9, 1766, *JP*, vol. XII, p. 38.

3. Marc Jetten, *Enclaves amérindiennes: les « réductions » du Canada 1637-1701*, Sillery, Septentrion, 1994, p. 10. Robert J. Surtees, "The Iroquois in Canada," *The History and Culture of Iroquois Diplomacy, op. cit.*, p. 67-68. William N. Fenton, Elizabeth Tooker, "Mohawk," *HNAI*, vol. 15, p. 469.

4. Pierre Margry, ed., *Mémoires et documents pour servir à l'histoire des origines françaises des pays d'outre-mer*, 1879, t.1, p. 174. Daniel Claus, "Journal of Indian Affairs," July 26, 1773, *JP*, vol. XIII, p. 624. Petition from François Lotono *et al.* to Matthew Lord Aylmer, Trois-Rivières, July 22, 1831, RG 10, vol. 83, p. 32484.

5. The *Jesuit Relations* are quite clear on this subject: In it there are frequent references to the Indigenous people from the "réductions" of New France and to the close ties they had with the missionaries regarding religion.

6. Denys Delâge, *Discours et pratiques coloniales, discours et pratiques autochtones*, 1996, p. 26-27.

7. "Conseil adressé à Mr Le Colonel Campbell Supr : int : des affaires sauvages & &," Kahnawake, October 7,1791, *RG* 10, vol. 8, p. 8202-8203.

8. "Paroles des Abénakis a leurs frères Algonquins et Nipissingues, au Lac des deux Montagnes." This document likely pre-dates 1804; *RG 10*, vol. 99, p. 41090. Petition from François Lotono *et al.* to Matthew Lord Aylmer, Trois-Rivières, July 22, 1831, *RG 10*, vol. 83, p. 32484.

9. In the French and English documents, the village is called "Lorette" or "Loreto," in tribute to the Italian chapel Casa Sancta da Loreto. "Wendake" means "where the Huron live."

10. The Abenaki village is called "Saint-François" or "St. Francis" in reference to the Saint-François River close to where the village stands and dedicated to the patron saint François de Sales. The people who lived there were usually referred to as the Abenaki and Sokoki of Saint-François.

11. In the literature, the village is known as "Bécancour." The Abenaki called it "Damiso Rantik."

12. References are usually to the village established near Trois-Rivières or to the Indigenous communities on the shores of Lac Saint-Pierre. The Indigenous peoples who lived there were collectively known as the "domiciled natives of Trois Rivières" or "Three Rivers Indians" or, more precisely, the "Algonquin of Trois-Rivières."

13. The French written tradition refers to "Saint-François-Xavier-du-Sault-Saint-Louis," while in English it was called "Caughnawaga." According to the oral tradition of the domiciled nations, the village was named "Gahnawage," "Gana8age," or "Kahnawake." This name means "at the rapids," in reference to the Lachine Rapids. The Indigenous people of this village were called "gens du Sault," "Iroquois du Sault," "Indians of Caughnawaga," or just "Caghnawaga."

14. This name means, literally, "the village on the hill." It refers to the relief of the Montérégie region where the Oka complex is located. In the archival documents, the village is referred to as "Lac des Deux Montagnes," "Lake of Two Mountains," "Oka," "Canasadaga," "Ganegsadaga," or "Scawendadey."

15. The Indigenous word "Akwesasne" refers to the sound of the waterfalls on the Racquette, Saint-Régis, and St. Lawrence confluents, on the shores of which the Iroquois settled. In the English archives, the village is named "Akwesasne" or "Aughquisasne," and also sometimes as "St. Régis," the name used by the French in honour of the missionary Jean-François Régis. These domiciled people were generally known by the name "St Régis Indians" or "Aughquisasne."

16. The French documents mention the village of "La Présentation" or "La Galette," while the English documents refer to it as "Oswegatchie," "Oswegatchy," "Swegatchy," or "Swegatsy." The domiciled Iroquois were known as the "domiciled natives of La Présentation" or simply as "Oswegatchies."

17. Brian Connell, ed., [John Knox], *The Siege of Quebec and the campaigns in North America 1757-1760*, Pendragon House of Mississauga, 1980, p. 384. The "journal" of James Murray, September 5, 1760, *MG 23, GII, 1, (4)*, p. 164.

18. "Indian Conference," "Montreal," Kahnawake, September 16, 1760, *JP*, vol. XIII, p. 163-166.

19. "Message of the Canada to the Western Indians," August 25, 1763, *IIADH*, bob. 25. "Messages sent by Eight Nations of Canada to the western nations," August 25, 1763, *IIADH*, bob. 26.

20. William Johnson, "Memorandum on Six Nations and Other Confederacies," November 11, 1763, *JP*, vol. IV, p. 243. *Ibid., DRCHNY*, vol. VIII, p. 244.

21. Alain Beaulieu, (Jean-Pierre Sawaya) "Qui sont les Sept Nations du Canada ?" *RAAQ*, vol. XXVII, no. 2 (Fall 1997), p. 43-51. In this important research note, the author identifies a number of ambiguities relating to the term "Seven Nations" over the course of history.

22. Daniel Claus to William Johnson, Montreal, September 30, 1760, *JP*, vol. III, p. 547.

23. "Proceedings of Sir William Johnson with the Indians," German Flats, July 18, 1770, *DRCHNY*, vol. VIII, p. 229, 244.

24. "Paroles des Sept Villages adressées au Lieutenant Colonel John Campbell Surintendant de ces Sauvages," Montreal, October 20, 1779, *IIADH*, bob. 35. John Campbell to Frederick Haldimand, Montreal, October 25, 1779, *HP*, add. mss. 21771, fo 170vo.

25. "Réponse de Son Exellence le Lord Dorchester, aux Sept Villages du Bas Canada venus en députation de la part de toutes les Nations du pays d'en

haut excepté les Chaouanons, Miamis et Loups, rendue en Conseil au Chateau de St. Louis à Québec le 10e. Février, 1794," *RG 10*, vol. 8, p. 8571.

26. Testimonial of Nicolas Vincent Tsaouenhohoui, House of Assembly of Lower Canada, Committee Chamber, Quebec, February 2, 1819, *JCA*, vol. XXVIII, 59 Geo. III, appendix (R), A. 1819.

27. Petition by Martin Ze Kanasentic *et al.* to Archibald Earl Gosford, Sault-Saint- Louis, February 3, 1837, *RG 10*, vol. 93, p. 39031.

28. Petition by Martin Tekanasontie *et al.* to James Bruce Earl Elgin, Sault-Saint-Louis, September 18, 1850, *RG 10*, vol. 607, p. 51855.

29. Petition by Joseph Kentarontie *et al.* to Sir Edmund Walker Head, Kahnawake, August 8, 1856, *RG 10*, vol. 232, pt. 2, p. 138229.

30. Conference in Trois-Rivières between Louis-Juchereau Duchesnay, the Abenaki of Saint-François and Bécancour, the Huron of Lorette, and the Algonquin of Pointe-du-Lac, October 26, 1829, *RG 8*, vol. 268, p. 724-736. *Ibid., RG 10*, vol. 6750, file 420-10 B.

31. "An Indian Conference," Johnson Hall, July 29, 1768, *JP*, vol. XII, p. 570. Jean-Baptiste Destimauville to Alexander McKee, Saint-François, June 29, 1795, *RG 10*, vol. 9, p. 8957. Petition by Jean Jaksos *et al.* to James Henry Craig, Trois-Rivières, January 19, 1808, *RG 10*, vol. 487, p. 4285-4286. *Ibid., RG 10*, vol. 625, p. 182363-182365.

32. In this case, the problem concerning the Huron of Lorette having been settled; conference in Trois-Rivières between Louis-Juchereau Duchesnay, the Abenaki of Saint-François and Bécancour, the Huron of Lorette, and the Algonquin of Pointe-du-Lac, October 26, 1829, *RG 8*, vol. 268, p. 791-792.

33. "Report of Capt. Danl. Claus's proceedings at Canasadaga with the Indians," Montreal, March 15, 1762, *JP*, vol. X, p. 398. Carl F. Klinck, James J. Talman, *The Journal of Major John Norton*, 1816, Champlain Society 46, Toronto, Champlain Society, 1970, p. 243.

34. In the English documents, there are several mentions of the "Caneghsadarundax," likely meaning the Iroquois ("Caneghsada") and Algonquin ("Arundax") allies. The juxtaposition of these two proper nouns can be confusing. However, generally speaking, the term "Caneghsadagey" refers to the Iroquois of Lake of Two Mountains, as is the case in "Messages of the Canada to the Western Indians," *IIADH*, bob. 25 or "Messages sent by Eight Nations in Canada to the western Indians," August 25, 1763, *IIADH*, bob. 25. "Proceedings of Sir William Johnson with the Indians," German Flats, July 18, 1770, *DRCHNY*, vol. VIII, p. 228. See also on this topic: Maurice Ratelle, *Présence des Mohawks au Québec méridional de 1534 à nos jours*, 1991, p. 15-16.

35. This is especially true for the documents from the 18th century: Daniel Claus, "Journal of Indian Affairs," August 27, 1767, *JP*, vol. XIII, p. 428. "Account of Daniel Claus," July 20, 1769, *JP*, vol. XIII, p. 488. Daniel

Claus to William Johnson, Montreal, July 8, 1772, *JP*, vol. XII, p. 971. "Memorial of a Council held at the village of Caughnawaga," June 26, 1841, *RG 10*, vol. 596, p. 45996. "Answers of the Chiefs of the Caughnawaga to the correspondence between Mr S.Y. Chesley and the officers of the Indian Department at Albany in the State of New York," July 9, 1841, *RG 10*, vol. 596, p. 45999. In the 19th century, the Algonquin and Nipissing joined their voices more often than not, as evidenced by numerous petitions in the archives of the Department of Indian Affairs.

36. Sir William Johnson referred in 1763 to the "Skoghquanoghroonas,' whom we believe to have been Nipissing: William Johnson, "Memorandum on Six Nations and Other Confederacies," November 11, 1763, *JP*, vol. IV, p. 243. The ecclesiastic register of the parish of La Visitation maintained by Alexandre Dugré refers to Têtes-de-Boule and Montagnais: François De Lagrave, *Pointe-du-Lac: 1738-1988*, Pointe-du-Lac, Édition du 250e anniversaire, 1988, p. 101-102. In the 19th century, archival documents refer to the Algonquin and Têtes-de-Boule: Joseph De Niverville to John Johnson, Trois-Rivières, December 26, 1814, *RG 10*, vol. 487, p. 4544-4545. George Dyett to Duncan C. Napier, September 14, 1843, *RG 10*, vol. 721, p. 168251.

37. Louis-Juchereau Duchesnay to George Couper, Quebec, July 26, 1830, *RG 10*, vol. 25, p. 26269. Petition by Pierre Baptiste Mékinac *et al.* to George Lord Durham, Trois-Rivières, August 4, 1838, RG 10, vol. 99, p. 39476-39478.

38. Conference in Trois-Rivières between Louis-Juchereau Duchesnay, the Abenaki of St. François and Bécancour, the Huron of Lorette, and the Algonquin of Pointe-du-Lac, October 26, 1829, *RG 8*, vol. 268, p. 724-736.

39. "At a Treaty held at the City of New York, by the United States, with the nations or tribes of Indians denominating themselves the Seven Nations of Canada," May 23, 1796, *The New American State Papers. Indian Affairs*, 1972, vol. 6, p. 155.

40. Archibald Maclean to François Deschambault, Cornwall, May 21, 1818, *RG 10*, vol. 489, p. 29345-29346. "Memorial of a Council held at the Village of Caughnawaga 26th June; For the Head Officer of the Indian Department on the Treaty of 1796," Kahnawake, June 26, 1841, *RG 10*, vol. 596, p. 45996-45998. In 1851, the creation of Indigenous reserves in Eastern Canada definitively marked the division between the two political councils of the Iroquois of Akwesasne.

41. Testimonial of Nicolas Vincent Tsaouenhohoui, House of Assembly of Lower Canada, Committee Chamber, Quebec, January 29, 1824, *JCA*, 5 Geo. IV, appendix (A), A. 1824.

42. Jean-Baptiste Delorimier, "I certify that on the 13th. of August 1796 I was called to a council held at Caughnawaga, of the Seven Nations of Lower Canada, the Courtes oreilles or Odawas of Michilimackinac, Mickmacs,

Muskrats &c. of which the following are the true Speeches addressed to His Excellency General Prescott," Montreal, August 27, 1796, *RG 8*, vol. 249, pt. 2, p. 301-304.

43. In his correspondence dated July 26, 1830, with the military secretary of Quebec, the superintendent of Indian Affairs, Louis-Juchereau Duchesnay, mentions that the "Têtes de Boulle" were very upset by the decisions made by the Grand Council of the Seven Nations about hunting grounds. Does this suggest that these people were part of the Seven Nations? Not necessarily. However, the reference to their reaction shows that they were aware of the decisions reached by the Grand Council of the Confederacy: Louis-Juchereau Duchesnay to George Couper, Quebec, July 26, 1830, *RG 10*, vol. 25, p. 26269.

44. In a petition dated 1838 that was presented jointly to Governor Durham by the Algonquin of Pointe-du-Lac and the Têtes-de-Boule of the Saint-Maurice River, the Algonquin presented their petition on behalf of the Têtes-de-Boule and explained that they were mandated to represent them before the colonial government; that both groups had participated in the military expeditions alongside Louis de Salaberry at the Battle of Châteauguay in 1813; and that their ancestors had also been military allies of the British Crown during the American Revolution: petition by Pierre Baptiste Mékinac *et al.* to George Lord Durham, Trois-Rivières, August 4, 1838, *RG 10*, vol. 99, p. 39476-39478 ; Duncan C. Napier to George Dyett, Montreal, November 3, 1843, RG 10, vol. 114, pt. 2, p. 167452. The Montagnais, on the other hand, had not taken part in the wars leading to the Conquest of Canada, as they were allied militarily with neither the French nor the English. In a speech by a group of Montagnais representatives from Saguenay, the chiefs pointed out that during the war, they were "tranquil" and went about their hunting "without concerning ourselves with who was at peace or at war:" Claude Godefroy Coquart, Tadoussac, March 12, 1765, *RG 10*, vol. 625, p. 182548-182552.

45. We personally compiled all the following data from archival documents and various demographic, historical, and other studies. Between 1665 and 1685, the population of domiciled people continued to increase, climbing from 300 to 2,100, before dropping to 1,900 in 1685. By 1705, it had climbed once again to 2,500, then to 3,000 in 1710, before declining to 2,300 in 1715. From that time, the population continued to grow, with census numbers showing 2,500 inhabitants in 1725 and 2,700 in 1735. And by 1737, that number nearly doubled, reaching 5,000. This is the highest figure we came across. Eight years later, in 1745, the population of domiciled people plummeted to 3,500. Between 1755 and 1763, the Indigenous population of the Seven Fires increased. In 1755, there were 4,100 habitants, and that number had risen to 4,850 by 1763. In 1765, only two years later, it had sunk to 3,100. From 1768 to 1823, the population fluctuated enormously,

going from 3,600 inhabitants in 1768, to 3,000 in 1800, 3,727 in 1820, and three years later, in 1823, dropping again to 2,925. Between 1823 and 1832, the population of the Seven Fires hovered around 3,000. By 1833, it had declined to 2,682, only climbing again in 1839, to 3,331. The population dropped once again in 1840, with the census reporting 3,070 Indigenous inhabitants. Between 1840 and 1846, the population rose from 3,070 to 3,495. However, as of 1846, that number never ceased to shrink, progressively declining from that point on. From 3,495 inhabitants in 1846, the population was only 2,994 in 1854. See graphs on the Seven Nations of Canada: Population of the Allied Villages, 1655-1854.

46. Claude-Charles Le Roy De Bacqueville La Potherie, *Histoire de l'Amérique septentrionale*, Paris, Brocas, 1753 (1722) t. I, p. 360.

47. *Ibid.*, p. 542.

48. William Johnson, "Memorandum on Six Nations and Other Confederacies," November 11, 1763, *JP*, vol. IV, p. 240-246.

49. Many Iroquois emigrated to Ohio or to Western Canada, signing up as *voyageurs* for Montreal merchants. In the 19th century, many Abenaki turned to making handicrafts for tourists, and relocated to the United States.

50. John A. Dickinson, Jan Grabowski, "Les populations amérindiennes de la vallée laurentienne, 1608-1765," *Annales de démographie historique* (1993), p. 51, 60-61. Bruce G. Trigger, "Nouveaux établissements indigènes, 1635-1800," Cole R. Harris, ed., *Atlas historique du Canada*, Montreal, Presses de l'Université de Montréal, 1987, vol. I, p. 122-123. Gunther Michelson, "Iroquois Population Statistics," *Man in the Northeast*, no. 14 (Fall 1977), p. 3-17. Elizabeth Tooker, "The League of The Iroquois. Its History, Politics, and Rituals," *HNAI*, vol. 15, p. 418-419. See the six volumes of Henry R. Schoolcraft's *History of the Indian Tribes of the United States*, Philadelphia, J.P. Lippincolt, 1856.

51. In his journal, French officer Louis-Antoine de Bougainville recounts one of his visits to see the inhabitants at Lake of Two Mountains, noting that the domiciled people would pray at the church, "each in their own language": *RAPQ*, 1924, p. 271.

52. Louis Franquet, *Voyages et mémoires sur le Canada, Institut Canadien de Québec*, Quebec, Côté, 1889, p. 41-49 *passim*. From the 19th century on, Nipissing would prevail in discussions between the Algonquin communities of the St. Lawrence: Gordon N. Day, "Nipissing," *HNAI*, vol. 15, p. 787.

53. David S. Blanchard, *Kahnawake : aperçu historique*, series on the history of Kahnawake no. 1, Kahnawake, Kanien'kehaka Raotitiohkwa, 1980, p. 1. Henri Béchard, *The Original Caughnawaga Indians*, Montreal, *International Publisher's Representatives*, 1976 (1975), p. 38. Fenton, Tooker, "Mohawk," *HNAI*, vol. 15, p. 473.

54. The chiefs of the Iroquois Council of Lake of Two Mountains, September 1, 1829, *RG 10*, vol. 23, p. 25292.
55. "Journal of Indian Affairs," March 24-30, 1762, *JP*, vol. X, p. 410.
56. "Conference with Indians," Niagara, July 9, 1764, *JP*, vol. XI, p. 262.
57. "An Indian Conference," Johnson Hall, July 28 to August 11, 1770, *IIADH*, bob. 30.
58. "At a Council called by the three Outawa Chiefs at Sault St Louis," February 1786, *IIADH*, bob. 38.
59. Petition by Ignace [Kaindatiron ?] *et al.* to George Provost, Kahnawake, September 18, 1811, *RG 10*, vol. 627, p. 182882-182883.
60. The chiefs of the councils of Lake of Two Mountains, Saint-Régis, Saint-François, Bécancour, and Lorette to James Kempt, Lorette, October 8, 1828, *RG 8*, vol. 267, p. 293.
61. Duncan C. Napier to T.W.C. Murdock, Montreal, June 28, 1841, *RG 10*, vol. 6, p. 2683.
62. Ignace Giasson to James Bruce Lord Elgin, Saint-Philomène, March 11, 1848, *RG 10*, vol. 123, p. 6458-6460.
63. On April 30, 1835, the missionary wrote to the secretary of Indian Affairs that he was working on an Iroquois grammar and a French-Iroquois dictionary: "I am determined to complete, as a complement to the Iroquois grammar and the French-Iroquois dictionary that took me nearly half a sheaf of paper, another French-Iroquois dictionary that my successor, whomever that shall be, will certainly not be able to complete, as no one is truly well-acquainted with this language.": Joseph Marcoux to Duncan C. Napier, Sault-Saint-Louis, April 30, 1835, *RG 10*, vol. 89, p. 36094-36101.
64. One such list of Department of Indian Affairs expenses can be consulted in "Account against the Crown," Johnson Hall, September 25, 1770, *JP*, vol. XII, p. 867.
65. "Conference between M. de Vaudreuil and the Indians," December 13 to 30, 1756, *IIADH*, bob. 20. "Indian Conference," "Montreal," Kahnawake, September 16, 1760, *JP*, vol. XIII, p. 166. Daniel Claus to William Johnson, Montreal, June 2, 1762, *JP*, vol. III, p. 752. Pertuis received an official commission from the British government on March 24, 1765: "Perthuis appointment as Interpreter," March 24, 1765, *RG 10*, vol. 15, p. 61-62.
66. Édouard Delorimier to William Johnson, Lachine, July 5, 1766, *JP*, vol. V, p. 305-306. Duncan C. Napier to T.W.C. Murdock, Montreal, June 28, 1841, *RG 10*, vol. 6, p. 2683.
67. Jean-Baptiste Destimauville to Alexander McKee, Saint-François, June 29, 1795, *RG 10*, vol. 9, p. 8956.
68. Daniel Claus, "Complaint of Indians," September 8, 1764, *IIADH*, bob. 27.
69. James Hughes to Duncan C. Napier, Montreal; this document possibly dates from March 12, 1828, *RG 10*, vol. 21, p. 14486-14487.

70. James Kempt to George Murray, Quebec, May 20, 1830, P. Ford *et al.*, *Correspondence and Other Papers Relating to Aboriginal Tribes in British Possessions. 1834*, 1969, vol. 3, p. 95.

71. James Hughes to Duncan C. Napier, Montreal, February 4, 1837, *RG 10*, vol. 93, p. 38048-38049.

72. Council at Lake of Two Mountains, October 7, 1843, *RG 10*, vol. 598, p. 46979.

73. Eleazar Wheelock to William Johnson, Dartmouth College, February 27, 1773, *JP*, vol. XII, p. 1012.

74. William Johnson to Eleazar Wheelock, Johnson Hall, March 23, 1773, *JP*, vol. VIII, p. 743-744.

75. "Conseil adressé à Mr Le Colonel Campbell Supr : int : des affaires sauvages," Kahnawake, October 7, 1791, *RG 10*, vol. 8, p. 8201-8202.

76. Journal de Bougainville, *RAPQ*, 1924, p. 284, 373.

77. "Memorandum on the Indian Department," Quebec, February 16, 1828, *RG 10*, vol. 791, p. 7177-7191. Joseph-Vincent Quiblier to the Iroquois, June 11, 1839, *RG 10*, vol. 95, p. 39344-39345. Nicolas Dufresne to Nicholas Tekanatoken, Lake of Two Mountains, June 15,1840, *RG 10*, vol. 100, p. 41466. P. Billaudèle to Richard Bruce, Montreal, July 6, 1852, *RG 10*, vol. 609, p. 52922-52923.

78. Jean-Baptiste Destimauville, Quebec, January 10, 1797, *RG 8*, vol. 250, pt. 1, p. 66-69.

79. "Conseil adressé à Mr Le Colonel Campbell Supr : int : des affaires sauvages & &.,", Kahnawake, October 7, 1791, *RG 10*, vol. 8, p. 8202.

80. Journal de Bougainville, *RAPQ*, 1924, p. 259.

81. *Ibid.*, p. 270-271.

82. Journal of Warren Johnson, November 1760, *JP*, vol. XIII, p. 190. Letter from the secrétaire de la Propagation de la Foi, A. M. Campbell, Cornwall; this document predates 1850; *RG 10*, vol. 118, p. 169441.

83. Brief about Lake of Two Mountains. This document predates 1842; *RG 10*, vol. 118, p. 169715. We also consulted a document dating from 1865, an ecclesiastic book for the use of the three domiciled nations of Lake of Two Mountains. The work is entitled *Le livre des sept nations ou paroissien iroquois.* « *Auquel on a ajouté, pour l'usage de la mission catholique du Lac des Deux-Montagnes, quelques cantiques en langue algonquine* » and also bears the Iroquois title *Tstatak nthonon8entstake onk8e on8e akoiatonsera.* It includes a chart of religious holidays, a processional containing Iroquois and Algonquin hymns and songs (with musical scores and texts in Latin), and a book of prayers drafted by Joseph Marcoux, a missionary posted at Sault-Saint-Louis: Jean-André Cuoq, *Le livre des sept nations ou paroissien iroquois*, Tiohtiake, Tehoristorarakon, John Lovell, 1865.

84. "Articles of the Capitulation of Montreal," September 8, 1760, Adam Shortt, Arthur G. Doughty, *Documents relatifs à l'histoire constitutionnelle*

du Canada 1759- 1791, Ottawa, Thomas Mulvey, 1921, vol. 1, p. 18.

85. We were unable to locate the text of the Treaty of Oswegatchie; the document has likely been lost. However, we are able to reconstruct its content through subsequent allusions. For an exhaustive report of all the documentary references relating to the Treaty of Oswegatchie and Article 40, as well as references to these agreements by the Indigenous peoples of the Seven Fires, see Delâge, Sawaya, *Les Sept Feux et les traités avec les Britanniques*, 1996.

86. "Paroles des Sept Villages adressées au Lieutenant Colonel John Campbell Surintendant de ces Sauvages," Montreal, October 20, 1779, *IIADH*, bob. 35.

87. *Ibid.*

88. *Ibid.*

89. *Ibid.*

90. William Johnson to Lord Hillsborough, Johnson Hall, August 14, 1770, *DRCHNY*, vol. VIII, p. 226.

91. Petition by Nicolas Vincent Tsaouhenhoui *et al.* to Joseph-Octave Plessis, Lorette, April 18, 1816, *RG 10*, vol. 488, p. 28900-28902.

92. "A Memorial concerning the Iroquois," New York, October 1, 1771, *IIADH*, bob. 30.

93. Daniel Claus to William Johnson, Montreal, May 24, 1761, *JP*, vol. III, p. 394.

94. William Johnson to Daniel Claus, Castle Cumberland, June 11, 1761, *JP*, vol. X, p. 281.

95. William Johnson, "Journal of Indian Affairs," March 30, 1762, *JP*, vol. X, p. 415.

96. "An Indian Conference," Johnson Hall, July 29, 1768, *JP*, vol. XII, p. 571.

97. Denys Delâge, "Les Iroquois chrétiens des réductions, 1667-1770, I: Migration et rapports avec les Français," *RAAQ*, vol. XXI, no. 1-2 (1991), p. 61.

98. "Indian Proceedings," Carrying Place camp, August 21, 1755, *JP*, vol. II, p. 379.

99. "Johnson's Proceedings with Deputies," Fort Johnson, February 13 to 14, 1760, *JP*, vol. III, p. 189.

100. "Journal of Indian Affairs." May 6, 1762, *IIADH*, bob. 23.

101. Daniel Claus to William Johnson, Montreal, August 30, 1765, *JP*, vol. XI, p. 917.

102. "Answer to a Speech to the Caughnawagas, or Canadian Tribes of Indians, near Montreal, sent by the Stockbridge Indians - returned 15th June," 1775, *IIADH*, bob. 31.

103. "At a Treaty held at the City of New York, by the United States, with the nations or tribes of Indians denominating themselves the Seven Nations of Canada," May 23, 1796, *The New American State Papers. Indian Affairs*, 1972, vol. 6, p. 157.

104. Testimonial of Nicolas Vincent Tsaouenhohoui before the House of Assembly of Lower Canada, Quebec, January 29, 1824, *Journals of the House of Assembly of Lower-Canada*, Quebec, Bibliothèque de l'Assemblée nationale, 5 Geo. IV, Appendix (R).

105. Council at the village of the Iroquois of Saint-Régis, August 6-7, 1830, *RG 10*, vol. 25, p. 26312.

106. "Conseil adressé à Mr Le Colonel Campbell Supr : int : des affaires sauvages," Kahnawake, October 7, 1791, *RG 10*, vol. 8, p. 8203.

107. *Ibid.*

108. Pierre Pouchot, *Mémoires sur la dernière guerre de l'Amérique Septentrionale*, Yverdon, 1781, t. 2, p. 223.

109. "I am certify that on the 13th. of August 1796 I was called to a council held at Caughnawaga, of the Seven Nations of Lower Canada, the Courtes oreilles or Ottawas of Michilimackinac, Mickmacs, Muskrats &c. of which the following are the true Speeches addressed to His Excellency General Prescott," *RG 8*, vol. 249, pt. 2, p. 301.

110. *Ibid.*

111. Jean-Baptiste Destimauville, Quebec, January 10, 1797, *RG 8*, vol. 250, pt. 2, p. 66.

112. Daniel Claus, "Journal of Indian Affairs," October 4, 1767, *JP*, vol. XIII, p. 431-432.

113. Daniel Claus to William Johnson, Montreal, August 30, 1765, *JP*, vol. XI, p. 918.

114. Gilles Havard, *La Grande Paix de Montréal de 1701 : les voies de la diplomatie franco-amérindienne*, Signes des Amériques, Montreal, *RAAQ*, 1992, p. 138. "Propositions of the Five Nations to the Commissioners of Indian Affairs," June 30, 1700, *DRCHNY*, vol. IV, p. 694. "Report of Captain John Bleeker and Mr. David Schuyler's journey to the Onondagas, in August and September" September 22, 1700, *DRCHNY*, vol. IV, p. 918-919. "French intrigues with the Indians," October 4, 1700, *DRCHNY*, vol. IV, p. 709. Baqueville de la Potherie to Jérôme Phélypeaux de Pontchartrain, Quebec, October 16, 1700, MG 1, C11A, vol. 18, ff. 150-151, 155. "The Lieut Govr John Nanfan Esqr met the 5 Nations & made á Speech to them wch is not recorded. They Answer," Albany, July 14, 1701, Charles H. McIlwain ed., *An Abridgement of Indian Affairs*, 1915, p. 39. "Ratification de la Paix faitte au mois de septembre dernier, entre la Colonie de Canada, les Sauvages ses alliéz, et les iroquois dans une assemblée géneralle des chefs de chacune de ces nations convoquée par monsieur le Chevalier de Callières gouverneur et Lieutenant general pour le Roy en la nouvelle France," Montreal, August 4, 1701, *MG 1*, C11A, vol. 19, ff. 41-44.

115. "Copie d'une lettre que les Sauvages du Sault St Louis ecrive aux Mohawks et addresse á Joseph Brant." This document appears to date from 1798; *RG 10*, vol. 10, p. 9202-9303.

116. "Paroles des chefs du Sault St Louis adresser á l'honorable Baronet Sir John Johnson, superintendant General, et Inspecteur General des Affairs Sauvages," Lachine, April 6, 1798, *RG 10*, vol. 10, p. 9295.

117. See Map 1: Seven Fires Hunting Grounds. For the precise boundaries of these hunting grounds, as reconstructed using colonial documents, see Sawaya, *Les sept nations du Canada: traditions d'alliance dans le Nord-Est*, 1995. See also Delâge, Sawaya, *Les Sept Feux et les traités avec les Britanniques*, 1996.

118. "Conseil adressé à Mr Le Colonel Campbell Supr : int : des affaires sauvages," Kahnawake, October 7, 1791, *RG 10*, vol. 8, p. 8205.

119. *Ibid.*

120. *Ibid.*, p. 8206.

121. *Ibid.*

122. "Conseils tenus a notre Pere Colonel Campbell par les Algonkins et Nepissingues," Montreal, July 14, 1791, *RG 10*, vol. 625, p. 182292.

123. Council between Louis-Juchereau Duchesnay, the Huron of Lorette, the Algonquin of Pointe-du-Lac, and the Abenaki of St. François and Bécancour; Trois-Rivières, October 26, 1829, *RG 10*, vol. 6750, file 420-10 B.

124. Proceedings from a conference, Montreal, August 25, 1827, *RG 10*, vol. 20, p. 14184.

125. "Proceedings of a Grand Council held with the Chiefs of the undermentioned Tribes at the Government House in the Village of Caughnawaga on Friday the 5th of October 1827," *RG 10*, vol. 20, p. 14244.

126. *Ibid.*, p. 14250-14251.

127. Proceedings of a council with the Iroquois of Saint-Régis, August 6-7, 1830, *RG 10*, vol. 25, p. 26317.

128. C. Leonard to William Mackay, "Notes sur la situation actuelle des Sauvages Iroquois du Lac des Deux Montagnes [...] Discours d'un des principaux Chefs," Lake of Two Mountains, August 18, 1830, RG 10, vol. 25, p. 26365.

129. Petition by Pierre Constant Peninsi *et al.* to James Kempt, Montreal, July 8, 1830, *RG 10*, vol. 25, p. 26247-26249.

130. For instance, it is possible to consult the argument of the Abenaki of Saint-François and Bécancour against that of the Algonquin of Pointe-du-Lac in the following document: council between Louis-Juchereau Duchesnay, the Huron of Lorette, the Algonquin of Pointe-du-Lac, and the Abenaki of Saint-François and Bécancour; Trois-Rivières, October 26, 1829, *RG 10*, vol. 6750, file 420-10 B.

131. "Report of the Proceedings of a Grand Council held at the Village of Caughnawaga," Kahnawake, July 5, 1830, *RG 10*, vol. 25, p. 26185-26190.
132. List of documents illustrating these disputes: George Couper to William Mackay, Quebec, July 31, 1830, *RG 10*, vol. 590, no 499. William Mackay to George Couper, Montreal, August 2, 1830, *RG 10*, vol. 25, p. 26283-26284. Petition by Simon Obomsawine *et al.* to Matthew Lord Aylmer, Saint-François, December 10, 1830, *RG 10*, vol. 25, p. 26552-26555. William Mackay to Duncan C. Napier, Montreal, December 22, 1830, *RG 10*, vol. 25, p. 26557-26558. Duncan C. Napier to William Mackay, Quebec, January 10, 1831, *RG 10*, vol. 590, no. 548.

CHAPTER TWO. Rules, Operations, and Political Relations

1. "Proceedings of Sir William Johnson with the Indians," March 1768, *DRCHNY*, vol. VIII, p. 45. The term "Caughnawagas," which appears frequently in the British colonial archives, is often employed as a figure of speech, in the manner of an understatement signifying the political alliance of the Indigenous Peoples of Canada.
2. "At a meeting of Captain Brant and other Chiefs from the Grand River, and the Chiefs and principal men of the Missassagui nation," Credit River, September 18, 1798, *IIADH*, bob. 44.
3. "Evidence of the Revd. J. Marcoux Missionary at Caughnawaga having reference to the Iroquois of that settlement;" this document likely dates from January 1843; *RG 10*, vol. 115, p. 167884-167891.
4. Petition by the Iroquois of Kahnawake to Sir James Henry Craig, Montreal, July 15, 1809, *RG 10*, vol. 625, p. 182283.
5. Pierre Roubaud to William Johnson, Saint-François, October 30, 1761, *JP*, vol. III, p. 555.
6. "At a council held at Montreal," August 14, 1778, *IIADH*, bob. 34.
7. Jean-Baptiste Destimauville to Francis, Baron of Rottenburg, Lorette, February 26, 1811, *RG 10*, vol. 487, p. 4399.
8. Louis de Salaberry to Sir John Sherbrooke, Beauport, October 1, 1816, *RG 10*, vol. 785, p. 181461-181462.
9. "Conseil adressé à Mr Le Colonel Campbell Supr : int : des affaires sauvages," Kahnawake, October 7, 1791, *RG10*, vol. 8, p. 8203.
10. See Map 2: Geopolitical Organization of the Indigenous World
11. Daniel Claus to William Johnson, Montreal, June 2, 1762, *JP*, vol. III, p. 752.
12. Daniel Claus to William Johnson, Lachine, August 25, 1769, *JP*, vol. VII, p. 128. This speech was given on August 21 to remind the British of the terms of the agreements reached between the Seven Nations and the British in Oswegatchie in August 1760, and of the content of the Royal Proclamation of King George III in October 1763: "A Meeting with Aughquisasnes," Kahnawake, August 21, 1769, *JP*, vol. VII, p. 109-112.

13. John Campbell to Frederick Haldimand, Montreal, July 19, 1781, *IIADH*, bob. 36.

14. John Johnson to Peregrine Maitland, Montreal, August 9, 1824, *RG10*, vol. 588.

15. The Seven Nations chiefs to Archibald Earl Gosford, Kahnawake, February 3, 1837, *RG 10*, vol. 93, p. 38031-38039.

16. Henry C. Darling to Duncan C. Napier, Quebec, September 1, 1827, *RG 10*, vol. 20, p. 14200.

17. Henry C. Darling to James Givens, Quebec, October 27, 1827, *RG 10*, vol. 586, p. 24590.

18. "Proceedings of a Grand Council held with the Chiefs of the undermentioned Tribes at the Government House in the Village of Caughnawaga," Kahnawake, October 5, 1827, *RG 10*, vol. 20, p. 14240-14252. "Extract of an Address by Major General Darling Deputy Superintendent General to the Chiefs of the Algonquins and Nipissings from the Lake of the Two Mountains, the Iroquois of Sault St Louis and St Régis: & the Abenaquois of St Francis," Kahnawake, October 5, 1827, *RG 10*, vol. 44, p. 23418-23423.

19. Henry C. Darling, Quebec, July 24, 1828, P. Ford *et al.*, *Correspondence and Other Papers, op. cit.*, p. 25.

20. "Extract from Return of Lands," March 31, 1845, *RG 10*, vol. 600, p. 48030.

21. Frank G. Speck, "The Eastern Algonkian Wabanaki Confederacy," *American Anthropologist*, vol. 17 (1915), p. 496.

22. Louis de Salaberry to George Earl Dalhousie, Beauport, August 25, 1822, *RG 10*, vol. 492, p. 30288. Louis de Salaberry to John Johnson, Beauport, August 27, 1822, *RG 10*, vol. 492, p. 30290.

23. R. Symes to Duncan C. Napier, Quebec, August 17, 1844, *RG 10*, vol. 599, p. 47843-47844.

24. H.L. Ingall to D'Urban, September 14, 1850, *RG 10*, vol. 607, p. 51844-51845. Duncan C. Napier, Montreal, September 16, 1850, *RG 10*, vol. 607, p. 51847.

25. Jean-Baptiste Delorimier, "Suivant le deSir de son Excelence le Lord Dorches- ter, qui est de remetre au gouvernement les remarques qui sont fait sur differans objets concernant les affairs sauvages," Quebec, October 22, 1793, *RG 8*, vol. 247, p. 42-44.

26. Petition by Nicolas Vincent Tsaouenhohoui *et al.* to Charles, Duke of Richmond, Lorette, January 21, 1819, *RG 10*, vol. 625, p. 182441-182446.

27. Daniel Claus, "Journal of Indian Affairs," August 25, 1767, *JP*, vol. XIII, p. 428.

28. "An Indian Conference," Johnson Hall, July 29, 1768, *JP*, vol. XII, p. 570. William Johnson blamed this delay of several days on his busy agenda: "An Indian Congress," August 5, 1768, *JP*, vol. XII, p. 579.

29. Daniel Claus, "Journal of Indian Affairs," July 26, 1773, *JP*, vol. XIII, p. 626.

30. *Ibid.*, July 28, 1773, *JP*, vol. XII, p. 630.

31. *Ibid.*, June 9, 1773, *JP*, vol. XIII, p. 621.

32. Thomas Teiohatekon *et al.* to the chiefs and warriors of the Abenaki of St. Francis, Kahnawake, August 28, 1853, *RG 10*, vol. 610, p. 53359.

33. Daniel Claus, "Journal of Indian Affairs," August 28, 1767, *JP*, vol. XIII, p. 429.

34. The Abenaki proceeded to appoint two other chiefs the same day: Bernard Saint-Germain to John Johnson, Saint-François, December 14, 1824, *RG 10*, vol. 16, p. 12893.

35. Édouard-Narcisse Delorimier to Duncan C. Napier, Sault-Saint-Louis, February 3, 1842, *RG 10*, vol. 597, p. 46142.

36. James Hughes to Duncan C. Napier, Montreal, February 10, 1842, *RG 10*, vol. 597, p. 46148.

37. François Boucher to Charles Theophilus Metcalf, Saint-Ambroise, April 3, 1845, *RG 10*, vol. 600, p. 48043.

38. Petition by the council chiefs of the Huron of Lorette to James Henry Craig; this document dates from 1807-1811; *RG 10*, vol. 611, p. 153919.

39. Daniel Claus to William Johnson, Lachine August 3, 1771, *JP*, vol. VIII, p. 214-215.

40. "Memoire on behalf of the Indians of S. Louis." This document likely dates from October 1829; *RG 10*, vol. 118, p. 169593.

41. Testimonial of Nicolas Vincent Tsaouenhohoui, House of Assembly of Lower Canada, Committee Chamber, Quebec, February 2, 1819, *JCA*, vol. XXVIII, 59 Geo. III, appendix (R), A. 1819.

42. Petition by André Tsonhahissen *et al.* to Duncan C. Napier, Lorette, November 13, 1844, *RG 10*, vol. 599, p. 47652.

43. June Helm, Eleanor Burke Leacock, "The Hunting Tribes of Subarctic Canada," *North American Indians in Historical Perspective*, Prospect Heights (Illinois), Waveland Press, 1988 (1971), p. 367-368. When referring to the "Indigenous nations in the Northeast," we are aware of the vast difference that exists between the Algonquin (hunter-gatherers north of and along the St. Lawrence River/semi-sedentary farmers in New England) and the Iroquoian peoples (consisting of sub-groups of domiciled Catholics, nations of the League, Huron, and others).

44. Jennings, ed., "Glossary of Figures of Speech in Iroquois Political Rhetoric," *The History and Culture of Iroquois Diplomacy, op. cit.*, p. 122.

45. Daniel K. Richter, "Iroquois Versus Iroquois: Jesuit Missions and Christianity in Village Politics, 1642-1686," *Ethnohistory*, vol. 32, no.1 (1985), p. 10.

46. Daniel Claus, "Journal of Indian Affairs," July 7, 1773, *JP*, vol. XIII, p. 619.

47. *Ibid.*, August 10, 1773, *JP*, vol. XIII, p. 633.

48. Joseph Marcoux, Sault-Saint-Louis, March 17, 1851, *RG 10*, vol. 608, p. 52168.

49. "Extract of a narrative & remarks made by a gentleman who left Canada on the 14th of June Last," 1775, *IIADH*, bob. 31.

50. Druke, "Iroquois Treaties: Common Forms, Varying Interpretations," *The History and Culture of Iroquois Diplomacy, op. cit.*, p. 93-94.

51. Petition by Simon Obomsawine *et al.* to Matthew Lord Aylmer, Saint-François, March 1, 1833, *RG 10*, vol. 87, p. 34461.

52. "Report of an Indian Conference," Montreal, January 30, 1762, *JP*, vol. X, p. 373.

53. "Letter from Benjamin Franklin, Samuel Chase and Charles Carroll, about Council at Fort George with the Seven Nations of Canada returning from Conference at Onondaga," May 6, 1776, *IIADH*, bob. 32.

54. *Ibid.*

55. "Coll Louis's Information," Philadelphia, May 3, 1792, *IIADH*, bob. 41.

56. "At a Treaty held at the City of New York, by the United States, with the nations or tribes of Indians denominating themselves the Seven Nations of Canada," May 23, 1796, *The New American State Papers. Indian Affairs*, 1972, vol. 6, p. 157.

57. "Answer to a Speech to the Caughnawagas, *or* Canadian *Tribes of* Indians, *near* Montreal, *sent by the* Stockbridge Indians - *returned* 15th June," 1775, *IIADH*, bob. 31.

58. "Proceedings of Sir William Johnson with the Indians," German Flats, July 19, 1770, *DRCHNY*, vol. VIII, p. 232.

59. *Ibid.*, July 20, 1770, *DRCHNY*, vol. VIII, p. 234.

60. Petition by Sosa8atis saan8entsio8ane *et al.* to Sir Edmund Walker Head, Kahnawake, March 20, 1854, *RG 10*, vol. 209, p. 123659-123660.

61. *Ibid.*, p. 123658.

62. Jean Papino, Ignace Chawanabe, Amable Wisken, Sault-Saint-Louis, February 9, 1842, *RG 10*, vol. 597, p. 46144.

63. Joseph Marcoux to John Simpson, Sault-Saint-Louis, February 12, 1842, *RG 10*, vol. 597, p. 46238.

64. "Proceedings of a Court of Inquiry held by order of His Excellency Sir John Sherbrooke Governor General and Commander in Chief," September 25, 1817, *RG 10*, vol. 13, p. 11108-11109.

65. Petition by Ignace N. Kanawaka *et al.* to George Earl Dalhousie, Kahnawake, February 21, 1828, *RG 10*, vol. 659, p. 181420.

66. "Extract from Return of Lands," March 31, 1845, *RG 10*, vol. 600, p. 48032.

67. Joseph Marcoux to George Vardon, Sault-Saint-Louis, November 5, 1846, *RG 10*, vol. 602, p. 49007.

68. Petition by Thomas Teohatekon *et al.* to James Bruce Lord Elgin, Sault-Saint- Louis, December 28, 1847, *RG 10*, vol. 604, p. 50097.

69. "The 6 Nations Answer to the Gov^rs Speech," Albany, September 20, 1735, McIlwain ed., *op. cit.*, p. 195.

70. "A Meeting with Canajoharies," Canajoharie, March 10, 1763, *JP*, vol. IV, p. 56.

71. "Indian Conference," "Montreal," Kahnawake, September 20, 1760, *JP*, vol. XIII, p. 166.

72. "Proceedings of Sir William Johnson with the Mohawks," July 29, 1772, *DRCHNY*, vol. VIII, p. 307.

73. As noted, for example, by Marius Barbeau in the early 20th century about the Huron and other Indigenous peoples of Canada: "Indian Lorette, like other noted Canadian Villages, has its legend of old; its Sachems have carefully preserved it and handed down with embellishments to the budding papooses.": Marius Barbeau, *Huron and Wyandot Mythology: With an Appendix Containing Earlier Published Records*, Ottawa, Government Printing Bureau, 1915, p. 354.

74. "Proceedings of Sir William Johnson with the Mohawks," July 29, 1772, *DRCHNY*, vol. VIII, p. 307.

75. "At a Congress held on Tuesday the 19th April," 1774, *IIADH*, bob. 31.

76. "Conference held at Deerfield in the County of Hampshire between Jonathan Belcher and chiefs of the Caughnawaga, St. Francis, Hossatonoc, Seautacook and Moheegs," August 28, 1735, *IIADH*, bob. 10.

77. William Johnson, "Journal of Indian Affairs," Johnson Hall, February 7, 1764, *JP*, vol. XI, p. 47.

78. P. Langan to Daniel Claus, Montreal, August 12, 1779, *MG 19, F 1*, vol. 25, p. 114. *Ibid.*, vol. 26, p. 120. Daniel Claus to Frederick Haldimand, Montreal, August

30, 1779, *IIADH*, bob. 34. This request was even more imperative given that the Iroquois population were exposed to the ravages of the American Army, which torched the villages of the Iroquois of the League that had decided to provide military support to the King of England: "At a Conference with the Five Nations Deputies being Two Onondagoe and three Cayouga Indians," Quebec, August 20, 1779, *IIADH*, bob. 34.

79. "Paroles des Sept Villages adressées au Lieutenant Colonel John Campbell Surintendant de ces Sauvages," Montreal, October 20, 1779, *IIADH*, bob. 35.

80. William N. Fenton, "Northern Iroquois Culture Patterns," *HNAI*, vol. 15, 1978, p. 309.

81. "Response to the words of the Abenaki," 1780, *IIADH*, bob. 35.

82. "An Indian Council," Fort Johnson, July 21, 1758, *JP*, vol. IX, p. 950.

83. Daniel Claus, "Journal of Indian Affairs," July 7, 1773, *JP*, vol. XIII, p. 619.

84. *Ibid.*, p. 620.

85. "At a meeting with the four warriours of the *Six Nations* who were sent by the Commissioners (appointed by the *Twelve United Colonies*) of *Indian Affairs*, after the treaty held with the *Six Nations* at *Albany*, to the *Caughnawagas*," Albany, September 30, 1775, *IIADH*, bob. 32.

86. "Proceedings of Sir William Johnson with the Indians," Johnson Hall, September 7, 1763, *DRCHNY*, vol. VII, p. 559.

87. "Narration by Hendrick Aupaumut of journey to Western Nations to convince them to make peace with Americans [between 1777 & 1788]," *IIADH*, bob. 33.

88. *Ibid.*

89. "Col¹ Louis's Information," Philadelphia, May 3, 1792, *IIADH*, bob. 41.

90. "Proceedings of a General Council of the Several Indian Nations mentioned underneath, held at the Glaize," October 4, 1792, *IIADH*, bob. 41.

91. American anthropologist Mary A. Druke makes the same comment about diplomatic representation among the Iroquois nations of the League: Druke, "Iroquois Treaties: Common Forms, Varying Interpretations," *The History and Culture of Iroquois Diplomacy, op. cit.*, p. 94.

92. Samuel Jones *et al.* to George Clinton, New York, March 6, 1795, *IIADH*, bob. 43.

93. "At a Treaty held at the City of New York, by the United States, with the nations or tribes of Indians denominating themselves the Seven Nations of Canada," May 23, 1796, *The New American State Papers. Indian Affairs*, 1972, vol. 6, p. 157.

94. Daniel Claus, "Journal of Indian Affairs," July 9, 1773, *JP*, vol. XIII, p. 620-621. The name Saghtaghroana appears in the proceedings of several international conferences: "Proceedings of Sir William Johnson with the Indians," German Flats, July 22, 1770, *DRCHNY*, vol. VIII, p. 240. "An Indian Conference," July 28, 1770, *JP*, vol. XII, p. 838.

95. "An Indian Conference," July 28, 1770, *JP*, vol. XII, p. 843.

96. The Seven Nations chiefs to Daniel Claus, Kahnawake, July 31, 1770, *JP*, vol. VII, p. 318. Incidentally, the Iroquois of Akwesasne ended up expelling the Abenaki from their village following mediation, not by the Grand Council of the Seven Fires, but rather by Superintendent Johnson.

97. "At a meeting with the four warriors of the *Six Nations* who were sent by the Commissioners (appointed by the *Twelve United Colonies*) of *Indian Affairs*, after the treaty held with the *Six Nations* at *Albany*, to the *Caughnawagas,*" Albany, September 30, 1775, *IIADH*, bob. 32.

98. "The Deputies of the *Six Nations*, sent to *Canada*, returned this day, and make the following report," Ticonderoga, September 24, 1775, *IIADH*, bob. 32.

99. Daniel Claus to William Johnson, June 2, 1762, *JP*, vol. III, p. 752. Daniel Claus to William Johnson, Lachine, September 12, 1770, *IIADH*, bob. 30. Daniel Claus to William Johnson, Montreal, July 8, 1772, *JP*, vol. XII, p. 971.

100. Journal de Bougainville, *RAPQ*, 1924, p. 285.

101. Conference between Pierre de Rigaud de Vaudreuil-Cavagnal and the natives, December 13-30, 1756, *IIADH*, bob. 20.

102. "Proceedings of Sir William Johnson with the Indians," German Flats, July 22, 1770, *DRCHNY*, vol. VIII, p. 240.

103. *Ibid.*

104. "Message of the Canada to the Western Indians," August 25, 1763, *IIADH*, bob. 25. "Messages sent by Eight Nations of Canada to the western nations," August 25, 1763, *IIADH*, bob. 26.

105. William Printup to William Johnson, Fort Ontario, August 27, 1763, *JP*, vol. XIII, p. 299.

106. Daniel Claus to William Johnson, Montreal, May 30, 1764, *JP*, vol. IV, p. 435.

107. Thomas Gage to William Johnson, New York, July 16, 1764, *JP*, vol. IV, p. 484.

108. Jean-Baptiste Destimauville, Quebec, January 10, 1797, *RG 8*, vol. 250, pt. 1, p. 68.

109. Jennings, ed., "Introduction." *The History and Culture of Iroquois Diplomacy, op. cit.*, p. xv.

110. Fenton, "Structure, Continuity, and Change in Process of Iroquois Treaty Making," *The History and Culture of Iroquois Diplomacy, op. cit.*, p. 13-14.

111. *Relation* de 1640-1641, *JR*, vol. XX, p. 221-227. *Relation* de 1643-1644, *JR*, vol. XVI, p. 63. "Notes to vol. LXI," *JR*, vol. LXI, p. 272.

112. *Relation* de 1664-1665, *JR*, vol. XLIX, p. 229-231. *Relation* de 1667-1668, *JR*, vol. LI, p. 245. "Lettres de l'Église des Hurons à Lorette, en la Nouvelle-France, au Chapitre de Chartres »," Lorette, November 11, 1680, *JR*, vol. LXI, p. 261. "Decree of the Royal Council. The Missionairies of Sault St. Louis," 1722, *JR*, vol. LXVII, p. 77.

113. Louis-Armand de Lom d'Arce, baron de Lahontan, *Nouveaux Voyages en Amérique Septentrionale, op. cit.*, œuvres I, p. 117.

114. Léon Gérin, "La seigneurie de Sillery et les Hurons de Lorette," *Mémoires et comptes rendus de la société royale du Canada*, Ottawa, Hope, 2nd series, vol. 6 (May 1900), p. 107.

115. Cadwallader Colden, *The History of the Five Indian Nations of Canada*, London, T. Osborne, 1747, p. 31-32.

116. "An Indian Congress," October 20, 1763, *JP*, vol. X, p. 903.

117. Journal de Bougainville, *RAPQ*, 1924, p. 272.

118. Denis Vaugeois, *La fin des alliances franco-indiennes*, Montreal/Sillery, Boréal/ Septentrion, 1995, p. 46.

119. "The United States in Congress," Fort Stanwix, October 3, 1784, *IIADH*, bob. 36.

120. Milton W. Hamilton, "Sir William Johnson: Interpreter of the Iroquois," *Ethnohistory*, vol. 10, no. 3 (Summer 1963), p. 270-286. William Johnson to Phineas Lyman, Albany, July 27, 1755, *JP*, vol. I, p. 732.

121. "An Indian Congress," Johnson Hall, November 13-23,1764, *JP*, vol. XI, nt. 1, p. 479.

122. Daniel Claus, "Memorandum," Montreal, March 11, 1784, *RG 10*, vol. 654, p. 181400.

123. "Guy Johnson, Chronology," *JP*, vol. IV, p. xii. Guy Johnson to Cadwallader Colden, Johnstown, September 17, 1774, *JP*, vol. VIII, nt. 2, p. 1200.

124. Daniel Claus, "Memorandum," Montreal, March 11, 1784, *RG 10*, vol. 654, p. 181400.

125. *Ibid*. Petition by 8ishe Tagariontie *et al.* to Duncan C. Napier, Akwesasne, April 25, 1842, *RG 10*, vol. 101, p. 42329.

126. "Report of a Talk with the Indian Chiefs of the Lake of the Two Mountains, on delivering Two Brass Filed pieces to them from the Commander of the Forces," November 23, 1831, *RG 10*, vol. 83, p. 32712-32713.

127. "An Indian Congress," October 20, 1763, *JP*, vol. X, p. 903.

128. Daniel Claus, "Journal of Indian Affairs," October 4, 1767, *JP*, vol. XIII, p. 431-432.

129. "Discours qu'on se propose de faire aux différentes Nations d'Indiens assem- blé à Pittsbourg par un Officier François, accompagné d'un ceinturon à chaque Nation," 1778, *IIADH*, bob. 33. "Récit d'un Conseil Tenù par le Marquis de la fayette au village des Honoyotts, Parlant aux Sept Villages du Canada, 15 jours après celuy du Gouverneur de Nouvel York," 1784, *RG 10*, vol. 14, p. 191.

130. "Speech of a Caughnawaga Chief in answer to that of the Marquis De la Fayette," October 4, 1784, *IIADH*, bob. 38.

131. Denys Delâge, "L'alliance franco-amérindienne, 1660-1701," *RAAQ*, vol. XIX, no. 1 (1989), p. 3-15 *passim*.

132. "Conference between M. de Longueuil, Commandant at Detroit, and the Indians," 1700, *DRCHNY*, vol. IX, p. 705.

133. "Parolles des Sauvages du party commandé par Monsieur de Ramezay," August, 2, 1709, *MG 1, C11A*, vol. 30, fo 128-128vo.

134. "Laurence Claasse the Interpreter & others who was sent to the Sennekas Country to watch the Motions of the French, return & report," Albany, June 11, 1721, McIlwain ed., *op. cit.*, p. 135.

135. Petition by Ignace N. Kanawaka *et al.* to George Lord Dalhousie, Sault-Saint- Louis, February 21, 1828, *RG 10*, vol. 659, p. 181418.

136. Pierre Roubaud to William Johnson, Saint-François, November 13, 1760, *JP*, vol. III, p. 281.

137. "An Indian Conference," July 28, 1770, *JP*, vol. XII, p. 841.

138. "Nous les chefs Capitaines, Et Guerriers du village de Sénaomsket Établit à Batiscan, où Rivière Chaudière, Et les autres émigrés du grand Village de Senaoueskèt sur les limites américaines," Quebec, August 5, 1810, *RG 10*, vol. 625, p. 182421-182422.

139. George Lord Dalhousie to Lord Bathurst, Quebec, December 16, 1822, P. Ford *et al.*, *Correspondence and Other Papers, op. cit.*, p.7.

140. Daniel Claus, "Journal of Indian Affairs," July 26, 1773, *JP*, vol. XIII, p. 625.

141. "Proceedings of Guy Johnson with the Six Nations," Guy Park, January 20-28, 1775, *IIADH*, bob. 31.

142. "Proceedings of a Grand Council," Kahnawake, October 5, 1827, *RG 10*, vol. 20, p. 14243.

143. "A meeting with Aughquisasnes," Kahnawake, August 21, 1769, *JP*, vol. VII, p. 110.

144. "Messages of the Canada to the Western Indians," *IIADH*, bob. 25. "Messages sent by Eight Nations in Canada to the western Indians," August 25, 1763, *IIADH*, bob. 25.

145. "Récit d'un Conseil Tenù par le Marquis de la fayette au village des Honoyotts, Parlant aux Sept Villages du Canada, 15 jours après celuy du Gouverneur de Nouvel York," 1784, *RG 10*, vol. 14, p. 191.

146. "Proceedings of a General Council of the Several Indian Nations mentioned underneath, held at the Glaize," October 4, 1792, *IIADH*, bob. 41.

147. Thomas Martin to Robert Shore Milnes, December 22, 1803, *RG 10*, vol. 486, p. 3924.

148. "Conceille des algonkin et Nepisainge du lac Des Deux-Montagnes," July 30, 1819, *RG 10*, vol. 625, p. 182438.

149. Jean-Baptiste Destimauville to Francis, Baron de Rottenburg, Lorette, February 26, 1811, *RG 10*, vol. 487, p. 4399.

150. *Ibid.*, p. 4400.

151. "Conference between M. de Vaudreuil and the Indians," December 1756, *IIADH*, bob. 20.

152. "Journal of Indian Affairs," March 28, 1762, *JP*, vol. X, p. 411.

153. Daniel Claus to William Johnson, Montreal, August 30, 1765, *JP*, vol. XI, p. 918-919.

154. "At a council held at Montreal," August 14, 1778, *IIADH*, bob. 34.

155. Frederick Haldimand to the ambassadors of the Seven Nations of Canada; this document appears to date from 1779; *IIADH*, bob. 34.

156. "Proceedings of a Grand Council," Kahnawake, October 5, 1827, *RG 10*, vol. 20, p. 14250-14251.

157. The Abenaki chiefs to William MacKay, Saint-François, November 23, 1830, *RG 10*, vol. 25, p. 26528.

158. Conference at Trois-Rivières between Louis-Juchereau Duchesnay, the Abenaki of St. Francis and Bécancour, the Huron of Lorette, and the Algonquin of Pointe-du-Lac, October 26, 1829, *RG 8*, vol. 268, p. 724.

159. *Ibid.*, p. 729, 730-731.

160. Petition by Pierre Constant Peninsi *et al.* to James Kempt, Montreal, July 8, 1830, *RG 10*, vol. 25, p. 26248.

161. "Minutes of the Proceedings of an Inquiry Holden at La Chine," April 11, 1840, *IIADH*, bob. 48.

162. "An Indian Congress," Fort Pitt, May 10, 1765, *JP*, vol. XI, p. 727.

163. "A Speech of the Onnondages & Cajouga Sachems made in the Court House at Albany," August 2, 1684, McIlwain ed., *op. cit.*, 11.

164. "Governor Fletcher's Speech to the Indian Sachems," "Answer of the Five Nations to Governor Fletcher," Albany, February 25, 1693, *DRCHNY*, vol. IV, p. 20, 22.

165. "Propositions of Canada Praying Indians and the Answers thereunto," Albany, June 28, 1700, *IIADH*, bob. 6.

166. "Minutes of N.Y. Commissioners for Indian Affairs," Albany, August 1, 1735, *IIADH*, bob. 10. "Sundry Sachems of the Cacknawaga Canada Indians arrive at Albany & desire a Meeting from the Commissrs ," Albany, August 1, 1735, McIlwain ed., *op. cit.*, p. 193.

167. "Conference held at Deerfield in the County of Hampshire between Jonathan Belcher and chiefs of the Caughnawaga, St. Francis, Hossatonoc, Seautacook and Moheegs," August 28, 1735, *IIADH*, bob. 10.

168. "At a Meeting of yè. Commissionrs. of yè. Indian Affairs," Albany, March 13, 1724, *IIADH*, bob. 9. "At a Meeting of the Comrs. of In. Affairs," Albany, June 26, 1724, *IIADH*, bob. 9.

169. "Conference held at Deerfield in the County of Hampshire between Jonathan Belcher and chiefs of the Caughnawaga, St. Francis, Hossatonoc, Seautacook and Moheegs," August 27, 1735, *IIADH*, bob. 10.

170. "Mon Père Comme tu est le seul maitre dans cette province, ainsi mon Père à l'égar de ce qui nous arives nous tes enfans au Lac des deux Montagnes." This document likely dates from 1828; *RG 8*, vol. 267, p. 286-290.

171. "Indian Conference," "Montreal," Kahnawake, September 16, 1760, *JP*, vol. XIII, p. 163-166. "Proceedings at a Meeting held at Albany," June 28, 1761, *IIADH*, bob. 24. In negotiations between brothers, the host must ensure the comfort of his other brothers. In the context of negotiations with the State of New York, the Americans pledged to pay certain expenses incurred by the embassy of the Seven Nations: the commissioners of the State of New York to the Seven Nations of Canada, Lake George, October 2, 1795, *RG 8*, vol. 248, p. 367-368.

172. "Proceedings of Sir William Johnson with the Indians," Johnson Hall, September 11, 1763, *DRCHNY*, vol. VII, p. 558. "Indian Proceedings," Johnson Hall, July 28, 1765, *JP*, vol. XI, p. 872-873.

173. "Proceedings of Sir William Johnson with the Indians," German Flats, July 22, 1770, *DRCHNY*, vol. VIII, p. 237-238.

174. "Speech to Caghnawageys," Johnson Hall, July 15, 1771, *JP*, vol. XIII, p. 504.

175. Daniel Claus, "Journal of Indian Affairs," Quebec, July 28, 1773, *JP*, vol. XIII, p. 628-629.

176. "At a Council held at Montreal," August 14, 1778, *IIADH*, bob. 34.

177. "Proceedings of Sir William Johnson with the Indians," Johnson Hall, September 11, 1763, *DRCHNY*, vol. VII, p. 558.

178. "Minutes of a Speech addressed to Sir John Johnson Bart: Superintendant General & Inspector General of Indian Affairs, by the principal Chiefs of the Village of Lake of Two Mountains assembled in Council," Montreal, February 8, 1788, *RG 10*, vol. 14, p. 235-238.

179. "Paroles des Sauvages des Sept vilages du Bas Canada, adressée à Mons : le Colonel Mc Ki Supr Intendant General, et yinspecter General des Affairs Sauvages &c &c &c," July 28, 1795, *RG 8*, vol. 248, p. 232.

180. "Recit d'un Conseil tenu par les Commissaires des 13 Provinces, pour Regler les affaires avec les 6 Nations, au fort Stanwix, en présence des Chaounon, Loup, Honoyoth & les 7 Villages du Canada 6 jours après Celuy du Marquis de la Fayette," October 1784, *RG 10*, vol. 14, p. 190-192.

181. "Speech of the Subscribers Agents for the State of New York to Col. Lewis and ten other St Regis Indians," New York, March 11, 1795, *RG 8*, vol. 248, p. 78-83.

182. John Jay to the Iroquois of Akwesasne, New York, August 10, 1795, *RG 8*, vol. 248, p. 263-264.

183. The Seven Nations of Canada chiefs to George Washington, Lake George, October 2, 1795, *RG 8*, vol. 248, p. 365-366.

184. "At a Treaty held at the City of New York, by the United States, with the nations or tribes of Indians denominating themselves the Seven Nations of Canada," May 23, 1796, *The New American State Papers. Indian Affairs*, 1972, vol. 6, p. 157.

185. "Report of the Commissioner, appointed by the Governor, on the Claim of the Iroquois Indians," Massana, June 20-21,1855, *IIADH*, bob. 49.

186. Timothy P. Redfield, "Memorial. Report on the claim of the Iroquois Indians upon the State of Vermont, for their Hunting Ground," 1854, *IIADH*, bob. 49.

187. "Journal of William Johnson proceedings with the Indians of Canajoharie," April 1759, *IIADH*, bob. 23. "Report of George Croghan," New York, January 18, 1767, *JP*, vol. XIII, p. 408-409. "A Literal Translation of the Message from the Six Nations Confederacy to the Shawanese &c," November 1774, *IIADH*, bob. 31. Jean-Baptiste Delorimier to Joseph Chew, Lachine, August 26, 1796, *RG 8*, vol. 249, pt. 2, p. 305-307.

188. Charles de Boische De Beauharnois to Jean-Frédéric Phélypeaux de Maurepas, Quebec, September 21, 1741, *MG 1, C11A*, vol. 75, f° 139-142v°.

189. "Conseil adressé à Mr Le Colonel Campbell Supr : int : des affaires sau-vages & & &," Kahnawake, October 7, 1791, *RG 10*, vol. 8, p. 8202.

190. *Ibid.*, p. 8204.

191. Conference at Trois-Rivières between Louis-Juchereau Duchesnay, the Abenaki of St. Francis and Bécancour, the Huron of Lorette, and the Algonquin of Pointe-du-Lac, October 26, 1829, *RG 8*, vol. 268, p. 728-732.

192. Jean Papino, Ignace Chawanabe, Amable Wisken, Sault-Saint-Louis, February 9, 1842, *RG 10*, vol. 597, p. 46144.

193. Edouard-Narcisse Delorimier to Duncan C. Napier, Sault-Saint-Louis, January 28, 1848, *RG 10*, vol. 600, p. 47866.

194. William Johnson, "Journal of Indian Affairs," May 6, 1762, *JP*, vol. X, p. 448.

195. "The same day the 6 Nations made answer to the above Speech of the Lieut Govrs," Albany, June 27, 1737, McIlwain ed., *op. cit.*, p. 201. "Proceedings of Sir William Johnson with the Indians," German Flats, July 18, 1770, *DRCHNY*, vol. VIII, p. 230. James Dean to Peter Schuyler, Oneida, March 18, 1776, *IIDAH*, bob. 32. "At a Council held at Montreal," August 14, 1778, *IIADH*, bob. 34.

196. John Deserontyon to Daniel Claus, Oghnyorege Island, May 9, 1780, *MG 19*, *F 1*, vol. 24, p. 7.

197. "Paroles des chefs du Sault St Louis adresser à l'honorable Baronet Sir John Johnson, superintendant General, et Inspecteur General des Affairs Sauvages &a &a &a ," Lachine, April 6, 1798, *RG 10*, vol. 10, p. 9293.

198. "Speech made by the Caughnawagas at their meeting with the Five Nations, at Caughnawaga," July 5, 1799, *RG 8*, vol. 252, p. 190. "Account of what passed at a Council held at Caghnawaga of the Five Nations, with the Seven Nations of Canada," July 5, 1799, *IIADH*, bob. 44.

199. "At a Meeting of the Chiefs of the Five Nations and Seven Nations, in Presence of Sir John Johnson Bart ," Lachine, July 12, 1799, *RG 8*, vol. 252, p. 183.

200. "Conference between M. de Vaudreuil and the Indians," Montreal, December 1756, *DRCHNY*, vol. X, p. 512.

201. Speck, "The Eastern Algonkian Wabanaki Confederacy," *loc. cit.*, p. 485.

202. Jean-Baptiste Destimauville, Quebec, January 10, 1797, *RG 8*, vol. 250, pt. 1, p. 68.

203. Journal de Bougainville, *RAPQ*, 1924, p. 261.

204. Normand Clermont, "La place de la femme dans les sociétés iroquoïennes de la période du contact," *RAAQ*, vol. XIII, no. 4 (1983), p. 287-288. Francis Jennings writes that, in the 18th century, the Iroquois of the League attributed this term to certain Delaware of Pennsylvania. It is unclear whether it held the same meaning for the Algonquian of the Northeast: "Glossary of Figures of Speech in Iroquois Political Rhetoric," *The History and Culture of Iroquois Diplomacy, op. cit.*, p. 124.

CHAPTER THREE. Forest Diplomacy: Indigenous Rituals and Protocols

1. So wrote Israel Pemberton, a Philadelphia merchant and religious leader of the Quakers in Pennsylvania, in 1756. In explaining the meetings he held with the Indigenous people, he pointed out to the superintendent that he had obtained prior permission from the governor of the colony: Israel Pemberton to William Johnson, Philadelphia, April 25, 1756, *JP*, vol. XI, p. 442.

2. "An Indian Conference," Johnson Hall, March 24, 1764, *JP*, vol. XI, p. 135.
3. The Europeans manipulated the Indigenous people by borrowing their language, speaking to them in their cultural terms, and other tactics. This ability to objectify, i.e., to manipulate the culture of the other, is more powerful than military capacity, according to Tzvetan Todorov (trans. Richard Howard), *The Conquest of America*, New York, Harper & Row, 1984.
4. Robert Hunter Morris to William Johnson, Philadelphia, April 24, 1756, *JP*, vol. II, p. 442-443.
5. "Journal of Indian Affairs," Niagara, May 31, 1764, *JP*, vol. XI, p. 208.
6. Wilbur Jacobs, "Wampum, the Protocol of Indian Diplomacy," *William and Mary Quarterly*, vol. 6 (1949), p. 596-604. Michael K. Foster, "Another Look at the Function of Wampum in Iroquois-White Councils," *The History and Culture of Iroquois Diplomacy, op. cit.*, p. 99-114. Bernard Assiniwi, *Histoire des Indiens du Haut Canada et du Bas Canada*, Ni-t'chawama/Mon ami/Mon frère, Montreal, Leméac, 1973-74, vol. 1, p. 124-151 *passim*. Lynn Ceci, "The Value of Wampum Among the New York Iroquois: A Case Study in Artifact Analysis," *Journal of Anthropological Research*, vol. 38, no. 1 (1982), p. 97-105. Pauline Joly de Lotbinière, "Des Wampums et des 'Petits humains:' Récits historiques sur les wampums algonquins," *RAAQ*, vol. XXIII, no. 2-3 (1993), p. 55.
7. "An Indian Congress," Niagara, July 29, 1764, *JP*, vol. XI, p. 306.
8. William Johnson to Arent Stevens, May 1755, *JP*, vol. IX, p. 185.
9. "Journal of Indian Affairs," March 24, 1766, *JP*, vol. XII, p. 61-62.
10. "An Indian Conference," Johnson Hall, July 29, 1768, *JP*, vol. XII, p. 569.
11. Jean-Baptiste Destimauville to George De Salaberry, Quebec, April 6, 1811, *RG 10*, vol. 11, p. 10112.
12. "Brothers of Kaghnawaga attend." This document likely dates from 1775. *IIADH*, bob. 30.
13. "An Indian Conference," Johnson Hall, July 4, 1770, *JP*, vol. XII, p. 831.
14. Journal of Henry Hamilton, June 24 to July 13, 1777, *IIADH*, bob. 35.
15. "Speech of His Excellency George Provost Baronet Governor in Chief and Commander of the Forces in British North America, to the deputation of Chiefs and Warriors of the Western Nations," Quebec, March 17, 1814, *RG 10*, vol. 136, pt. 1, p. 77642-77643.
16. William Johnson to Thomas Gage, Johnson Hall, November 13, 1768, *JP*, vol. XII, p. 636.
17. "At a Congress held on Tuesday the 19th of April," 1774, *IIADH*, bob. 31.
18. "Henry Balfour's Conference with Indians," September 29, 1761, *JP*, vol. III, p. 539.
19. Eyre Massy to William Johnson, Quebec, August 20, 1767, *JP*, vol. V, p. 628.
20. "An Indian Congress," August 5, 1768, *JP*, vol. XII, p. 581.

21. "Journal of Sir William Johnson's Proceedings with Indians," Canajoharie, April 21, 1759, *DRCHNY*, vol. VII, p. 392.

22. "William Johnson sends message to Canada via the Indians of Caughnawaga," July 24, 1763, *IIADH*, bob. 26.

23. "Proceedings of Sir William Johnson with the Indians," Johnson Hall, March 4, 1768, *DRCHNY*, vol. VIII, p. 39.

24. "A Meeting with Aughquisasnes," Kahnawake, August 21, 1769, *JP*, vol. VII, p. 109.

25. "Paroles des Sept Villages adressées au Lieutenant Colonel John Campbell Surintendant de ces Sauvages," Montreal, October 20, 1779, *IIADH*, bob. 35.

26. "Conference between M. de Vaudreuil and the Indians," December 13, 1756, *DRCHNY*, vol. X, p. 505.

27. "An Indian Conference," February 25, 1756, *JP*, vol. IX, p. 380.

28. "Conference with Indians," Niagara, July 14, 1764, *JP*, vol. XI, p. 271.

29. "Journal of Sir William Johnson's Proceedings with the Indians," Canajoharie, April 16, 1759, *DRCHNY*, vol. VII, p. 385.

30. "Proceedings at a Meeting held at Albany," June 28, 1761, *IIADH*, bob. 24.

31. "An Indian Congress," Niagara, July 29, 1764, *JP*, vol. XI, p. 307.

32. Benedict Arnold to Peter Schuyler, Montreal, June 10, 1776, *IIADH*, bob. 32.

33. "Paroles de Théorgointé Chef Yroqui des Cinq Nation prononcez devant le Lieut : Colonel Campbell," June 19, 1777, *IIADH*, bob. 34.

34. *Ibid.*

35. "An Indian Conference," Johnson Hall, July 28, 1770, *IIADH*, bob. 30.

36. William Johnson to Daniel Claus, June 26, 1774, *JP*, vol. XII, p. 1107.

37. "Statement of the Prices at which the following Articles required to complete the Mississague Purchase are to be procured in Montreal," Lachine, February 22, 1808, *RG 10*, vol. 11, p. 8780.

38. Jennings, "Descriptive Treaty Calendar," *The History and Culture of Iroquois Diplomacy, op. cit.,* p. 189.

39. "Journal of Indian Affairs," October 17, 1763, *JP*, vol. X, p. 898.

40. "Narration by Hendrick Aupaumut of journey to Western Nations to convince them to make peace with Americans [between 1777 & 1788]," *IIADH*, bob. 33. Is it possible that the fourteenth and fifteenth colonies represented on the necklace symbolized Florida and Canada?

41. "At a General Meeting with the Six Nations, Shawanese Delawares Nanticokes," Niagara, March 28, 1780, *RG 10*, vol. 12, p. 227.

42. William Johnson to Thomas Gage, Johnson Hall, February 19, 1764, *JP*, vol. IV, p. 330-331. In her study on the protocols surrounding the treaties between Indigenous people and European colonists, Mary A. Druke analyzes the importance of wampum exchanges: "Euramericans were usually careful to see that wampum was exchanged for matters important to them,

in much the same way that the Iroquois often insisted that a written copy of treaty minutes be given to them": Druke, "Iroquois Treaties: Common Forms, Varying Interpretations," *The History and Culture of Iroquois Diplomacy, op. cit.*, p. 89.

43. "An Indian Conference," Fort Johnson, February 13, 1757, *JP*, vol. IX, p. 604.
44. "Journal of Niagara Campaign," October 11, 1759, *JP*, vol. XIII, p. 155-156.
45. *Ibid.*, p. 156.
46. "Report of an Indian Conference," Montreal, January 30, 1762, *JP*, vol. X, p. 374.
47. Petition by the Abenaki of Bécancour chiefs to James Henry Craig, Quebec, August 5, 1810, *RG 10*, vol. 625, p. 182420.
48. Charles de Boische De Beauharnois to Jean-Frédéric Phélypeaux de Maurepas, Quebec, September 21, 1741, *MG 1, C11A*, vol. 75, f° 138-142.
49. "Minutes of a Speech addressed to Sir John Johnson Bart Superintendant General & Inspector General of Indian affairs, by the principal Chiefs of the Village of the Lake of Two Mountains," Montreal, February 8, 1788, *RG 10*, vol. 14, p. 232-233.
50. "Indian Proceedings," Johnson Hall, July 28, 1765, *JP*, vol. XI, p. 874-876.
51. Duncan C. Napier to Samuel P. Jarvis, October 10, 1838, *RG 10*, vol. 69, p. 64975.
52. Referring to the wampum kept in museums and that were originally exchanged at treaty signings between Indigenous nations and Europeans, anthropologist William N. Fenton writes: "When the belt and the verbal stream became separated from the written transactions at treaties which repose in archives, as happened with belts kept in museums, a reading became less probable and in time virtually impossible": "Structure, Continuity, and Change in Process of Iroquois Treaty Making," *The History and Culture of Iroquois Diplomacy, op. cit.*, p. 18.
53. "Proceedings of Sir William Johnson with the Indians," German Flats, July 22, 1770, *DRCHNY*, vol. VIII, p. 237-238.
54. "Proceedings of a General Council of the Several Indian Nations mentioned underneath, at the Glaize," October 4, 1792, *IIADH*, bob. 41.
55. *Ibid.*
56. "Paroles des Sept Villages adressées au Lieutenant Colonel John Campbell Surintendant de ces Sauvages," Montreal, October 20, 1779, *IIADH*, bob. 35.
57. "Proceedings of Sir William Johnson with the Indians," Johnson Hall, March 11, 1768, *DRCHNY*, vol. VIII, p. 52.
58. "Quebec. Saturday July 17th 1779. Coll Johnson arrived (in a sloop he had purchased for that purpose) at Quebec and paid his respect to General Haldimand Commdr in Chief," July 18, 1779, *RG 10*, vol. 12, p. 2.

59. Conference at Trois-Rivières between Louis-Juchereau Duchesnay, the Abenaki of St. Francis and Bécancour, the Huron of Lorette, and the Algonquin of Pointe- du-Lac, October 26, 1829, *RG 8*, vol. 268, p. 727.

60. Speck, "The Eastern Algonkian Wabanaki Confederacy," *loc. cit.*, p. 496.

61. Druke, "Iroquois Treaties: Common Forms, Varying Interpretations," *The History and Culture of Iroquois Diplomacy, op. cit.*, p. 90. Sir William Johnson wrote about this subject on March 28, 1772, in an analysis of the workings of the chiefdom among the Iroquois Six Nations: "This Chief of a Whole Nation has the Custody of the Belts of Wampum &ca [...] which are as [...] Records [...] of publk. Transactions. & he prompts the Speaker [...] to time at all Treaties & proposes [...] Affairs of Consequence, he sits with the rest of the Sachems who form the Grand Council [...] the Sachems of each Tribe often deliberate apart on the Affairs of their Tribe." William Johnson to Arthur Lee, Johnson Hall, March 28, 1772, *JP*, vol. XII, p. 952.

62. "Les Principaux, et Chefs Subalternes, et Guerriers du Village du Sault St Louis se plaignent contre une partie du Conseil du dit Village," Sault-Saint-Louis, July 28, 1834, *RG 10*, vol. 88, p. 35559.

63. "Journal of Indian Affairs," Johnson Hall, June 4, 1765, *JP*, vol. XI, p. 770.

64. Petition by Ignace Kawawaha *et al.* to Charles, Duke of Richmond, October 1818, *RG 10*, vol. 489, p. 29405-29412.

65. "Journal to Detroit," July 21, 1761, *JP*, vol. XIII, p. 224.

66. "Journal of Indian Affairs," March 6, 1762, *JP*, vol. X, p. 446.

67. "Indian Proceedings," Johnson Hall, July 28, 1765, *JP*, vol. XI, p. 875.

68. "Proceedings of Sir William Johnson with the Indians," Johnson Hall, March 6, 1768, *DRCHNY*, vol. VIII, p. 49-50. The document is entitled "Treaty of Peace, Friendship and Alliance Entered into the Six United Nations and Seven Confederate Nations of Canada, and the Cherokees Deputys sent from their Nation to enter into the same."

69. William N. Fenton, "Northern Iroquois Culture Patterns," *HNAI*, vol. 15, p. 315. Druke, "Iroquois Treaties: Common Forms, Varying Interpretations," *The History and Culture of Iroquois Diplomacy, op. cit.*, p. 92-94. Fenton, "Structure, Continuity, and Change in Process of Iroquois Treaty Making," *The History and Culture of Iroquois Diplomacy, op. cit.*, p. 12-13.

70. "A Deputation from the Cacknawaga, Skawendes & Orondax Indians living in & about Canada arrive & told the Commiss^rs that they had often been desired to come & renew the Treaty between them say they were come to do it," Albany, September 28, 1742, McIlwain ed., *op. cit.*, p. 229.

71. "The information of Lewis a Cagnuago Indian who is lately returned from Canada." This document likely dates from 1778; *IIADH*, bob. 34.

72. "At a Treaty held at the City of New York, by the United States, with the nations or tribes of Indians denominating themselves the Seven Nations

of Canada," May 23, 1796, *The New American State Papers. Indian Affairs*, 1972, vol. 6, p. 158.

73. Conference at Trois-Rivières between Louis-Juchereau Duchesnay, the Abenaki of St. Francis and Bécancour, the Huron of Lorette, and the Algonquin of Pointe-du-Lac, October 26, 1829, *RG 8*, vol. 268, p. 728-732.

74. Daniel Claus to William Johnson, Montreal, March 19, 1761, *JP*, vol. III, p. 362.

75. "Report of an Indian Conference," Montreal, January 30, 1762, *JP*, vol. X, p. 374.

76. Petition by Ignace Kawawaha *et al.* to Charles, Duke of Richmond, October 1818, *RG 10*, vol. 489, p. 29405-29412.

77. Jean-Baptiste Destimauville to Alexander McKee, Saint-François, June 29, 1795, *RG 10*, vol. 9, p. 8957.

78. "At a Treaty held at the City of New York, by the United States, with the nations or tribes of Indians denominating themselves the Seven Nations of Canada," May 23, 1796, *The New American State Papers. Indian Affairs*, 1972, vol. 6, p. 159.

79. John Chew to Herman W. Ryland, Montreal, November 30, 1801, *RG 10*, vol. 486, p. 3847.

80. "Memorandum of a Conference between Sir George Murray, the Secretary of State for the Colonial Department, and Two Deputies of the Iroquois Nation, with an Interpreter of that Tribe," Downing Street, January 15, 1830, *RG10*, vol. 659, p. 181426.

81. C. Léonard to William Mackay, Lake of Two Mountains, August 18, 1830, *RG 10*, vol. 25, p. 26367.

82. Solomon Y. Chesley to Duncan C. Napier, Saint-Régis, April 4, 1836, *RG 10*, vol. 91, p. 37118-37129. The Indigenous people kept manuscripts in their village, be it deeds of grant or treaties: Solomon Y. Chesley to Duncan C. Napier, Saint-Régis, March 23, 1843, *RG 10*, vol. 598, p. 46684.

83. Timothy P. Redfield, "Report on the Claim of the Iroquois Indians upon the State of Vermont, for their Hunting Ground," Montpellier, 1854, *IIADH*, bob. 49.

84. The Iroquois affirmed: "We say that we have in our possession volumes of treaties published by the general government, and other official documents, from which we learn the date of each treaty, with whom made, the amount ceded to the United States in acres, the sum paid in consideration of said cessions, from the origin of government to A.D. 1840:" "Report of the Commissioner, appointed by the Governor, on the Claim of the Iroquois Indians," Montpellier, November 3, 1855, *IIADH*, bob. 49.

85. According to Mary A. Druke, the procedural rules for negotiations between Europeans and Indigenous nations were such that both traditions were followed: "In cross-cultural negotiations, therefore, the presence or absence of wampum, on the one side, or of signed and sealed written

articles on the other could make a difference in whether an agreement was considered valid, not by virtue of any intrinsic nature of the forms themselves, but rather because of the meanings of the forms in the context of council procedure," Druke, "Iroquois Treaties: Common Forms, Varying Interpretations," *The History and Culture of Iroquois Diplomacy, op. cit.,* p. 85.

86. "Proceedings of Sir William Johnson with the Indians," German Flats, July 18, 1770, *DRCHNY*, vol. VIII, p. 229-230.

87. Daniel Claus, "Journal of Indian Affairs," August 27, 1767, *JP*, vol. XIII, p. 428-429.

88. "Proceedings at a Meeting held at Albany," June 28, 1761, *IIADH*, bob. 24.

89. "Indian Proceedings" Johnson Hall, December 15, 1764, *JP*, vol. XI, p. 503.

90. Fenton, "Structure, Continuity, and Change in Process of Iroquois Treaty Making," *The History and Culture of Iroquois Diplomacy, op. cit.,* p. 12-16. In April 1774, a spokesman for the Shawnee noted, during a meeting with Sir William Johnson, that grieving chiefs cannot address a gathering: "At a Congress held on Tuesday the 19th of April 1774," *IIADH*, bob. 31. Anthropological studies attribute this to the division into "halves" that characterize most of the social organizations of the Iroquoian-speaking nations: Fenton, "Northern Iroquois Culture Patterns," *HNAI*, vol. 15, p. 310-312. Tooker, "The League of The Iroquois. Its History, Politics, and Rituals," *HNAI*, vol. 15, p. 418-441.

91. "Indian Proceedings," Johnson Hall, December 1764, *JP*, vol. XI, p. 503.

92. "Proceedings of Sir William Johnson with the Indians," Johnson Hall, March 4, 1768, *DRCHNY*, vol. VIII, p. 39.

93. Daniel Claus, "Journal of Indian Affairs," May 6, 1762, *JP*, vol. X, p. 445.

94. All the more so since these deaths were attributed to a group of Seneca from the Iroquois League of Six Nations: "Journal of Indian Affairs," Johnson Hall, March 23, 1764, *JP*, vol. XI, p. 113.

95. "Conference between M. de Vaudreuil and the Indians," December 13, 1756, *DRCHNY*, vol. X, p. 505.

96. "Journal to Detroit," September 12, 1761, *JP*, vol. XIII, p. 255.

97. "Proceedings of Sir William Johnson with the Indians," German Flats, July 18, 1770, *DRCHNY*, vol. VIII, p. 230.

98. *Ibid.,* July 19, 1770, *DRCHNY*, vol. VIII, p. 231.

99. Guy Johnson to Thomas Gage, Johnson Hall, July 12, 1774, *JP*, vol. XII, p. 1122.

100. Guy Johnson to Thomas Gage, Guy Park, September 29, 1774, *JP*, vol. XIII, p. 681.

101. Louis-Armand de Lom d'Arce, Baron de Lahontan, *Nouveaux Voyages en Amérique Septentrionale, op. cit.,* œuvres I, p. 102.

102. "Copy of the Indian Councill held near Detroit between the Deputys of the Six Nations, & the Western Indians," June 1761, *IIADH*, bob. 24.

103. "Proceedings of a Grand Council held at Caughnawaga," Kahnawake, October 5, 1827, *RG 10*, vol. 20, p. 14245.

104. "Sundry Sachems of the Cacknawaga Canada Indians arrive at Albany & desire a Meeting from the Commiss.ʳˢ," Albany, August 1, 1735, McIlwain ed., *op. cit.,* p. 193.

105. *"Answer to a Speech to the Caughnawagas, or Canadian Tribes of Indians, near Montreal, sent by the Stockbridge Indians - returned 15th June,"* 1775, *IIADH*, bob. 31. The tree metaphor is central, and William N. Fenton explains its scope: "A tree is uprooted to bury the hatchet, to cast the weapons of war into the underground stream that carries off the pollution of war, and then the tree of peace is replanted:" cited in Tooker, "The League of The Iroquois. Its History, Politics, and Rituals," *HNAI*, vol. 15, p. 429.

106. "A conference held with the Mohock Indians at Caughnawaga," November 10, 1776, *IIADH*, bob. 33.

107. "Proceedings of a General Council of the Several Indian Nations mentioned underneath, at the Glaize," October 4, 1792, *IIADH*, bob. 41.

108. Jennings, "Glossary of Figures of Speech in Iroquois Political Rhetoric," *The History and Culture of Iroquois Diplomacy, op. cit.,* p. 122.

109. "Speech delivered by the Wyandots, in behalf of themselves, Mohawks, Chippewas, Powtewatamies and Mingoes to the Kickapoes Chiefs from the Wabash," Detroit River, July 23, 1788, *IIADH*, bob. 39.

110. "An Indian Conference," Johnson Hall, July 28, 1770, *JP*, vol. XII, p. 838.

111. "At a Council called by the three Outawa Chiefs at Sault Sᵗ Louis in behalf of their Chiefs of Michilimackinac," February 1786, *IIADH*, bob. 38.

112. "An Indian Congress," July 15, 1764, *JP*, vol. XI, p. 275.

113. Journal de Bougainville, *RAPQ*, 1924, p. 271.

114. Petition by Amable Chevalier *et al.* to John Colborne, Lake of Two Mountains, May 31, 1831, *RG 10*, vol. 83, p. 32288-32289.

115. "An Indian Conference," Fort Johnson, February 13, 1757, *JP*, vol. IX, p. 605.

116. "Journal of Indian Affairs," Johnson Hall, February 21, 1765, *JP*, vol. XI, p. 597-598.

117. "Journal of Indian Affairs," July 13, 1767, *JP*, vol. XII, p. 344.

118. "Journal of Indian Affairs," January 3, 1768, *JP*, vol. XII, p. 452.

119. "Proceedings of Sir William Johnson with the Indians," Johnson Hall, March 4, 1768, *DRCHNY*, vol. VIII, p. 40. The proceedings note that Sir William presented these offerings after each nation shouted their cries of approval.

120. "List of articles Send by Genᶦ Darling to the Chiefs assembled at the Grand Council at Caughnawaga on the 5th October 1827," *RG 10*, vol. 20, p. 14234-14235.

121. "Proceedings of a Grand Council held at Caughnawaga," October 5, 1827, *RG 10*, vol. 20, p. 14245.
122. "An Indian Congress," Johnson Hall, August 11, 1770, *JP*, vol. XII, p. 847.
123. Daniel Claus, "Journal of Indian Affairs," September 12, 1770, *JP*, vol. VII, p. 947.
124. Daniel Claus, "Journal of Indian Affairs," July 26, 1773, *JP*, vol. XIII, p. 626.
125. "Journal of Indian Affairs," Johnson Hall, June 5-6,1764, *JP*, vol. XI, p. 234.
126. Robert Matthews, Quebec, March 31, 1783, *IIADH*, bob. 36.
127. François Deschambault to John Johnson, Montreal, February 1, 1815, *RG 10*, vol. 487, p. 4523-4524.
128. John Johnson to Noah Freer, Montreal, February 3, 1815, *RG 10*, vol. 487, p. 4518-4519.
129. Petition by the warrior chiefs of the Huron of Lorette to Sir James Henry Craig. This document dates from 1807-1811; *RG 10*, vol. 611, p. 53920.
130. Petition by Charles Kana8ato *et al.* to Matthew Lord Aylmer, Lake of Two Mountains, June 18, 1831, *RG 10*, vol. 83, p. 32297.
131. "Report of a Talk with the Indian Chiefs of the Lake of the Two Mountains, on delivering Two Brass Field pieces to them from the Commander of the Forces, Lord Aylmer," November 23, 1831, *RG 10*, vol. 83, p. 32711-32713.
132. Petition by Atonwa Sonatsiowane *et al.* to James Kempt, Lorette, October 8, 1828, *RG 8*, vol. 267, p. 292.
133. James Kempt to George Murray, Quebec, May 16, 1829, P. Ford *et al.*, *Correspondence and Other Papers, op. cit.*, p. 38-39.
134. "Memorandum," Thomas Wilson to Lord Howick, March 29, 1832, *ibid.*, p. 140.
135. The Seven Nations to Archibald Lord Gosford, Kahnawake, February 3, 1837, *RG 10*, vol. 93, p. 38031-38039.
136. Journal de Bougainville, *RAPQ*, 1924, p. 277.
137. William Johnson to Daniel Claus, Castle Cumberland, May 20, 1761, *JP*, vol. X, p. 269-270.
138. "Proceedings at a Meeting held at Albany," June 28, 1761, *IIADH*, bob. 24.
139. "An Indian Conference," Johnson Hall, July 28, 1770, *JP*, vol. XII, p. 837-838.
140. Thomas Gage to Lord Hillsborough, November 10, 1770, *IIADH*, bob. 30.
141. William Johnson, "Expenses of Indian Department," Johnson Hall, August 27, 1768, *JP*, vol. VI, p. 340-341.
142. William N. Fenton writes: "The Indians were great eaters and persons of all ages attended both as witnesses and to share the great event:" "Structure,

Continuity, and Change in Process of Iroquois Treaty Making," *The History and Culture of Iroquois Diplomacy, op. cit.,* p. 25.

143. The archives of Sir William Johnson and Daniel Claus include tables from the years 1766 to 1775 compiling the expenditures of the superintendent and his representative for diplomacy with the Seven Nations representatives: "Account of Daniel Claus," March 24, 1766, *JP*, vol. V, p. 96-97. "Account of Daniel Claus," July 20 to September 21, 1769, *JP*, vol. XIII, p. 488-489. "Account with Daniel Claus," March 18, 1772 to April 4, 1775, *JP*, vol. XIII, p. 705-706. "Daniel Claus' Account of Indian Expenses," August 28, 1770 to September 25, 1775, *JP*, vol. XIII, p. 707-722.

144. Joseph Marcoux to Duncan C. Napier, Sault-Saint-Louis, February 12, 1845, *RG 10*, vol. 598, p. 46629.

145. Édouard-Narcisse Delorimier to Duncan C. Napier, Sault-Saint-Louis, January 28, 1848, *RG 10*, vol. 600, p. 47866. Delorimier noted that "it appears that this gathering of different villages came about due to the fact that the Government decided to no longer donate any annual equipment to the children born since the previous first of May, and to the subject of the *métisses* for the same reason."

146. Journal de Bougainville, *RAPQ*, 1924, p. 216.

147. *Ibid.*, p. 272.

148. *Ibid.*

149. "Instructions to Daniel Claus," February 10, 1764, *JP*, vol. XI, p. 53.

150. "Journal of Indian Affairs," Johnson Hall, June 8, 1764, *JP*, vol. XI, p. 236.

CHAPTER FOUR. Diplomatic Relations Stretching from the Atlantic to the Great Lakes

1. Journal de Bougainville, *RAPQ*, 1924, p. 212.

2. "The United States in Congress," Fort Stanwix, October 1784, *IIADH*, bob. 36.

3. We have arbitrarily refrained from describing certain key diplomatic sites.

4. Charles de Boische De Beauharnois to Jean-Frédéric Phélypeaux de Maurepas, Quebec, September 21, 1741, *MG 1, CIIA*, vol. 75, fo 141.

5. "Sundry Sachems of the Cacknawaga Canada Indians arrive at Albany & desire a Meeting from the Commissrs," Albany, August 1, 1735, McIlwain ed., *op. cit.,* p. 193.

6. Pierre-Jacques de Taffanel De La Jonquière to Antoine-Louis de Rouillé, Quebec, October 17, 1751, *MG 1, CIIA*, vol. 97, fo 118-188vo. On October 19, he reiterated this observation: Quebec, October 19, 1751, *ibid.,* vol. 97, fo 127-128vo.

7. Jennings, "Descriptive Treaty Calendar," *The History and Culture of Iroquois Diplomacy, op. cit.,* p. 188.

8. Daniel Claus to Richard Peters, Canajoharie, July 10, 1755, *JP*, vol. IX, p. 194.

9. "Journal of Indian Affairs," May 5, 1758, *JP*, vol. XIII, p. 111.

10. "Journal of Indian Affairs," January 27, 1762, *JP*, vol. X, p. 9.

11. William Johnson to Thomas Gage, Johnson Hall, February 19, 1764, *JP*, vol. XII, p. 330.

12. "Journal of Indian Affairs," March 29, 1762, *JP*, vol. X, p. 412.

13. "An Indian Conference," Guy Park, May 24-27,1768, *JP*, vol. XII, p. 515-516. "Proceedings of Colonel Guy Johnson with the Six Nations," Guy Park, December 1774, *DRCHNY*, vol. VIII, p. 518-520. "Proceedings of Colonel Guy Johnson with the Six Nations," Guy Park, January 20-2, 1775, *DRCHNY*, vol. VIII, p. 534-542.

14. "Proceedings of Commissioners Appointed to Treat with the Six Nations of Indians," German Flats, August 15, 1775, *IIADH*, bob. 32. There had also been talk of this the previous month: "A Speech to the Six Confederate Nations, Mohawks, Oneidas, Tuscaroras, Onondagas, Cayugas, Senecas, from the Twelve United Colonies, convened in Council at Philadelphia," July 13, 1775, *IIADH*, bob. 31.

15. "An Indian Congress," Fort Pitt, May 11, 1765, *JP*, vol. XI, p. 732.

16. "Discours qu'on se propose de faire aux différentes Nations d'Indiens assemblé à Pittsbourg par un Officier François, accompagné d'un ceinturon à chaque Nation," 1776, *IIADH*, bob. 33. "Conference with Indians at Fort Pitt," July 6, 1776, *IIADH*, bob. 32.

17. "Niagara and Detroit Proceedings," Detroit, September 15, 1761, *JP*, vol. III, p. 494. "Speech of Three Indians," Detroit, May 9, 1773, *JP*, vol. VIII, p. 789.

18. "Journal to Detroit," July 21, 1761, *JP*, vol. XIII, p. 223.

19. "Conference with Indians at Fort Pitt," July 6, 1776, *IIADH*, bob. 32. "Proceedings of a Meeting with the Deputies of the Six Nations on their Return from the Southward," Niagara, June 17, 1780, *IIADH*, bob. 34.

20. "Parolles de Tsioüeoüy et de [?genenraguere ?], deputez des iroquois a monsieur le chler de caillieres gouverneur et lieutenant general pour le roy en toute la nouvelle france. Reponses de monsieur le chler de calliere aux parolles des deux deputez cy a costé," Quebec, March 2, 1701, *MG 1*, *C11A*, vol. 30, f° 230-230v°.

21. "Réponse de Son Exellence le Lord Dorchester, aux Sept Villages du Bas Canada venus en députation de la part de toutes les Nations du pays d'en haut excepté les Chaouanons, Miamis et Loups, rendue en Conseil au Chateau de St. Louis à Québec le 10e. Février, 1794," *RG 10*, vol. 8, p. 8571.

22. "At a Conference with the Five Nations Deputies being two Onondagoe and three Cayouga Indians," Quebec, August 20, 1779, *IIADH*, bob. 34. Frederick Haldimand, "Answer to a Speech addressed by His Excellency before Capt. Fraser Commanding at Carleton Island & the Indian Officer of the 6 Nation Department & others by the Mohawk, Onondago, Cayouga & Delaware Indians," Quebec, May 1780, *MG 19*, *F 1*, vol. 26, p. 203-207.

23. "Speech of His Excellency George Provost Baronet Governor in Chief and Commander of the Forces in British North America, to the deputation of Chiefs and Warriors of the Western Nations," Quebec, March 17, 1814, *RG 10*, vol. 136, pt. 1, p. 77640.

24. "Ratification de la Paix faitte au mois de septembre dernier, entre la Colonie de Canada, les Sauvages ses alliéz, et les iroquois dans une assemblée géneralle des chefs de chacune de ces nations convoquée par monsieur le Chevalier de Callières gouverneur et Lieutenant general pour le Roy en la nouvelle France," Montreal, August 4, 1701, *MG 1, C11A*, vol. 19, f° 41-44.

25. Baron de Lahontan, *Nouveaux Voyages en Amérique Septentrionale, op. cit.*, œuvres I, p. 122. We are unable to determine how long this practice continued.

26. Charles de Boische De Beauharnois to Jean-Frédéric Phélypeaux de Maurepas, Quebec, September 21, 1741, *MG 1, C11A*, vol. 75, fo 139.

27. *Ibid.*, fo 139vo.

28. "Copy of the Indian Councill held near Detroit between the Deputys of the Six Nations, & the Western Indians," Detroit, June 1761, *IIADH*, bob. 23.

29. "Congress at Fort Stanwix," October 5, 1768, *JP*, vol. XII, p. 619.

30. "Journal of Indian Affairs," May 5, 1758, *JP*, vol. XIII, p. 111.

31. "Proceedings of a Congress held by the Six Nations with their Dependants at Onondaga," November 1774, *IIADH*, bob. 31.

32. "At a meeting of the Commissioners for Indian affairs in the Northern Department," Albany, August 15, 1778, *IIADH*, bob. 34.

33. Jennings, "Gazetteer," *The History and Culture of Iroquois Diplomacy, op. cit.*, p. 210-211. John Johnson to Frederick Haldimand, Montreal, March 19, 1784, *IIADH*, bob. 37.

34. Henry Tekarihigan *et al.* to William Claus, Onondaga, November 9, 1806, *RG 10*, vol. 103, p. 189. The following documentary reference contains information about the Great Fire of the Iroquois of the League at Buffalo Creek: "At a Council with the Six Nations of Indians," Fort George, August 3, 1826, *RG 10*, vol. 103, p. 402.

35. Jean-Baptiste Delorimier, Lachine, August 26, 1796, *RG 8*, vol. 249, pt. 2, p. 306-307.

36. "Proceedings of a Council of the Six Nation Indians held at the Onondaga Council fire at the Grand River, June 9, 1832, *RG 10*, vol. 51, p. 56379. Dating from as early as the period between April 30, 1803, and February 24, 1804, there are references to the presence of several Indigenous chiefs from the nations of the Great Lakes and the southern United States: "Chippewa," "Ottawa," "Shawanoe," "Potewatomie," "Wyandott," "Munsey," "Nanticoke," "Mingoe," "Mohawk," "Miami," "Massissaque," "Matouchtata," "Missouri," "Mohigan," "Delaware," "Kikapou," and "Cherokee": "Return of Indians who have visited the Post of Amherstburg,

with the supposed number of their Nations &c. from 30th. April 1803 to 24th. February 1804," February 1804, *MG 19, F 1*, vol. 25, p. 24-26.

37. Speck, "The Eastern Algonkian Wabanaki Confederacy, *loc. cit.*, p. 492.

38. Frank G. Speck, "Culture Problems in the Northeastern North America," *Proceedings of the American Philosophical Society*, vol. 65, n° 4 (1926), p. 282.

39. Speck, "Culture Problems in the Northeastern North America," *loc. cit.*, p. 282. Speck, "The Eastern Algonkian Wabanaki Confederacy," *loc. cit.*, p. 492-494. Dean R. Snow, "Eastern Abenakis," *HNAI*, vol. 15, p. 143, 147. According to the Penobscot elder Newell Lyon, who was interviewed by Speck, the alliance dated back to the 1700s. Speck and Snow are more conservative in their estimates, suggesting that the agreement dated instead from around 1749.

40. This tradition was recorded in the 20th century by Speck after speaking with Wabanaki "traditionalists" who provided the anthropologist with valuable information on the type of wampum that was exchanged between the Seven Fires, the Odawa, and the Wabanaki. Facsimiles of these objects appear in his works: Speck, "The Eastern Algonkian Wabanaki Confederacy," *loc. cit.*, p. 492. Speck, "The Eastern Algonkian Wabanaki Confederacy," *loc. cit.*, p. 500-501. The Jennings collection also includes such information: "Penobscot Council Belt," *IIADH*, no. 61, bob. 50. "Photograph by F.G. Speck of Penobscot, Micmac, Passamaquoddy, and Iroquois Wampum Belts," *IIADH*, no. 142, bob. 50.

41. Speck, "The Eastern Algonkian Wabanaki Confederacy," *loc. cit.*, p. 499-500, 505. The Mi'kmaq occupied a special place in the alliance, and Speck explains why: "The Micmac, who were designated in the confederacy as the 'younger brothers,' owing perhaps to their extreme easterly location and being so widely scattered, seem to have occupied a position somewhat apart from their allies.".

42. Leslie F.S. Upton, *Micmacs and Colonists: Indian-White Relations in the Maritime Provinces, 1713-1867*, Vancouver, University of British Columbia Press, 1979, p. 144.

43. Speck, "The Eastern Algonkian Wabanaki Confederacy," *loc. cit.*, p. 506.

44. Delâge, "Les Iroquois chrétiens des réductions, 1667-1770, II: Rapports avec la Ligue iroquoise, les Britanniques et les autres nations autochtones," *loc. cit.*, p. 47.

45. Ephraim Tucker, *Five Months in Labrador Newfoundland, Summer 1838* in Dorothy Catherine Anger, *Where the Sand Blows: Vignette of Bay St. George Micmacs*, Bay St. George Regional Indian Council, Port au Port East, Newfoundland, 1988, p.7.

46. Speck, "The Eastern Algonkian Wabanaki Confederacy," *loc. cit.*, p. 507.

47. *"A Talk of one of the St. John's Tribe, attended by two of the* Passamaquoddy Indians, *with His Excellency General* Washington," Cambridge, January 31, 1776, *IIADH*, bob. 32. The following documents recount the same event:

George Washington to the President of Congress, Cambridge, January 30, 1776, *IIADH*, bob. 32. "*The Talk of sundry Sachems and Warriors of the* Caughnawaga Nations, *with His Excellency General* Washington," Cambridge, January 31, 1776, *IIADH*, bob. 32. Peter Schuyler to George Washington, Albany, January 5, 1776, *IIADH*, bob. 32. To Peter Schuyler, Cambridge, January 7, 1776, *IIADH*, bob. 32.

48. *Royal Gazette*, Fredericton, July 17, 1839, *IIADH*, bob. 48.

49. Dean R. Snow, "Eastern Abenakis," *HNAI*, vol. 15, p. 143.

50. Speck, "The Eastern Algonkian Wabanaki Confederacy," *loc. cit.*, p. 493.

51. Was this role played by the Odawa an extension of the French alliance in the Great Lakes in which, at least from 1660 onwards, the Odawa occupied the key position? Delâge, "L'alliance franco-amérindienne, 1660-1701," *loc. cit.*, p. 3-15 *passim*.

52. Speck, "The Eastern Algonkian Wabanaki Confederacy," *loc. cit.*, p. 490-496 *passim*.

53. *Ibid.*, p. 497-498. Willard Walker *et al.*, "A Chronological Account of the Wabanaki Confederacy," *Political Organization of Native North Americans*, Washington, D.C., University Press of America, 1980, p. 69-74 *passim*.

54. Craig Maclaine, Michael S. Baxendale, *This Land is Our Land. The Mohawk Revolt at Oka*, Montreal/Toronto, Optimum Publishing International, 1990, p. 99-121. John N. B. Hewitt, "Legend of the Founding of the Iroquois League," *American Anthropologist*, vol. 5, no. 2 (1892), p. 131-148. Anthony F.C. Wallace, "The Tuscarora: Sixth Nation of the Iroquois Confederacy," *Proceedings of the American Philosophical Society*, vol. 93, no. 2 (1949), p. 159-165. "An Indian Conference," Hartford, May 28, 1763, *JP*, vol. IV, p. 124.

55. "An Indian Conference," Hartford, May 28, 1763, *JP*, vol. IV, p. 124.

56. Tooker, "The League of The Iroquois. Its History, Politics, and Rituals," *loc. cit.*, p. 430-437.

57. "At a Council held at Philadelphia," March 31, 1755, *IIADH*, bob. 17.

58. "Journal of Sir William Johnson's Proceedings with the Indians," Canajoharie, April 21, 1759, *DRCHNY*, vol. VII, p. 392.

59. "Johnson's Proceedings with Deputies," Fort Johnson, February 13, 1760, *JP*, vol. III, p. 188-189.

60. "We think it necessary to tell you." This document appears to date from the 1760s; *IIADH*, bob. 23.

61. Daniel Claus to William Johnson, 1762, *MG 19, F 1*, vol. 1, p.69.

62. "Proceedings of Sir William Johnson with the Indians," Johnson Hall, September 8, 1763, *DRCHNY*, vol. VII, p. 553-554.

63. "Proceedings of Sir William Johnson with the Indians," German Flats, July 22, 1770, *DRCHNY*, vol. VIII, p. 240.

64. "Proceedings of Commissioners appointed to Treat with the Six Nations of Indians," German Flats, August 15, 1775, *IIADH*, bob. 32.

65. Starting in the summer of 1776, deep divisions began to emerge between the members of the Iroquois League of Six Nations: some wanted to remain neutral, others wished to side with the American Congress, and others still preferred to align themselves with the British Crown. The Iroquois were unable to reach a consensus on the matter: conference between the Iroquois Six Nations and the American commissioners, August 1776, *IIADH*, bob. 32.

66. "At a Council held at Montreal 14ᵗʰ August 1778. Present Colonel Campbell the Superintendant, the Deputy Superintend: General of the Indian Affairs," *IIADH*, bob. 34.

67. "Conseil des Sonontoins tenû aux Sept Vilages accompagné d'un grand Colier de porcelaine au nom des Cinq Nations," Montreal, August 10, 1779, *IIADH*, bob. 34.

68. John Deserontyon to Daniel Claus, Oghnyorege Island, May 9, 1780, *MG 19, F 1*, vol. 24, p. 7."At a Meeting held at Niagara the 6th March 1784 at the request of the Sachems and Chiefs of the Six Nations, in consequence of a Speech sent by General Schuyler, in answer to the Six Nations Speech sent to him last fall by Peterus and Little Beard," Niagara, March 7, 1784, *IIADH*, bob. 37.

69. Jennings, "Iroquois Alliances in American History," *The History and Culture of Iroquois Diplomacy, op. cit.,* p. 38. Complete this analysis with Francis Jennings, "The Constitutional Evolution of the Covenant Chain," *Proceedings of the American Philosophical Society*, vol. 115, no. 2 (April 1971), p. 88-96.

70. "Journal of Sir William Johnson's Proceedings with the Indians," Canajoharie, April 18, 1759, *DRCHNY*, vol. VII, p. 388.

71. "Sundry Sachems of the Cacknawaga Canada Indians arrive at Albany & desire a Meeting from the Commissrs," Albany, August 1, 1735, McIlwain ed., *op. cit.,* p. 193.

72. *Ibid.*, p. 193-194.

73. "A Deputation from the Cacknawaga, Schawendes & Orondax Indians living in & about Canada arrive," Albany, September 28, 1742, McIlwain, dir., *op. cit.,* p. 229.

74. "At a Meeting of the Commissioners of Indians affairs at the House of Robert Loterage in the City of Albany," October 30, 1753, *IIADH*, bob. 15.

75. "An Indian Conference," Johnson Hall, September 10, 1762, *JP*, vol. X, p. 506.

76. "Indian Conference," "Montreal," Kahnawake, September 16, 1760, *JP*, vol. XIII, p. 163, 166.

77. "Proceedings of Sir William Johnson with the Indians," Johnson Hall, September 7, 1763, *DRCHNY*, vol. VII, p. 554.

78. Jennings, "Iroquois Alliances in American History," *The History and Culture of Iroquois Diplomacy, op. cit.,* p. 58.

79. To localize the geographic sites occupied by these nations, consult the maps in the *Atlas of Great Lakes Indian History* by Helen H. Tanner, published in 1987.

80. Lyle M. Stone, Donald Chaput, "History of the Upper Great Lakes Area," *HNAI*, vol. 15, 1978, p. 603.

81. Bruce G. Trigger, "Indians and Ontario's History," *Ontario History*, vol. LXXIV, no. 4 (1982), p. 250. Delâge, "L'alliance franco-amérindienne, 1660-1701," *loc. cit.*, p. 3-10 *passim*.

82. "The Lieut Govr John Nanfan Esqr met the 5 Nations & made á Speech to them wch is not recorded. They Answer," Albany, July 14, 1701, McIlwain, ed., *op. cit.*, p. 39. Synonyms for these names are also found in Hodge, ed., "Synonymy," *HAINM*, vol. 2.

83. Daniel Claus to Richard Peters, Canajoharie, July 10, 1755, *JP*, vol. IX, p. 194.

84. Denys Delâge, "Les premiers contacts dans 'History of the Ojibway People' de William Warren. Un récit de transition entre l'oral et l'écrit," *RAAQ*, vol. XXII, no. 2-3 (1992), p. 57.

85. Louis-Antoine De Bougainville, "Mémoire sur l'état de la Nouvelle-France," *RAPQ*, 1924, p. 46.

86. *Ibid.*, p. 287-288.

87. *Ibid.*, p. 208-209, 216.

88. Havard, *op. cit.*, p. 138.

89. "Message of the Canada to the Western Indians," August 25, 1763, *DRCHNY*, vol. VII, p. 544.

90. "Correspondence from Henry Bouqyet and proceedings of councils at the Forks of Muskingum," November 2, 1764, *IIADH*, bob. 27.

91. "Indian Proceedings," Johnson Hall, December 15, 1764, *JP*, vol. XI, p. 503.

92. Journal de Bougainville, *RAPQ*, 1924, p. 287-288.

93. Daniel Claus, "Journal of Indian Affairs," July 26, 1773, *JP*, vol. XIII, p. 624.

94. John Johnson to Robert Matthews, Montreal, April 3, 1783, *HP*, add. mss. 21774, f° 97.

95. "The information of Lewis a Cagnuago Indian who is lately returned from Canada." This document likely dates from 1778; *IIADH*, bob. 34.

96. "Réponse de Son Exellence le Lord Dorchester, aux Sept Villages du Bas Canada venus en députation de la part de toutes les Nations du pays d'en haut excepté les Chaouanons, Miamis et Loups, rendue en Conseil au Chateau de St. Louis à Québec le 10e. Février, 1794," *RG 10*, vol. 8, p. 8571.

97. "Translation of a Report made by Mr Lorimier of the proceedings of a Council held at Caughnawaga the 6th and 7th August 1796, by the Indians of the Seven Nations of Lower Canada," Kahnawake, August 6, 1796, *RG 8*, vol. 249, pt. 2, p. 308-309. Jean-Baptiset Delorimier, "I am certify that on the 13th. of August 1796 I was called to a council held at Caughnawaga,

of the Seven Nations of Lower Canada, the Courtes oreilles or Ottawas of Michilimackinac, Mickmacs, Muskrats &c. of which the following are the true Speeches addressed to His Excellency General Prescott," *RG 8*, vol. 249, pt. 2, p. 301-304.

98. Jean-Baptiste Delorimier, Lachine, August 26, 1796, *RG 8*, vol. 249, pt. 2, p. 307.

99. Testimonial of Nicolas Vincent Tsaouenhohoui before the House of Assembly of Lower Canada, Quebec, January 29, 1824, *Journals of the House of Assembly of Lower-Canada*, Quebec, 5 Geo. IV, appendix (R). According to Tsaouenhohoui's speech, the alliance appears to date back to 1624; in fact, this is a dating error, as the description the Grand Chief gives of these seven nations refers to the domiciled nations living in the Indigenous villages between Montreal and Quebec.

100. Daniel Claus, "Journal of Indian Affairs," July 26, 1773, *JP*, vol. XIII, p. 624.

101. "Conseil adressé à Mr Le Colonel Campbell Supr : int : des affaires sau-vages," Kahnawake, October 7, 1791, *RG10*, vol. 8, p. 8201-8202.

102. *Ibid.*, p. 8203.

103. "Paroles des Sauvages des Sept vilages du Bas Canada, adressee á Mons : le Colonel Mc Ki Supr Intendant General, et yinspecteur Genreral des Affairs Sauvages," July 28, 1795, *RG 8*, vol. 248, p. 230.

104. "Substence of á Letter Received by Joseph Chew S.I.A. the 7th. of August 1795 from the Algonkine, Iroquois and Nipissing Indian Nations of the Lake of the Two Mountains," *RG 8*, vol. 248, p. 254.

105. Joseph K. Gabriel *et al.* to the Minister of the Interior, Lake of Two Mountains, November 10, 1919, *RG 10*, vol. 6750, file 420-10.

106. Petition by François Lotono *et al.* to Matthew Lord Aylmer, Trois-Rivières, July 22, 1831, *RG 10*, vol. 83, p. 32484.

107. "Paroles des Abénakis á leurs frères Algonquins et Nipissingues, au Lac des deux Montagnes." This document predates 1804; *RG 10*, vol. 99, p. 41090.

108. *Ibid.*, p. 41090-41091.

109. "Journal of William Johnson's Proceedings with the Indians," April 4-21, 1759, *DRCHNY*, vol. VII, p. 392-393. "Journal of Niagara Campaign," October 11, 1759, *JP*, vol. XIII, p. 155-156. "Johnson's Proceedings with Deputies," Fort Johnson, February 13-14, 1760, *JP*, vol. III, p. 188-193.

110. "A Meeting with Aughquisasnes," Kahnawake, August 21, 1769, *JP*, vol. VII, p. 109.

111. "Indian Conference," "Montreal," Kahnawake, September 16, 1760, *JP*, vol. XII, p. 163-166.

112. See Delâge, Sawaya, *Les Sept-Feux et les traités avec les Britanniques*, 1996.

Bibliography

Printed and Manuscript Sources

Anger, Dorothy Catherine. *Where the Sand Blows: Vignettes of Bay St. George Micmacs*. Bay St. George Regional Indian Council. Port au Port East, Newfoundland, 1988.

Boehm, Randolph, ed. *Records of the British Colonial Office. Westward Expansion, 1760-1783; the Board of Trade; the French and Indian War.*

Canada. *Indian Treaties and Surrenders, from 1680 to 1890*. Toronto, Coles Publishing Company, 1971 (1912), 3 vols.

Canada. Archives nationales du Canada/ National Archives of Canada. Ottawa.

Record Group 8: British Military and Naval Records

A 1: "Correspondence of the Military Secretary of the Commander of the Forces, 1767-1870 - Subject Files 1767-1870"

B 13: "Records of the Canadian Command, 1785-1883 - Memorials and Petitions, 1808-1811"

D 8: "Miscellaneous Records, 1757-1896 - Militia Records Accumulated by the Claus Family, 1787-1794, 1802- 1808"

Record Group 10: Indian Affairs

A: "Administration Records - Imperial Control, 1755-1860"

B: "Administration Records - Ministerial Control after 1860"

C: "Records of the Field Offices of the Indian Department"

D: "Land Records"

Manuscript Group 1: Archives Nationales, Paris, Archives des Colonies C11A: "Correspondance générale, Canada, 1540-1784" *Manuscript Group 19: Fur Trade and Indians 1763-1867 F1*: "Fur Trade Indians - Claus Papers"

Manuscript Group 23: Late Eighteenth Century Papers

GII1: "Quebec and Lower Canada Political Figures - Murray, James"

Carter, Clarence Edwin, ed. *The Correspondence of General Thomas Gage with the Secretaries of State 1763-1775*. Archon Books, 1969, 2 vols.

Cochran, Thomas C., ed., *The New American State Papers. 1789-1860. Indian Affairs. Northwest*. Wilmington, Delaware, Scholarly Resources Inc., 1972, vol. 4.

Collin, Jacques. [Louis-Armand de Lom d'Arce, Baron de Lahontan]. *Nouveaux Voyages en Amérique septentrionale, Œuvres I*. Montreal, L'Hexagone/ Minerve, 1983, 346 p.

Connell, Brian, ed. [John Knox]. *The Siege of Quebec and the Campaigns in North-America 1757-1760*. Pendragon House of Mississauga, 1980.

Cruikshank, Ernest A. *The Administration of Lieut.-Governor Simcoe, Viewed in His Official Correspondence*. Transactions of the Canadian Institute.

Cruikshank, Ernest A., ed. *The Correspondence of Lieutenant Governor John Graves Simcoe, 1792-1796*. Toronto, The Ontario Society, 1931, 5 vol.

Ford P., *et al.*, ed. *Correspondence and Other Papers Relating to Aboriginal Tribes in British Possessions. 1834*. British Parliamentary Papers series, Anthropology-Aborigines. Shannon, Ireland, Irish University Press, vol. 3, 1969, 147 p.

Franquet, Louis. *Voyages et mémoires sur le Canada*. Institut canadien de Québec. Quebec, Côté, 1889, 213 p.

[Haldimand, Frederick]. *Sir Frederick Haldimand: Unpublished Papers and Correspondence 1758-84*. London, England. World Microfilms Publications, 115 bob.

Jennings, Francis, ed. *Iroquois Indians: A Documentary History of the Diplomacy of the Six Nations and their League. The Microfilm Collection*. The D'Arcy McNickle Center for the History of the American Indian. The Newberry Library. Woodbridge, Connecticut; Reading, England. Research Publications, 1984, 50 bob.

Kidder, Frederick. *Military Operations in Eastern Maine and Nova Scotia During the Revolution Chiefly Compiled from the Journals and Letters of Colonel John Allan, with Notes and a Memoir of Col. John Allan*. Albany, Joel Munsell, 1867.

Klinck, Carl F., James J. Talman, *The Journal of Major John Norton, 1816*. The Champlain Society 46. Toronto, Champlain Society, 1970, cxxiv-391 p.

[Labouchere]. *Copies or Extracts of Correspondence Since 1st April 1835 between the Secretary of State for the Colonies and the Governors of the British American Provinces, Respecting the Indians in those Provinces*. Toronto, Canadiana House, 1973, 171 p.

La Potherie, Claude-Charles Le Roy, dit Bacqueville de. *Histoire de l'Amérique septentrionale*. Paris, Brocas, 1753 (1722) 4 t.

Lincoln, Charles Henry, ed. *Correspondence of William Shirley Governor of Massachusetts and Military Commander in America 1731-1760.* New York, The Macmillan Company, 1912, 2 vols.

Margry, Pierre, ed. *Mémoires et documents pour servir à l'histoire des origines françaises des pays d'outre-mer.* Paris, Maisonneuve, 1879, t. 1.

McIlwain, Charles Howard, ed. [Peter Wraxall]. *An Abridgment of the Indian Affairs: Contained in Four Folio Volumes, Transacted in the Colony of New York, from the Year 1678 to the Year 1751 by Peter Wraxall.* Harvard Historical Studies no. 21. Cambridge, Massachusetts. Harvard University Press, 1915, cxviii-251 p.

[Murray, James]. *Governor Murray's Journal of Quebec - From 18th September, 1759, to 25th May 1760.* Quebec and Montreal, Literary and Historical Society of Quebec.

O'Callaghan, Edward B., ed. *The Documentary History of the State of New York.* Albany, Weed, Parsons and Co., 1849-1851, 4 vols.

O'Callaghan, Edward B., ed. *Documents Relative to the Colonial History of the State of New York.* Albany, Weed, Parsons and Co., 1856-1887, 15 vols.

Pouchot, Pierre. *Mémoires sur la dernière guerre de l'Amérique Septentrionale entre la France et l'Angleterre. Suivis d'Observations, dont plusieurs sont relatives au théatre actuel de la guerre, & de nouveaux détails sur les mœurs & les usages des Sauvages, avec des cartes topographiques.* Yverdon, 1781, 3 vols.

Quebec. *Journals of the House of Assembly of Lower-Canada.* Quebec, Bibliothèque de l'Assemblée nationale, 1795-1837.

Quebec. *Rapport de l'archiviste de la Province de Québec pour 1932-1933.* "Les Départements du Secrétaire de la Province," Rédempti Paradis. Quebec, Imprimeur de Sa Majesté Le Roi, 1933.

Roy, Pierre-Georges. *Rapport de l'archiviste de la Province de Québec pour 1923-1924.* Quebec, Imprimerie du roi, 1924, xiv-426 p.

Shortt, Adam, Arthur G. Doughty, *Documents relatifs à l'histoire constitutionnelle du Canada 1759-1791.* Ottawa, Thomas Mulvey, vol. 1, 1921, xix-1064 p.

Sullivan, James, *et al.*, ed. [William Johnson]. *The Papers of Sir William Johnson.* Albany, University State of New York, 1921-1962, 14 vols.

Thwaites, Reuben Gold, ed. *The Jesuit Relations and Allied Documents: Travels and Explorations of the Jesuit Missionaries in New-France, 1610-1791.* Burrows Bros. Company. Cleveland, Ohio, 1896-1901, 73 vols.

Webster, J. Clarence, ed. [Jeffery Amherst]. *The Journal of Jeffery Amherst, Recording the Military Career of General Amherst in America from 1758 to 1763.* Toronto, The Ryerson Press, 1931.

Reference Works

Abler, Thomas Struthers, *et al. A Canadian Indian Bibliography. 1960-1970.* Toronto, University of Toronto Press, 1974, xii-732 p.

Cruikshank, Ernest. *Inventory of the Military Documents in the Canadian Archives.* Ottawa, Government Printing Bureau, 1910.

Desrosiers, André. *France. Archives des Colonies, Série CIIA Correspondance générale, Canada. MG 1, Série CIIA. Instrument de recherche no 856/ Finding Aid No 856 (volumes 1-20, 50-65).* Ottawa, Archives nationales du Canada, Division des Manuscrits/Public Archives of Canada, Manuscript Division, 1989.

Dominique, Richard, Jean-Guy Deschênes. *Cultures et sociétés autochtones du Québec. Bibliographie critique.* Collection "Instruments de travail." Quebec, Institut québécois de recherche sur la culture, 1985, 221 p.

Gillis, Peter *et al. Archives ayant trait aux Affaires indiennes (R.G.10).* Division des archives fédérales. Collection de l'inventaire général. Ottawa, Archives publiques Canada, 1975, xi-47 p.

Halpenny, Francess G., Jean Hamelin, ed. *Dictionnaire biographique du Canada/Dictionary of Canadian Biography.* Quebec/Toronto, Les Presses de l'Université Laval/Toronto University Press, 1965-1990, 12 vols.

Harris, R. Cole, ed. *Historical Atlas of Canada.* French edition: Louise Deschêne, ed. Montreal, Presses de l'Université de Montréal, 1987, vol. 1, xviii-198p.

Hodge, Frederick Webb, ed. *Handbook of American Indians North of Mexico.* Smithsonian Institution. Bureau of American Ethnology. Bulletin 30. New York, Pageant Books, 1960 (1907), 2 vols.

IROBEC. *Bibliographie sur les Iroquoïens du Québec.* Quebec/Montreal, Ministère des Affaires culturelles / Département d'Anthropologie de l'Université de Montréal, 1985, 110 p.

Jennings, Francis, ed. *Iroquois Indians: A Documentary History of the Diplomacy of the Six Nations and their League. Guide to the Microfilm Collection.* The D'Arcy McNickle Center for the History of the American Indian. The Newberry Library. Woodbridge, Connecticut; Reading, England, Research Publications, 1984, 718 p.

McCardle, Bennett Ellen. *Indian History and Claims: A Research Handbook. Volume Two: Research Methods.* Treaties and Historical Research Center. Research Branch. Corporate Policy. Indian and Northern Affairs Canada, Ottawa, December 1982, p. 233-249.

Murdock, George P., *et al. Bibliography of Native North Americans on Disc.* Santa Barbara, California, Electronic ABC-CLIO Library, 4th edition (1975), 1992.

Public Archives of Canada. *Record Group 10, Indian Affairs, Preliminary Inventory*. Ottawa, Manuscript Division, 1951, xiii-13 p.

Public Archives of Canada. *Record Group 8, British Military and Naval Records, Preliminary Inventory*. Ottawa, Manuscript Division, 1954, 28 p.

Public Archives of Canada. *General Inventory, Manuscripts, MG 17-MG 21*. Ottawa, Manuscript Division, 1974, p. 157-159.

Sturtevant, William C., ed. *Handbook of North American Indians*. vol. 6, June Elm, ed. *Subarctic*. Washington, D.C., Smithsonian Institution, 1978, 837 p.

—, ed. *Handbook of North American Indians*. vol. 15, Bruce G. Trigger, ed. *Northeast*. Washington, D.C., Smithsonian Institution, 1978, 924 p.

Tanner, Helen Hornbeck, *et al. Atlas of Great Lakes Indian History*. The Newberry Library. Norman, University of Oklahoma Press, 1987, xv- 222 p.

Tooker, Elizabeth. *The Indians of the Northeast: A Critical Bibliography*. The Newberry Library Center for the American Indian. Bloomington, Indiana University Press, 1978, xi-77 p.

Historical Studies

Albers, Patricia C. "New Directions in Scholarship on American Indians: The Convergence of Anthropology with History and Other Social Science Disciplines." *Reviews in Anthropology*, vol. 14, no. 3 (Summer 1987), p. 221-235.

Aquila, Richard. *The Iroquois Restoration. Iroquois Diplomacy on the Colonial Frontier, 1701-1754*. Detroit, Wayne State University Press, 1983, 285 p.

Assiniwi, Bernard. *Histoire des Indiens du Haut Canada et du Bas Canada*. Ni-t'chawama / Mon ami / Mon frère. Montréal, Leméac, 1973-1974, 3 vols.

Axtell, James. "Ethnohistory: An Historian's Viewpoint." *Ethnohistory*, vol. 26, no. 1 (Winter 1979), p. 1-13.

Barbeau, Marius. "Huron and Wyandot Mythology." *Geological Survey*, Ottawa, Department of Mines, Memoir 80, no. 11 (1915), p. 375-392.

Beauchamp, William Martin. *The Iroquois Trail, or Foot-prints of the Six Nations: In Customs, Traditions and History*. Fayetteville, New York, Beauchamp, 1892, viii-154 p.

Beaulieu, Alain. *Convertir les fils de Caïn. Jésuites et Amérindiens nomades en Nouvelle-France, 1632-1642*. Québec, Nuit Blanche, 1994, 177 p.

Beaulieu, Alain, (Sawaya, Jean-Pierre). "Qui sont les Sept Nations du Canada?" *Recherches amérindiennes au Québec*, vol. XXVII, no. 2 (Fall 1997) p. 43-51.

Béchard, Henri. *The Original Caughnawaga Indians*. Montreal, International Publisher's Representatives, 1976 (1975), xv-258 p.

Blanchard, David Scott. *Kahnawake: aperçu historique*. Série sur l'histoire de Kahnawake no. 1. Kahnawake, Kanien'kehaka Raotitiohkwa, 1980, vii- 32 p.

—, *Tecaughretanego. Éléments du leadership Mohawk*. Série sur l'histoire de Kahnawake no. 2. Kahnawake, Kanien'kehaka Raotitiohkwa, 1980, 27 p.

—, "The Other Side of the Sky: Catholicism at Kahnawake, 1667-1700."

Anthropologica, vol. XXIV (1982), p. 77-102.

—, *Kahnawake: aperçu historique*. Série sur l'histoire de Kahnawake no. 1.

Kahnawake, Kanien'kehaka Raotitiohkwa, 1980, vii-32 p.

—, "The Seven Nations of Canada: an alliance and a treaty." *American Indian Culture and Research Journal*, vol. 7, no. 2 (1983), p. 3-23.

Boiteau, Georges. *Les Chasseurs hurons de Lorette*. Université Laval, département d'Histoire, faculté des Arts et des Sciences, 1954.

Boyce, Douglas W. "A Glimpse of Iroquois Culture History Through the Eyes of Joseph Brant and John Norton." *Proceedings of the American Philosophical Society*, vol. 117, no. 4 (1973), p. 286-294.

Brown, George, Ron Maguire. *Indian Treaties in Historical Perspective*. Research Branch. Ottawa, Department of Indian and Northern Affairs, 1979, xxviii-49 p.

Calloway, Colin Gordon. *Crown and Calumet: British-Indian Relations, 1783-1815*. Norman, University of Oklahoma Press, 1987, xiv-345 p.

Clermont, Normand. "La place de la femme dans les sociétés iroquoïennes de la période du contact." *Recherches amérindiennes au Québec*, vol. XIII, no. 4 (1983), p. 286-290.

Conkling, Robert. "Legitimacy and Conversion in Social Change: The Case of French Missionaries and the Northeastern Algonkian." *Ethnohistory*, vol. 21, no. 1 (Winter 1974), p. 1-24.

Couture, Yvon Hermann. *Les Algonquins*. Racines amérindiennes. Val d'Or, Hyperborée, 1983, 184 p.

Delâge, Denys. "Les Iroquois chrétiens des réductions, 1667-1770, I: Migration et rapports avec les Français." *Recherches amérindiennes au Québec*, vol. XXI, no. 1-2 (1991), p. 59-70.

—, "Les Iroquois chrétiens des réductions, 1667-1770, II: Rapports avec la Ligue iroquoise, les Britanniques et les autres nations autochtones." *Recherches amérindiennes au Québec*, vol. XXI, no. 3 (1991), p. 39-50.

—, *Le pays renversé : Amérindiens et Européens en Amérique du Nord-Est, 1660-1664*. Montréal, Boréal, 1991.

—, "L'alliance franco-amérindienne, 1660-1701." *Recherches amérindiennes au Québec*, vol. XIX, no. 1 (1989), p. 3-15.

—, "Les premiers contacts selon un choix de récits amérindiens publiés aux xixᵉ et xxᵉ siècles." *Recherches amérindiennes au Québec*, vol. XXII, no. 2-3 (1992), p. 101-116.

—, "Les premiers contacts dans 'History of the Ojibway People' de William Warren. Un récit de transition entre l'oral et l'écrit." *Recherches amérindiennes au Québec*, vol. XXII, no. 4 (1992), p. 49-59.

—, *Discours et pratiques coloniales, discours et pratiques autochtones.* Commission royale d'enquête sur les peuples autochtones, ed., Ottawa, Service de l'approvisionnement, July 1996 (CD-ROM, December 1996), p. 1-49.

Delâge, Denys, Jean-Pierre Sawaya. *Les Sept-Feux et les traités avec les Britanniques.* Commission royale d'enquête sur les peuples autochtones, ed., Ottawa, Service de l'approvisionnement, July 1996 (CD-ROM, December 1996).

De Lagrave, François. *Pointe-du-Lac: 1738-1988.* Pointe-du-Lac, Édition du 250ᵉ anniversaire, 1988.

Deschênes, Jean-Guy. "La contribution de Frank G. Speck à l'anthropologie des Amérindiens du Québec." *Recherches amérindiennes au Québec*, vol. XI, no. 3 (1978), p. 205-220.

Dickason, Olive Patricia. *Les Premières Nations du Canada. Depuis les temps les plus lointains jusqu'à nos jours.* Sillery, Septentrion, 1996.

Dickinson, John A., Jan Grabowski. "Les populations amérindiennes de la vallée laurentienne, 1608-1765." *Annales de démographie historique* (1993), p. 51-65.

Dufour, Jules. "Les revendications territoriales des peuples autochtones au Québec.' *Cahier de Géographie du Québec*, vol. 37, no. 101 (September 1993), p. 263-290.

Feest, Christian F. *Indians of Northeastern North America.* Iconography of Religions. Section X, North America. Fasc. 7. Leiden, E.J. Brill, 1986.

Fenton, William N. "Problems Arising from the Historic Northeastern Position of the Iroquois." *Smithsonian Miscellaneous Collections*, no. 100 (1940), p. 159-252.

—, "Seth Newhouse's Traditional History and Constitution of the Iroquois Confederacy." *Proceedings of the American Philosophical Society*, vol. 93, no. 2 (1949), p. 141-158.

Foster, Michael K., *et al. Extending the Rafters: Interdisciplinary Approaches to Iroquoian Studies.* The D'Arcy McNickle Center for the History of the American Indian. The Newberry Library. Albany, State University of New York, 1984.

Fraser, Alexander. *Fifth Report of the Bureau of Archives for the Province of Ontario. Huronia.* Toronto, L. K. Cameron, 1909.

Gérin, Léon. "La seigneurie de Sillery et les Hurons de Lorette." *Mémoires et comptes rendus de la société royale du Canada*, Ottawa, Hope, 2ᵉ série, tome 6 (May 1900), p. 73-115.

Grabowsky, Jan. "Les Amérindiens domiciliés et la 'contrebande' des fourrures en Nouvelle-France." *Recherches amérindiennes au Québec*, vol. XXIV, no. 3 (1994), p. 45-52.

Graymont, Barbara. *The Iroquois in the American Revolution.* Syracuse, New York, Syracuse University Press, 1972.

Hamilton, Milton W. "Sir William Johnson: Interpreter of the Iroquois." *Ethnohistory*, vol. 10, no. 3 (Summer 1963), p. 270-286.

Havard, Gilles. *La Grande Paix de Montréal de 1701: les voies de la diplomatie franco-amérindienne.* Signes des Amériques. Montréal, Recherches amérindiennes au Québec, 1992.

Hewitt, John Napoleon B. "Legend of the Founding of the Iroquois League." *American Anthropologist*, vol. 5, no. 2 (1892), p. 131-148.

Jacobs, Wilbur R. "Wampum, the Protocol of Indian Diplomacy." *William and Mary Quarterly*, vol. 6 (1949), p. 596-604.

Jennings, Francis. *The Invasion of America.* Chapel Hill, University of North Carolina Press, 1975.

Jennings, Francis. *The Ambiguous Iroquois Empire: The Covenant Chain Confederation of Indian Tribes with English Colonies from its Beginnings to the Lancaster Treaty of 1744.* New York, Norton, 1984.

Jennings, Francis, ed. *The History and Culture of Iroquois Diplomacy: An Interdisciplinary Guide to the Treaties of the Six Nations and their League.* The D'Arcy McNickle Center for the History of the American Indian. The Newberry Library. Syracuse, New York, Syracuse University Press, 1985.

Jennings, Francis. *Empire of Fortune: Crowns, Colonies and Tribes in the Seven Years War in America.* Ontario/New York, Penguin Books Canada/W.W. Norton, 1988.

Jetten, Marc. *Enclaves amérindiennes : les « réductions » du Canada 1637-1701.* Sillery, Septentrion, 1994.

Joly de Lotbinière, Pauline. "Des wampums et des 'Petits humains.' Récits historiques sur les wampums algonquins." *Recherches amérindiennes au Québec*, vol. XXIII, no. 2-3 (1993), p. 53-68.

Lanctôt, Gustave. *Histoire du Canada*, Montréal, Beauchemin, 1959, 3 vols.

Leacock, Eleanor, Oestreich Lurie, Nancy. *North American Indians in Historical Perspective.* Prospect Heights, Illinois, Waveland Press, 1988 (1971).

Lynch, James. "The Iroquois Confederacy, and the Adoption and Administration of Non-Iroquoian Individuals and Groups Prior to 1756." *Man in the Northeast*, no. 30 (1985), p. 83-99.

Maclaine, Craig, Michael S. Baxendale. *This Land is Our Land. The Mohawk Revolt at Oka*. Montreal/Toronto, Optimum Publishing International, 1990.

Macleod, Peter D. "The Anishinabeg Point of View: The History of the Great Lakes Region to 1800 in Nineteenth-Century Mississauga, Odawa, and Ojibwa Historiography." *Canadian Historical Review*, vol. LXXIII, no. 2 (1992), p. 194-210.

Maurault, Olivier. "Oka, les Vicissitudes d'une Mission Sauvage." *Revue Trimestrielle Canadienne*, vol. XVI, no. 62 (June 1930), p. 121-149.

Michelson, Gunther. "Iroquois Population Statistics." *Man in the Northeast*, no. 14 (Fall 1977), p. 3-17.

Morgan, Lewis Henry. *League of the Ho-De-No-Sau-Nee, or, Iroquois*. Rochester, New York, Sage & Brother, 1851.

Nichols, Frances S. *Index to Schoolcraft's "Indian Tribes of the United States."* Smithsonian Institution. Bureau of American Anthropology. Bulletin no. 152. New York, Paladin Press, 1969.

Ostola, Lawrence. *The Seven Nations of Canada and the American Revolution 1774-1783*. Université de Montréal, département d'Histoire, faculté des Arts et des Sciences. Master's thesis presented to the Faculty of Graduate Studies in history, 1989.

Patterson, E. Palmer. *The Canadian Indian: A History Since 1500*. Don Mills, Ontario, Collier-Macmillan Canada, 1972.

Ratelle, Maurice. *Présence des Mohawks au Québec méridional de 1534 à nos jours*. "Les études autochtones." Québec, Gouvernement du Québec, February 1991.

Richter, Daniel K. "War and Culture: The Iroquois Experience." *William and Mary Quarterly*, vol. 40, no. 4 (1983), p. 528-549.

Richter, Daniel K. "Iroquois Versus Iroquois: Jesuit Missions and Christianity in Village Politics, 1642-1686." *Ethnohistory*, vol. 32, no. 1 (1985), p. 1-16.

Richter, Daniel K., James H. Merrell. *Beyond the Covenant Chain. The Iroquois and Their Neighbours in Indian North America, 1600-1800*. Syracuse, New York, Syracuse University Press, 1987.

Sawaya, Jean-Pierre. *Les Sept-Nations du Canada: traditions d'alliance dans le Nord-Est, XVIIIe-XIXe siècles*. Commission royale d'enquête sur les peuples autochtones, ed., Ottawa, Service de l'approvisionnement, September 1996 (CD-ROM, December 1996).

Schoolcraft, Henry Rowe. *History of the Indian Tribes of the United States, their Present Conditions and Prospects and a Sketch of their Ancient States.* Philadelphia, J. P. Lippincolt, 1856, 6 vols.

Schusky, Ernest Lester, ed. *Political Organization of Native North Americans.* Washington, D.C., University Press of America, 1980.

Sioui, Georges E. *Pour une autohistoire amérindienne. Essai sur les fondements d'une morale sociale.* Québec, Les Presses de l'Université Laval, 1989.

Smith, Donald Boyd. *Le « Sauvage» pendant la période héroïque de la Nouvelle-France (1534-1663) d'après les historiens canadiens-français des XIXᵉ et XXᵉ siècles.* Collection "Cultures amérindiennes." Ville LaSalle, Cahiers du Québec/Hurtubise HMH, 1974.

—, "Who are the Mississauga?" *Ontario History,* vol. LXVII, no. 4 (December 1975), p. 211-222.

Speck, Frank G. "The Eastern Algonkian Wabanaki Confederacy." *American Anthropologist,* vol. 17 (1915), p. 492-508.

—, *Family Hunting Territories and Social Life of Various Algonkian Bands of the Ottawa Valley.* Memoir 70, Anthropological Series No. 8. Ottawa, Department of Mines Geological Survey, 1915.

—, "Culture Problems in the Northeastern North America." *Proceedings of the American Philosophical Society,* vol. 65, no. 4 (1926), p. 272-311.

—, "Boundaries and Hunting Groups of the River Desert Algonquin." *Indian Notes,* vol. VI, no. 2 (April 1929), p. 97-120.

Speck, Frank G., Wendell S. Hadlock. "A Report on Tribal Boundaries and Hunting Areas of the Malecite Indian of New Brunswick." *American Anthropologist,* vol. 48 (1946), p. 355-374.

Stanley, George F.G. "The First Indian 'Reserves' in Canada." *Revue d'histoire de l'Amérique française,* vol. 4, no. 2 (September 1950), p. 178-210.

Surtees, Robert J. "The Development of an Indian Reserve Policy in Canada." *Historical Essays on Upper Canada,* J. K. Johnson & Bruce G. Wilson, ed. The Carleton Library no. 82. McClelland & Stewart, 1975, p. 262-277.

Trigger, Bruce Graham. "Indians and Ontario's History." *Ontario History,* vol. LXXIV, no. 4 (1982), p. 246-257.

—, *Les Enfants d'Aataentsic : l'histoire du peuple huron.*, trans. Jean-Paul Sainte-Marie and Brigitte Chabert Hacikyan. Montréal, Libre Expression, 1991.

—, *Les Indiens, la fourrure et les Blancs : Français et Amérindiens en Amérique du Nord.* trans. Georges Khall. Montréal-Paris, Boréal-Seuil, 1990.

Trudel, Marcel. *Histoire de la Nouvelle-France.* Montréal, Fides, 1963, 4 vols.
Todorov, Tzvetan. *La conquête de l'Amérique.* Paris, Éditions du Seuil, 1982.

Upton, Leslie F.S. "Colonists and Micmacs." *Journal of Canadian Studies*, vol. 10, no. 3 (1975), p. 44-56.

—, *Micmacs and Colonists: Indian-White Relations in the Maritime Provinces, 1713-1867*. Vancouver, University of British Columbia Press, 1979.

Vaugeois, Denis. *La fin des alliances franco-indiennes. Enquête sur un sauf-conduit de 1760 devenu un traité en 1990*. Montréal-Sillery, Boréal-Septentrion, 1995.

Viau, Roland. "Premier colloque sur l'ethnohistoire des groupes autochtones au Québec, 21-22 novembre 1987." *Recherches amérindiennes au Québec*, vol. XVIII, no. 1 (1988), p. 85-87.

Vieni, Frank. *Québec Indian Communities Guide*. Ottawa, Ministry of Supply and Services Canada, 1990.

Villeneuve, Larry. *Historiques des réserves et villages indiens du Québec*. Updated by Daniel Francis. Ottawa, Indian and Northern Affairs Canada, Research Directorate, 1984.

Walker, Willard, *et al*. "A Chronological Account of the Wabanaki Confederacy." *Political Organization of Native North Americans*, Washington, D.C., University Press of America, 1980, p. 41-84.

Walker, Willard. "Wabanaki Wampum Protocol." *The Wampum Records. Wabanaki Traditional Laws*, Fredericton, Micmac-Maliseet Institute, 1990, p. 25-35.

White, Richard. *The Middle Ground. Empires and Republics in the Great Lakes Region, 1650-1815*. Cambridge, Cambridge University Press, 1991.

Also from Baraka Books

The Legacy of Louis Riel
Leader of the Métis Nation
John Andrew Morrow

Waswanipi
Jean-Yves Soucy

Let's Move On
Paul Okalik with Louis McComber

Journey to the Heart of the First Peoples Collections
Marie-Paul Robitaille

The Calf with Two Heads
Transatlantic Natural History in the Canadas
Louisa Blair

A Distinct Alien Race, The Untold Story of Franco-Americans
David Vermette

Stolen Motherhood, Surrogacy and Made-to-Order Children
Maria De Koninck

Still Crying for Help, The Failure of Our Mental Healthcare Services
Sadia Messaili

Pierre Trudeau's Darkest Hour
War Measures 1970
Guy Bouthillier, Édouard Cloutier, ed.

Montreal, City of Secrets
Confederate Operations in Montreal During the American Civil War
Barry Sheehy

Rwanda and the New Scramble for Africa
From Tragedy to Useful Imperial Fiction
Robin Philpot

Printed by Imprimerie Gauvin
Gatineau, Québec